A Roundelay of Fun and Merriment

Here is a sparkling and comprehensive collection of almost 700 poems of light verse, written by the leading practitioners of this art during the past five hundred years, selected by Oscar Williams, eminent poet and critic.

With a rich and tempting bill of fare ranging from nursery rhymes to well-turned sonnets, this book also includes famous ballads, lively limericks, poems for children, and even verses that gaily poke fun at well known poets and personalities. *The Hunting of the Snark* by Lewis Carroll is included in its entirety for the first time in paperbound form.

Offering selections from such diverse versifiers as Chaucer, Shakespeare, Ogden Nash and Dylan Thomas, this delightful volume is an ideal companion to F. T. Palgrave's *The Golden Treasury*, now also available in a Mentor edition which has been expanded and brought up-to-date by Oscar Williams.

In this treasury of well known favorites and hilarious discoveries are hours of fun for reading aloud and family relaxation as well as solitary enjoymen*

Books

by

OSCAR WILLIAMS

•

Books of Poems

The Golden Darkness
The Man Coming Toward You
That's All That Matters
Selected Poems

Anthologies

The New Poems Series
The War Poets
A Little Treasury of Modern Poetry
A Little Treasury of Great Poetry
A Little Treasury of American Poetry
A Little Treasury of British Poetry
Immortal Poems of the English Language
The Pocket Book of Modern Verse
The New Pocket Anthology of American Verse
*The Golden Treasury by Palgrave (Revised)
*The Silver Treasury of Light Verse

*Published by The New American Library

The
SILVER TREASURY
of
LIGHT VERSE

From Geoffrey Chaucer to Ogden Nash

Edited by
OSCAR WILLIAMS

Illustrations and Decorations by
**I. Rice Pereira, Walter Quirt,
Paul Lett, Mary Buckley and Ely Schless,
Tom Keogh, Barbara Tanner, Sylvia Carewe**

A MENTOR BOOK
Published by **THE NEW AMERICAN LIBRARY**

ACKNOWLEDGMENTS AND COPYRIGHT NOTICES
(The two pages following constitute an extension of this copyright page.)

The Editor has made a careful effort to secure permission from all holders of copyright material. Should there be a poet or publisher whose poems are represented from whom permission was not secured, the omission is inadvertent, not intentional. The Editor will be happy to correct such omissions in future printings. The Editor wishes to thank the following poets, publishers and agents:

Conrad Aiken for FROSTBITE and LIMBRICKER

Allen & Unwin Ltd. for THE CURSE from *Poems and Translations* by J. M. Synge

Phyllis Eleanor Armstrong for FORM 1040A

Edward Arnold Ltd. for POLITICAL ECONOMY, TENDERHEARTEDNESS, MISFORTUNES NEVER COME SINGLY, AUNT ELIZA, WASTE and AUNTIE, DID YOU FEEL NO PAIN? by Harry Graham

Mrs. George Bambridge and Macmillan Company of Canada Ltd. for SESTINA OF THE TRAMP-ROYAL and MANDALAY by Rudyard Kipling

George Barker for JUST A FISHING SMACK AT EMPSON; Roy Basler for EXODUS

Joseph Bennett for POINTILLISM from *Decembrist* (Clarke & Way), Copyright Joseph Bennett 1951; Ray Bradbury for A DUBLIN LIMERICK

Brandt & Brandt for FIRST FIG from *Collected Poems* by Edna St. Vincent Millay (Harper & Brothers), Copyright 1918, 1946, by Edna St. Vincent Millay, and for the following selections from *Poems 1923-1954* by E. E. Cummings (Harcourt, Brace and Company): "next to of course god america i," Copyright 1926, 1954, by E. E. Cummings; "it was a goodly co," "mr u will not be missed," and "a politician is an arse upon," Copyright, 1944, by E. E. Cummings; "i sing of Olaf glad and big," Copyright, 1931, by E. E. Cummings; "ponder darling, these busted statues," Copyright, 1926, by Horace Liveright, Copyright renewed, 1954, by E. E. Cummings

James Broughton for FRUITS OF EXPERIENCES and MRS. MOTHER HAS A NOSE, from *Musical Chairs*, Copyright 1950 by James Broughton

Curtis Brown Ltd. (New York) and the Estate of D. H. Lawrence for HOW BEASTLY THE BOURGEOIS IS from *Pansies* by D. H. Lawrence (Alfred A. Knopf), Copyright © 1929 by Frieda Lawrence Ravagli

Herbert Cahoon for THE ANGLEWORM POEM; Jonathan Cape Ltd. for CHARD WHITLOW and NAMING OF PARTS from *A Map of Verona and Other Poems* by Henry Reed

Chatto & Windus Ltd. for JUST A SMACK AT AUDEN from *Collected Poems of William Empson*; Robert Clairmont for THE ANSWERS

Miss D. E. Collins for THE LOGICAL VEGETARIAN and SONG OF THE QUOODLE from *Collected Poems of G. K. Chesterton*, Methuen & Co., Ltd. (London)

Frances Cornford for TO A FAT LADY; J. V. Cunningham for TWO EPIGRAMS from *Poems by American Poets*, Copyright 1953 by Ballantine Books, Inc.

David Daiches for FINAL THOUGHTS ON THE WEATHER IN ENGLAND DURING 1953, © 1953 The New Yorker Magazine, Inc., and THOUGHTS OF PROGRESS, © 1954 The New Yorker Magazine, Inc.

Dial Press, Inc., for ON SOME SOUTH AFRICAN NOVELISTS and THE DEATH OF POLYBIUS JUBB from *Adamastor* by Roy Campbell, Copyright 1931 by Roy Campbell; THE COMPLETE MISANTHROPE and EPITAPH FOR A FUNNY FELLOW from *A Bowl Of Bishop*, Copyright 1954, by Morris Bishop

Dodd, Mead & Company for THE LOGICAL VEGETARIAN and SONG OF THE QUOODLE from *The Collected Poems of G. K. Chesterton*, Copyright 1911, 1932, by Dodd, Mead & Company, Inc.; HEAVEN from *The Collected Poems of Rupert Brooke*, Copyright 1915 by Dodd, Mead & Company, Inc.

Doubleday & Company, Inc., for TO A THESAURUS from *Tobogganing On Parnassus* by F. P. Adams, Copyright 1911 by Doubleday & Company, Inc.; THE ARREST OF OSCAR WILDE from *Slick but Not Streamlined* by John Betjeman, Copyright 1947 by John Betjeman; SESTINA OF THE TRAMP-ROYAL and MANDALAY from *Departmental Ditties and Ballads & Barrack-Room Ballads* by Rudyard Kipling (also by permission of Mrs. George Bambridge); THE HONEY BEE from *Archy and Mehitabel* by Don Marquis, Copyright 1927 by Doubleday & Company, Inc.

Contents

Part Two: THE ANATOMY OF HAPPINESS

Part Three: RIGMAROLES, BURLESQUES AND TOURS DE FORCE

Part Four: LITERARY COCKTAIL PARTY

Part Five: *VERY MUCH OF THIS WORLD*

Part Six: INVECTIVES, IMPRECATIONS, AND OTHER BLASTS

Part Seven: THE BAWDY HOUSE

Part Eight: EAT, DRINK, AND BE MERRY

Part Nine: UNLIKELY TALES

Part Ten: ANIMAL FAIR

Part Eleven: YOUR P'S AND Q'S AND HAITCHES

Part Twelve: THE CHILDREN'S PLAYGROUND

Part Thirteen: SALLY IN OUR ALLEY

Part Fourteen: SONGS, LYRICS, AND BALLADS
FOR THE WEEKEND

Part Fifteen: THE READER'S PRIVATE ANTHOLOGY

Index of Authors: 415

Preface

This is a Companion Volume to *The Golden Treasury* edited
by Palgrave:
You'll recall he Devoted his Collection Only to Work which
was All grave—
(Perhaps there's nothing Funny about Victorians except their
Trite Verse)—
I take Pleasure, then, in presenting it: *The Silver Treasury of
Light Verse.*
(It's One of The Better Mentors, I know it, I've read It Myself,
Who Touches this Book Touches, not a man, but a Whole
Cut-up Shelf!)
Here, Forgive Me, if I don't Define "Light" though it's a
Heavy Omission,
But All my Life Long I have had a Rather Singular Ambition,
And That is never to get myself Caught Offering a Definition!)
But If you Must have One, look under "HUMOUR" in
Fowler's *English Usage;*
You'll be less likely to Indulge in the Verbiage of Abusage.

Now some People Call An Anthology a Nosegay, I call Mine
a Noose-ful
Which enables me to say, in Rhyme, I think you'll Find It
Useful:
From John Skelton to Ogden Nash, from Verse, Free, to
Rhymes, Feminine,
It Culls the Language closely, & Never, I think, lets a Lemon In;
From Light Verse which is Serious to Heavy Verse which is
Jabberwocky,
The World's Wide but this Book's Long on Double Meanings,
and Cocky.

So far that Thrilling Week-end which Threatens to become a
Disaster
Why not prove you have the Wit and the Soul of which you
are the Master
And dip into these Fifteen Sections, Hilarious to Discursive?
(Being the Life of *This* Party is not yet considered Subversive!)
There are Over 600 Choices, Ballads, Limericks and Blasts,
Up to the Topical Present the Place is Full of Amusing Repasts;
From Mother Goose to The Bawdy House and on to The
Animal Fair,
All over the lot you'll Spot the Couplet with a Delicate Air;
You can Trip the Step Fantastic or in The Children's
Playground dally,
And go from The Literary Cocktail Party right to Sally in
Our Alley,
And on till you come to the end with Week End Songs & Lyrics

And if by then you are tired of my, or the Contributors',
    Panegyrics,
Take Courage, there are a Number of Blank Pages and, as
    You Surmised,
You may add your Own Poems now and thus get Yourself
    Anthologized.

This brings me to an Embarrassing Matter which has Bothered
    the Literary Set;
Should an Editor who is a Poet Include his Own Poems Yet
    (or Not Yet)?
I'll bet you, or Should I say I'll Lay You a Monetary Wager,
That this was no problem for that Great Editor and Poet,
    Meleager,
Who used 130 of His Own Poems in the Greek Anthology,
And He Did It So Gracefully without a Single Greek Word
    for Apology.
I hate to think what might have happened to Literature
    in this Connection
If He Hadn't Included Himself So Generously in His
    Own Collection.
It's Usual for One who'd Build a Better Mousetrap in the Cold
    World of Letters
To step with Confidence onto Footpaths Beaten out for him
    by his Betters.
So you will see that I, for one, have been Remiss, not to say
    Reticent,
In Not Following that Ancient, Most Celebrated and Inviting
    Precedent,
Including only four (counting this Preface) of my Tours
    de Force,
And with this Modest Gesture I close this most difficult Dis-
    course.

But Not Before I've added a Postscript: I've Always Found
    it Hard to Curb
A Secret Desire to Write my Own Justly Extravagant
    Publisher's Blurb:
So: This Book's Shockingly Innocent, It's Clever, and Original,
    and Candid,
It's a Real Pleasure to Read, & It's Edited by a Charming Bandit.
(I Call Myself Names, to Forestall Those Rabid Rascals, the
    Reviewers,
Who're Sure to Send Me to Oblivion, or at Least on
    Skewers into Sewers.)
Now if you Don't Like This Book, Don't Get Hot Under
    Your Customer's Collar,
Don't Resort to Golden Silence, or Even Silver, Just Holler,
And Try to Get Back, IF YOU CAN, Your Highly
    Inflated Half Dollar!   *Oscar Williams*

The
SILVER TREASURY
of
LIGHT VERSE

PART ONE

Out of This World

Jabberwocky

'Twas brillig, and the slithy toves
  Did gyre and gimble in the wabe:
All mimsy were the borogoves,
  And the mome raths outgrabe.

"Beware the Jabberwock, my son!
  The jaws that bite, the claws that catch!
Beware the Jubjub bird, and shun
  The frumious Bandersnatch!"

He took his vorpal sword in hand;
  Long time the manxome foe he sought—
So rested he by the Tumtum tree,
  And stood awhile in thought.

And, as in uffish thought he stood,
  The Jabberwock, with eyes of flame,
Came whiffling through the tulgey wood,
  And burbled as it came!

One, two! One, two! And through and through
  The vorpal blade went snicker-snack!
He left it dead, and with its head
  He went galumphing back.

"And hast thou slain the Jabberwock?
   Come to my arms, my beamish boy!
O frabjous day! Callooh, Callay!"
   He chortled in his joy.

'Twas brillig, and the slithy toves
   Did gyre and gimble in the wabe:
All mimsy were the borogoves,
   And the mome raths outgrabe.

                   Lewis Carroll

From "The Westminster Drollery," 1671

I saw a peacock with a fiery tail
I saw a blazing comet drop down hail
I saw a cloud wrapped with ivory wand
I saw an oak creep upon the ground
I saw a pismire swallow up a whale
I saw the sea brimful of ale
I saw a Venice glass full fifteen feet deep
I saw a well full of men's tears that weep
I saw red eyes all of a flaming fire
I saw a house bigger than the moon and higher
I saw the sun at twelve o'clock at night
I saw the man that saw this wondrous sight.

                   Anonymous

Long John Brown and Little Mary Bell

Little Mary Bell had a Fairy in a Nut,
Long John Brown had the Devil in his Gut;
Long John Brown lov'd Little Mary Bell,
And the Fairy drew the Devil into the Nut shell.

Her Fairy skip'd out & her Fairy skip'd in;
He laugh'd at the Devil saying "Love is a Sin."
The Devil he raged & the Devil he was wroth,
And the Devil enter'd into the Young Man's broth.

He was soon in the Gut of the loving Young Swain,
For John eat and drank to drive away Love's pain;
But all he could do he grew thinner & thinner,
Tho' he eat & drank as much as ten Men for his dinner.

Some said he had a Wolf in his stomach day & night,
Some said he had the Devil & they guess'd right;

The Fairy skip'd about in his Glory, Joy & Pride,
And he laugh'd at the Devil till poor John Brown died.

Then the Fairy skip'd out of the old Nut shell,
And woe & alack for Pretty Mary Bell!
For the Devil crept in when the Fairy skip'd out,
And there goes Miss Bell with her fusty old Nut.

William Blake

In the Dumps

We're all in the dumps,
For diamonds are trumps;
The kittens are gone to St. Paul's!
The babies are bit,
The moon's in a fit,
And the houses are built without walls.

Anonymous

The Dying Airman

A handsome young airman lay dying,
And as on the aerodrome he lay,
To the mechanics who round him came sighing,
These last dying words he did say:

"Take the cylinders out of my kidneys,
The connecting-rod out of my brain,
Take the cam-shaft from out of my backbone,
And assemble the engine again."

Anonymous

Wolfram's Song

Old Adam, the carrion crow,
  The old crow of Cairo;
He sat in the shower, and let it flow
  Under his tail and over his crest;
    And through every feather
    Leaked the wet weather;
  And the bough swung under his nest;
For his beak it was heavy with marrow.
  Is that the wind dying? O no;
  It's only two devils, that blow
  Through a murderer's bones, to and fro,
    In the ghosts' moonshine.

Ho! Eve, my grey carrion wife,
  When we have supped on kings' marrow,
Where shall we drink and make merry our life?
  Our nest it is Queen Cleopatra's skull,
    'Tis cloven and cracked,
    And battered and hacked,
  But with tears of blue eyes it is full:
Let us drink then, my raven of Cairo!
  Is that the wind dying? O no;
  It's only two devils, that blow
  Through a murderer's bones, to and fro,
    In the ghosts' moonshine.

Thomas Lovell Beddoes

Four of a Kind

I. A CASE

As I was going up the stair
I met a man who wasn't there.
He wasn't there again today—
I wish to God he'd go away!

Anonymous

II. THE PERFECT REACTIONARY

As I was sitting in my chair
I *knew* the bottom wasn't there,
Nor legs nor back, but *I just sat*,
Ignoring little things like that.

Hughes Mearns

III. THE LADY WITH TECHNIQUE

As I was letting down my hair
I met a guy who didn't care;
He didn't care again today—
I *love* 'em when they get that way!

Hughes Mearns

IV. FRUSTRATED MALE

One night I met when stepping out
A gal who wasn't thereabout;
I said, "*Hel*-lo! And how are *you!*"
She didn't say; so I never knew.

Hughes Mearns

Taffy

Taffy was a Welshman, Taffy was a thief,
Taffy came to my house and stole a piece of beef;
I went to Taffy's house, Taffy wasn't in,
I jumped upon his Sunday hat, and poked it with a pin.

Taffy was a Welshman, Taffy was a sham,
Taffy came to my house and stole a leg of lamb;
I went to Taffy's house, Taffy was away,
I stuffed his socks with sawdust and filled his shoes with clay.

Taffy was a Welshman, Taffy was a cheat,
Taffy came to my house and stole a piece of meat;
I went to Taffy's house, Taffy was not there,
I hung his coat and trousers to roast before a fire.

Anonymous

The Man of Thessaly

There was a Man of Thessaly,
    And he was wondrous wise:
He jumped into a brier hedge
    And scratched out both his eyes.
But when he saw his eyes were out,
    With all his might and main
He jumped into another hedge
    And scratched them in again.

Anonymous

Folkways

Was Galahad hired,
    Artemis laid?
Was Hercules tired,
    Ajax afraid?

The Argo was scuttled
    And Jason fleeced?

Ulysses a cuckold,
    Aeneas beached?

O Totem O Wildwood
O Autumn of Childhood
No heroes? No glories?
O Eros O mores.

Isabella Gardner

On a Clergyman's Horse Biting Him

The steed bit his master;
    How came this to pass?
He heard the good pastor
    Cry, "All flesh is grass."

Anonymous

A Chronicle

Once—but no matter when—
    There lived—no matter
        where—
A man, whose name—but
        then
    I need not that declare.

He—well, he had been born,
    And so he was alive;
His age—I details scorn—
    Was somethingty and five.

He lived—how many years
    I truly can't decide;
But this one fact appears:
    He lived—until he died.

"He died," I have averred,
    But cannot prove 'twas so,
But that he was interred,
    At any rate, I know.

I fancy he'd a son,
    I hear he had a wife:
Perhaps he'd more than one,
    I know not, on my life!

But whether he was rich,
    Or whether he was poor,
Or neither—both—or which,
    I cannot say, I'm sure.

I can't recall his name,
    Or what he used to do:
But then—well, such is fame!
    'Twill so serve me and you.

And that is why I thus
    About this unknown man
Would fain create a fuss,
    To rescue, if I can

From dark oblivion's blow,
    Some record of his lot:
But, ah! I do not know
    Who—where—when—
        why—or what.

Moral

In this brief pedigree
    A moral we should find—
But what it ought to be
    Has quite escaped my
        mind!

Anonymous

Scylla Toothless

Scylla is toothless; yet when she was young,
She had both tooth enough, and too much tongue:
What should I now of toothless Scylla say?
But that her tongue hath worn her teeth away.

Anonymous

Death of My Aunt

My aunt she died a month ago,
   And she left me all her riches,
A feather-bed and a wooden leg,
   And a pair of calico breeches;
A coffee-pot without a spout,
   A mug without a handle,
A baccy box without a lid,
   And half a farthing candle.

Anonymous

The Persian Version

Truth-loving Persians do not dwell upon
The trivial skirmish fought near Marathon.
As for the Greek theatrical tradition
Which represents that summer's expedition
Not as a mere reconnaissance in force
By three brigades of foot and one of horse
(Their left flank covered by some obsolete
Light craft detached from the main Persian fleet)
But as a grandiose, ill-starred attempt
To conquer Greece—they treat it with contempt;
And only incidentally refute
Major Greek claims, by stressing what repute
The Persian monarch and the Persian nation
Won by this salutary demonstration:
Despite a strong defense and adverse weather
All arms combined magnificently together.

Robert Graves

Sonnet Found in a Deserted Madhouse

Oh that my soul a marrow-bone might seize!
For the old egg of my desire is broken,
Spilled is the pearly white and spilled the yolk, and
As the mild melancholy contents grease
My path the shorn lamb baas like bumblebees.
Time's trashy purse is as a taken token
Or like a thrilling recitation, spoken
By mournful mouths filled full of mirth and cheese.

And yet, why should I clasp the earthful urn?
Or find the frittered fig that felt the fast?
Or choose to chase the cheese around the churn?
Or swallow any pill from out the past?
Ah no, Love, not while your hot kisses burn
Like a potato riding on the blast.   *Anonymous*

The Big Nasturtiums

All of a sudden the big nasturtiums
Rose in the night from the ocean's bed,
Rested a while in the light of the morning,
Turning the sand dunes tiger red.

They covered the statue of Abraham Lincoln,
They climbed to the top of our church's spire.
"Grandpa! Grandpa! Come to the window!
Come to the window! Our world's on fire!"

Big nasturtiums in the High Sierras,
Big nasturtiums in the lands below;
Our trains are late and our planes have fallen,
And out in the ocean the whistles blow.

Over the fields and over the forests,
Over the living and over the dead—
"I never expected the big nasturtiums
To come in my lifetime!" Grandpa said.
   Robert Beverly Hale

Mind Over Matter

I. RELATIVITY

There was a young lady named Bright,
Who travelled much faster than light,
    She started one day
    In the relative way,
And returned on the previous night.

Anonymous

II. GENIUS

A scientist living at Staines
Is searching with infinite pains
    For a new type of sound
    Which he hopes, when it's found,
Will travel much faster than planes.

R. J. P. Hewison

III. FAITH-HEALER

There was a faith-healer in Deal
Who said, "Although pain isn't real,
    If I sit on a pin
    And it punctures my skin,
I dislike what I fancy I feel."

Anonymous

IV. ON MONSIEUR COUÉ

This very remarkable man
Commends a most practical plan;
    You can do what you want
    If you don't think you can't
So don't think you can't think you can.

Charles Inge

Evidence Read at the Trial of the Knave of Hearts

They told me you had been to her,
    And mentioned me to him:
She gave me a good character,
    But said I could not swim.

He sent them word I had not gone,
    (We know it to be true):
If she should push the matter on,
    What would become of you?

I gave her one, they gave him two,
    You gave us three or more;
They all returned from him to you,
    Though they were mine before.

If I or she should chance to be
    Involved in this affair,
He trusts to you to set them free,
    Exactly as we were.

My notion was that you had been
    (Before she had this fit)
An obstacle that came between
    Him, and ourselves, and it.

Don't let him know she liked them best,
    For this must ever be
A secret, kept from all the rest,
    Between yourself and me.

Lewis Carroll

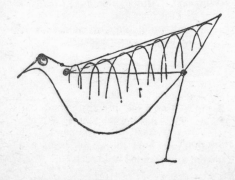

Humpty Dumpty's Recitation

In winter, when the fields are white,
I sing this song for your delight—

In spring, when woods are getting green,
I'll try and tell you what I mean.

In summer, when the days are long,
Perhaps you'll understand the song:

In autumn, when the leaves are brown,
Take pen and ink, and write it down.

I sent a message to the fish:
I told them "This is what I wish."

The little fishes of the sea
They sent an answer back to me.

The little fishes' answer was
"We cannot do it, Sir, because—"

I sent to them again to say
"It will be better to obey."

The fishes answered with a grin
"Why, what a temper you are in!"

I told them once, I told them twice:
They would not listen to advice.

I took a kettle large and new,
Fit for the deed I had to do.

My heart went hop, my heart went thump;
I filled the kettle at the pump.

Then some one came to me and said,
"The little fishes are in bed."

I said to him, I said it plain,
"Then you must wake them up again."

I said it very loud and clear;
I went and shouted in his ear.

But he was very stiff and proud;
He said "You needn't shout so loud!"

And he was very proud and stiff;
He said "I'd go and wake them, if—"

I took a corkscrew from the shelf:
I went to wake them up myself.

And when I found the door was locked,
I pulled and pushed and kicked and knocked.

And when I found the door was shut
I tried to turn the handle, but—

Lewis Carroll

The Voice of the Lobster

" 'Tis the voice of the Lobster; I heard him declare,
'You have baked me too brown, I must sugar my hair.'
As a duck with its eyelids, so he with his nose
Trims his belt and his buttons, and turns out his toes.
When the sands are all dry, he is gay as a lark,
And will talk in contemptuous tones of the Shark:
But, when the tide rises and sharks are around,
His voice has a timid and tremulous sound.

"I passed by his garden, and marked, with one eye,
How the Owl and the Panther were sharing a pie:
The Panther took pie-crust, and gravy, and meat,
While the Owl had the dish as its share of the treat.
When the pie was all finished, the Owl, as a boon,
Was kindly permitted to pocket the spoon:
While the Panther received knife and fork with a growl,
And concluded the banquet by—"

Lewis Carroll

An Old Looney of Rhyme

There was an old Looney of Rhyme
Whose candor was simply sublime:
    When they asked, "Are you there?"
    He said, "Yes, but take care,
For I'm never 'all there' at a time!"

Anonymous

If Everything

If everything around me is just air
Why can't I just fall up instead of down?
If yesterday was here, then when is where?
If I'm alone with dolls, then what's a town?
If streets and dogs are numbered, who counts why?
How many pennies jumping in a handful?
If birds are like black screams in the blue sky
How much gold sound is blowing in a bandful?

I touch a cat. It jumps. That means it's me.
The air's the world, but what I breathe is mine.
I'm looked at by the solid things I see.
If I speak to my watch and it says nine,
Because the sun climbs up and down all year,
Then where is when, how far from now is here?

Paul Engle

Mother Goose
(Circa 2054)

Humpty Dumpty sat on the wall,
A non-electro-magnetic ball.
All the Super's polariscopes
Couldn't revitalize his isotopes.

Irene Sekula

The Mad Gardener's Song

He thought he saw an Elephant,
    That practiced on a fife:
He looked again, and found it was
    A letter from his wife.
"At length I realize," he said,
    "The bitterness of Life!"

He thought he saw a Buffalo
    Upon the chimney-piece:
He looked again, and found it was
    His Sister's Husband's Niece.
"Unless you leave this house," he said,
    "I'll send for the Police!"

He thought he saw a Rattlesnake
    That questioned him in Greek:
He looked again, and found it was
    The Middle of Next Week.

"The one thing I regret," he said,
  "Is that it cannot speak!"

He thought he saw a Banker's Clerk
  Descending from the bus:
He looked again, and found it was
  A Hippopotamus.
"If this should stay to dine," he said,
  "There won't be much for us!"

He thought he saw a Kangaroo
  That worked a coffee-mill:
He looked again, and found it was
  A Vegetable-Pill.
"Were I to swallow this," he said,
  "I should be very ill!"

He thought he saw a Coach-and-Four
  That stood beside his bed:
He looked again, and found it was
  A Bear without a Head.
"Poor thing," he said, "poor silly thing!
  It's waiting to be fed!"

He thought he saw an Albatross
  That fluttered round the lamp:
He looked again, and found it was
  A Penny-Postage-Stamp.
"You'd best be getting home," he said,
  "The nights are very damp!"

He thought he saw a Garden-Door
  That opened with a key:
He looked again, and found it was
  A Double Rule of Three:
"And all its mystery," he said,
  "Is clear as day to me!"

He thought he saw an Argument
  That proved he was the Pope:
He looked again, and found it was
  A Bar of Mottled Soap.
"A fact so dread," he faintly said,
  "Extinguishes all hope!"

                                    Lewis Carroll

The Jumblies

They went to sea in a Sieve, they did,
In a Sieve they went to sea:
In spite of all their friends could say,
On a winter's morn, on a stormy day,
   In a Sieve they went to sea!
And when the Sieve turned round and round,
And every one cried, "You'll all be drowned!"
They called aloud, "Our Sieve ain't big,
But we don't care a button! we don't care a fig!
   In a Sieve we'll go to sea!"
      Far and few, far and few,
        Are the lands where the Jumblies live;
       Their heads are green, and their hands are blue,
        And they went to sea in a Sieve.

They sailed away in a Sieve, they did,
   In a Sieve they sailed so fast,
With only a beautiful pea-green veil
Tied with a riband by way of a sail,
   To a small tobacco-pipe mast;
And every one said, who saw them go,
"O won't they be soon upset, you know!
For the sky is dark, and the voyage is long,
And happen what may, it's extremely wrong
   In a Sieve to sail so fast!"
      Far and few, far and few,
        Are the lands where the Jumblies live;
       Their heads are green, and their hands are blue,
        And they went to sea in a Sieve.

The water it soon came in, it did,
   The water it soon came in;
So to keep them dry, they wrapped their feet
In a pinky paper all folded neat,
   And they fastened it down with a pin.
And they passed the night in a crockery-jar,
And each of them said, "How wise we are!
Though the sky be dark, and the voyage be long,
Yet we never can think we were rash or wrong,
   While round in our Sieve we spin!"
      Far and few, far and few,
        Are the lands where the Jumblies live;
       Their heads are green, and their hands are blue,
        And they went to sea in a Sieve.

And all night long they sailed away;
    And when the sun went down,
They whistled and warbled a moony song
To the echoing sound of a coppery gong,
    In the shade of the mountains brown.
"O Timballoo! How happy we are,
When we live in a Sieve and a crockery-jar,
And all night long in the moonlight pale,
We sail away with a pea-green sail,
    In the shade of the mountains brown!"
        Far and few, far and few,
            Are the lands where the Jumblies live;
            Their heads are green, and their hands are blue,
                And they went to sea in a Sieve.

They sailed to the Western Sea, they did,
    To a land all covered with trees,
And they bought an Owl, and a useful Cart,
And a pound of Rice, and a Cranberry Tart,
    And a hive of silvery Bees.
And they bought a Pig, and some green Jack-daws,
And a lovely Monkey with lollipop paws,
And forty bottles of Ring-Bo-Ree,
    And no end of Stilton Cheese.
        Far and few, far and few,
            Are the lands where the Jumblies live;
            Their heads are green, and their hands are blue,
                And they went to sea in a Sieve.

And in twenty years they all came back,
    In twenty years or more,
And every one said, "How tall they've grown!
For they've been to the Lakes, and the Torrible Zone,
    And the hills of the Chankly Bore";
And they drank their health, and gave them a feast
Of dumplings made of beautiful yeast;
And every one said, "If we only live,
We too will go to sea in a Sieve,—
    To the hills of the Chankly Bore!"
        Far and few, far and few,
            Are the lands where the Jumblies live;
            Their heads are green, and their hands are blue,
                And they went to sea in a Sieve.

                                        Edward Lear

Epitaphs

I. ON WILL SMITH

Here lies Will Smith—and, what's something rarish,
He was born, bred, and hanged, all in the same parish.

II. AT GREAT TORRINGTON, DEVON

Here lies a man who was killed by lightning;
He died when his prospects seemed to be brightening,
He might have cut a flash in this world of trouble,
But the flash cut him, and he lies in the stubble.

III. AT ABERDEEN

Here lie I, Martin Elginbrodde:
Have mercy o' my soul, Lord God,
As I wad do, were I Lord God,
And ye were Martin Elginbrodde.

IV. MIKE O'DAY

This is the grave of Mike O'Day
Who died maintaining his right of way.
His right was clear, his will was strong,
But he's just as dead as if he'd been wrong.

V

Beneath this stone, a lump of clay,
Lies Arabella Young,
Who on the twenty-fourth of May
Began to hold her tongue.

VI. A CHURCHYARD IN WALES

Our life is but a summer's day:
Some only breakfast, and away:
Others to dinner stay, and are full fed:
The oldest man but sups, and goes to bed.
Large his account who lingers out the day;
Who goes the soonest, has the least to pay.

VII. ON AN INFANT EIGHT MONTHS OLD

Since I have been so quickly done for,
I wonder what I was begun for.

VIII

Here lies poor stingy Timmy Wyatt,
Who died at noon and saved a dinner by it.

IX

Wha lies here?   Hoo! Johnny, is that you?
I, Johnny Dow.   Ay, man, but a'm dead now.

X

Here lies I and my three daughters,
Killed by drinking Cheltenham waters;
If we had stuck to epsom salts,
We'd not been a-lying in these here vaults.

XI. SUFFOLK EPITAPH

Stranger pass by and waste no time
On bad biography and careless rhyme.
For what I am, this humble dust encloses;
And what I was is no affair of yourses.   *Anonymous*

XII. HERE SKUGG LIES SNUG

Here Skugg lies snug
As a bug in a rug.   *Benjamin Franklin*

XIII. AN EPITAPH

Here lies a most beautiful lady:
Light of step and heart was she;
I think she was the most beautiful lady
That ever was in the West Country.
But beauty vanishes; beauty passes;
However rare—rare it be;
And when I crumble, who will remember
This lady of the West Country?   *Walter de la Mare*

Horror Movie

Dr. Unlikely, we love you so,
You who made the double-headed rabbits grow
From a single hare. Mutation's friend,
Who could have prophesied the end
When the Spider Woman deftly snared the fly
And the monsters strangled in a monstrous kiss
And somebody hissed, "You'll hang for this!"?

Dear Dracula, sleeping on your native soil
(Any other kind makes him spoil),
How we clapped when you broke the French door down
And surprised the bride in the overwrought bed!
Perfectly dressed for lunar research,
Your evening cape added much,
Though the bride, inexplicably dressed in furs,
Was a study in jaded jugulars.

Poor, tortured Leopard Man, you changed your spots
In the debauched village of the Pin-Head Tots;
How we wrung our hands, how we wept
When the eighteenth murder proved inept,
And, caught in the Phosphorous Cave of Sea,
Dangling the last of synthetic flesh,
You said, "There's something wrong with me."

The Wolf Man knew when he prowled at dawn
Beginnings spin a web where endings spawn.
The bat who lived on shaving cream,
A household pet of Dr. Dream,
Unfortunately, maddened by the bedlam,
Turned on the Doc, bit the hand that fed him.

And you, Dr. X, who killed by moonlight,
We loved your scream in the laboratory
When the panel slid and the night was starry
And you threw the inventor in the crocodile pit
(An obscure point: Did he deserve it?)
And you took the gold to Transylvania
Where no one guessed how insane you were.

We thank you for the moral and the mood,
Dear Dr. Cliché, Nurse Platitude.
When we meet again by the Overturned Grave
Near the Sunken City of the Twisted Mind
(In the Son of the Son of Frankenstein),
Make the blood flow, make the motive muddy:
There's a little death in every body.   *Howard Moss*

Exodus

Uranium cumulus mushrooms bursting sores
Upon empyrean lawns impressed Them there,
Beneath the wondrous tree; the poison spores
Of radiocirrus fungi spread fresh fare
For theoretic thought in triplicate.
In unison with single voice They spoke:
"Since Adam's day the sacrificial smoke
Has grown too lushy rank to tolerate;
Our primal verdict favoring industry
Took no account of this polluted air.
That notion of expanding space may be
The stretch of time to save Our triune neck;
Let's pick a spot of universe to spare,
Perhaps between the Great and Lesser Bear,
And out of here right quickly get the heck!"

Roy Basler

If All the World Were Paper

If all the world were paper,
And all the sea were ink;
And all the trees were bread and cheese,
What should we do for drink?

If all the world were sand 'o,
Oh, then what should we lack 'o;
If as they say there were no clay,
How should we make tobacco?

If all our vessels ran 'a,
If none but had a crack 'a;
If Spanish apes ate all the grapes,
What should we do for sack 'a?

If fryers had no bald pates,
Nor nuns had no dark cloisters,
If all the seas were beans and peas,
What should we do for oysters?

If there had been no projects,
Nor none that did great wrongs;
If fiddlers shall turn players all,
What should we do for songs?

If all things were eternal,
And nothing their end bringing;
If this should be, then how should we
Here make an end of singing?   *Anonymous*

PART TWO

The Anatomy of Happiness

The Anatomy of Happiness

Lots of truisms don't have to be repeated but there is one that
has got to be,
Which is that it is much nicer to be happy than it is not to be,
And I shall even add to it by stating unequivocally and with-
out restraint
That you are much happier when you are happy than when
you ain't.
Some people are just naturally Pollyanna,
While others call for sugar and cream and strawberries on
their manna.
Now, I think we all ought to say a fig for the happiness that
comes of thinking helpful thoughts and searching your soul,
The most exciting happiness is the happiness generated by
forces beyond your control,
Because if you just depend on your helpful thoughts for your
happiness and would just as soon drink buttermilk as champagne, and if mink is no better than lapin to you,

43

Why you don't even deserve to have anything nice and exciting happen to you.

If you are really Master of your Fate,

It shouldn't make any difference to you whether Cleopatra or the Bearded Lady is your mate,

So I hold no brief for the kind of happiness or the kind of unhappiness that some people constantly carry around in their breast,

Because that kind of happiness simply consists of being resigned to the worst just as that kind of unhappiness consists of being resentful of the best.

No, there is only one kind of happiness that I take the stump for,

Which is the kind that comes when something so wonderful falls in your lap that joy is what you jump for,

Something not of your own doing,

When the blue sky opens and out pops a refund from the Government or an invitation to a terrapin dinner or an unhoped-for Yes from the lovely creature you have been disconsolately wooing.

And obviously such miracles don't happen every day,

But here's hoping they may,

Because then everybody would be happy except the people who pride themselves on creating their own happiness who as soon as they saw everybody who didn't create their own happiness happy they would probably grieve over sharing their own heretofore private sublimity,

A condition which I could face with equanimity.

Ogden Nash

In Praise of Diversity

Since this ingenious earth began
   To shape itself from fire and rubble;
Since God invented man, and man
   At once fell to, inventing trouble,
One virtue, one subversive grace
Has chiefly vexed the human race.

One whimsical beatitude,
   Concocted for his gain and glory,
Has man most stoutly misconstrued
   Of all the primal category—
Counting no blessing, but a flaw,
That Difference is the mortal law.

Adam, perhaps, while toiling late,
   With life a book still strange to read in,
Saw his new world, how variegate,
   And mourned, "It was not so in Eden,"
Confusing thus from the beginning
Unlikeness with original sinning.

And still the sons of Adam's clay
   Labor in person or by proxy
At altering to a common way
   The planet's holy heterodoxy.
Till now, so dogged is the breed,
Almost it seems that they succeed.

One shrill, monotonous, level note
   The human orchestra's reduced to.
Man casts his ballot, turns his coat,
   Gets born, get buried as he used to,
Makes war, makes love—but with a kind
Of masked and universal mind.

His good has no nuances. He
   Doubts or believes with total passion.
Heretics choose for heresy
   Whatever's the prevailing fashion.
Those wearing Tolerance for a label
Call other views intolerable.

"For or Against" 's the only rule.
   Damned are the unconvinced, the floaters.
Now all must go to public school,
   March with the League of Women Voters
Or else for safety get allied
With a unanimous Other Side.

There's white, there's black; no tint between.
   Truth is a plane that was a prism.
All's Blanshard that's not Bishop Sheen.
   All's treason that's not patriotism.
Faith, charity, hope—now all must fit
One pattern or its opposite.

Or so it seems. Yet who would dare
   Deny that nature planned it other
When every freckled thrush can wear
   A dapple various from his brother,

When each pale snowflake in the storm
Is false to some imagined norm?

Recalling then what surely was
    The earliest bounty of Creation:
That not a blade among the grass
    But flaunts its difference with elation,
Let us devoutly take no blame
If similar does not mean the same.

And grateful for the wit to see
    Prospects through doors we cannot enter,
Ah! let us praise Diversity
    Which holds the world upon its center.
Praise *con amour* or *furioso*
The large, the little and the soso.

Rejoice that under cloud and star
    The planet's more than Maine or Texas.
Bless the delightful fact there are
    Twelve months, nine muses, and two sexes,
And infinite in earth's dominions
Arts, climates, wonders and opinions.

Praise ice and ember, sand and rock,
    Tiger and dove and ends and sources;
Space travelers, and who only walk
    Like mailmen round familiar courses;
Praise vintage grapes and tavern Grappas,
And bankers and Phi Beta Kappas;

Each in its moment justified,
    Praise knowledge, theory, second guesses;
That which must wither or abide;
    Prim men, and men like wildernesses;
And men of peace and men of mayhem
And pipers and the ones who pay 'em.

Praise the disheveled, praise the sleek;
    Austerity and hearts-and-flowers;
People who turn the other cheek
    And extroverts who take cold showers;
Saints we can name a holy day for
And infidels whom saints can pray for.

Praise youth for pulling things apart,
    Toppling the idols, breaking leases;

Then from the upset apple-cart
  Praise oldsters picking up the pieces.
Praise wisdom, hard to be a friend to,
And folly one can condescend to.

Praise what conforms and what is odd,
  Remembering, if the weather worsens
Along the way, that even God
  Is said to be three separate Persons.
Then upright or upon the knee,
Praise Him that by His courtesy,
For all our prejudice and pains,
Diverse His Creature still remains.

                                   Phyllis McGinley

Oh, to Be In England Now the Weather's There!

Ah, lovely Devon . . .
Where it rains eight days out of seven!

                                   Anonymous

Final Thoughts on the Weather in England During 1953

The bright earth moves in destined grooves:
The speed of light remains the same,
The full moon's rise is no surprise—
All is predictable and tame.
When Isaac Newt. was bumped by fruit,
The speed at which his apple sped
Was neither less nor more, I guess,
Than that which bumps a modern head.
No physicist has ever missed
The permanence of nature's laws;
Astronomers will all aver
That wandering planets never pause;
The doctors know—they'll tell you so—
That measles always has a rash,
That if you fall from something tall
There's bound to be a nasty smash.
It takes no skill to know that ill
Will come from drinking gin in quarts
Or if you take ground glass in cake
You'll soon be feeling out of sorts.
There is no flaw in Mendel's law,
And Euclid's propositions yet

Refer to truths that modern youths
Are not permitted to forget.
Wise men and fools are bound by rules;
The universe is standardized;
The universe's primal curse
Is that it cannot be surprised.
Its laws are strict, we can predict
What x will do when faced by y;
It's got a norm, it's uniform,
It doesn't change and doesn't try.
There's only one way it can act—
And that's a sci-en-tif-ic fact!

Yet here in England, months together,
Nobody can predict the weather.

David Daiches

USA

X marks the spot where the body lies in time,
Bloody blotch that fell through the howling air:

By love betrayed, the letter read and burned?
Darling, I'm sorry, can't we just be friends?
By grim phone call at night, the stranger's voice
Muffled through cloth, but harder than a fist?
By dark disease, hidden from family,
But X-rays absolute proof: look, that gray blur—
With antiseptic shrug and surgical smile—
Six months, maybe a year?
                                   Is there a note,
Scrawled like a scream on paper?
                                   I tried! I tried!
I thought it would work. Only myself to blame.
Best years of my life. I still can't figure out
Where it went wrong. Good-bye.
                                   Or a woman's name
Dropped on the pale page like dripping sound,
That one word loud as if it were live blood.

Or an address hinting it would tell all,
That proved his lodge, happy to send a wreath,
A bench of brothers to mourn.
                                   Or a paragraph
Neat as an order book, thought out for days,
A model to be used for the next man

Tagged for that territory, giving the car,
His guns and tackle, to his oldest boy,
And all insurance to his wife (he'd been
Well-covered, naturally).
                                       Or not one word,
Just silence leering from an empty room
To hint that after liquor, drugs, and girls
He'd given up and let the lesion take him—
Guilt like an old wound groaning with the weather.

Nothing to show the weasel, conscience, snarled
Once before he grabbed it, cage and all,
And jumped into the glittering cage of air?

Nothing: no next room salesman to report
He'd heard a yell, as if one heard the blind
Cyclops bellow in his astonished cave.

But look—The cops are calling. Give 'im air.
Let the poor bastard breathe. He's coming to.

He's tougher than we thought—some broken bones,
Not much for a fall like that, he'll soon be back
Good as ever, one of the boys, to bounce
History on his knee like a bold blonde.   *Paul Engle*

Thoughts on One's Head

(In Plaster, with a Bronze Wash)

A person is always self-conscious about his head.
It makes one nervous just to know it is cast
In enduring materials, and that when the real one is dead,
The cast one, if nobody drops it or melts it down, will last.

We pay more attention to the front end, where the face is,
Than to the interesting and involute interior:
The Fissure of Rolando and such queer places
Are parks for the passions and fears and mild hysteria.

The things that go on there! Erotic movies are shown
To anyone not accompanied by an adult.
The marquee out front maintains a superior tone:
Documentaries on Sharks and The Japanese Tea Cult.

The fronts of some heads are extravagantly pretty.
These are the females. Men sometimes blow their tops.

About them, launch triremes, sack a whole city.
The female head is mounted on rococo props.

Judgment is in the head somewhere; it keeps sums
Of pleasure and pain and gives belated warning;
This is the first place everybody comes
With bills, complaints, writs, summons, in the morning.

This particular head, to my certain knowledge
Has been taught to read and write, make love and money,
Operate cars and airplanes, teach in a college,
And tell involved jokes, some few extremely funny.

It was further taught to know and to eschew
Error and sin, which it does erratically.
This is the place the soul calls home just now.
One dislikes it of course: it is the seat of Me.

William Meredith

Atomic Courtesy

To smash the simple atom
All mankind was intent.
    Now any day
    The atom may
Return the compliment.   *Ethel Jacobson*

Brave Old World

When the last H-bomb blast has done its stuff
And stilled for good the geiger counter's voice,
When nothing's left but just a few of us
Will come the moment of my dreadful choice:
Invent the peaceful wheel? Oh dear me, no!
Let those who would, assuage the general woe—
I plan to freeze my neighbors to the marrow
By being the inventor of the bow and arrow.

Elisabeth Lambert

On Limited Warfare

Don'tcha worry, honey chile.
Don'tcha cry no more,
It's jest a li'l ole atom bomb
In a li'l ole lim'ted war.

It's jest a bitsy warhead, chile,
On a li'l ole tactical shell,
And all it'll do is blow us-all
To a li'l ole lim'ted hell.

Anonymous

This Age, This Faust

Proton, neutron, electron,
Spin their dervish dances on
Through the bulky mastodon
And the great Napoleon,
But at last they meet, head-on,
The prodigious cyclotron,
And all cannons are outdone
In the blast of bombardon.

In this age of diverse fun,
I am merely Faust, *dit-on*,
The late lamented, twelfth-hour-gone,
Sans your leave alive, *pardon*,
Of modernism the paragon,
Handyman and devil's son,
Ready with that sharp *frisson*
Of horror mixed with belladon
—To justify the end, *bon ton*.

George Reavey

Epitaph for a Funny Fellow

He always was one for a jeer and a jest,
    And was given to iconoclasm;
His smile was sardonic, and seemed to suggest:
    "Let others arouse 'em; I razz 'em!"

His phrases were likely to smolder and scald,
    And act like a blister to bluster;
By the name of "buffoon" he was commonly called,
    Though possibly "jester" were juster.

We recently met; he was clouded in gloom;
    His spirit was battered, embittered.
He asked me to chisel these words on his tomb:
    "The universe tottered; I tittered."

Morris Bishop

So-and-So Reclining on Her Couch

On her side, reclining on her elbow.
This mechanism, this apparition,
Suppose we call it Projection A.

She floats in air at the level of
The eye, completely anonymous,
Born, as she was, at twenty-one,

Without lineage or language, only
The curving of her hip, as motionless gesture,
Eyes dripping blue, so much to learn.

If just above her head there hung,
Suspended in air, the slightest crown
Of Gothic prong and practick bright,

The suspension, as in solid space,
The suspending hand withdrawn, would be
An invisible gesture. Let this be called

Projection B. To get at the thing
Without gestures is to get at it as
Idea. She floats in the contention, the flux

Between the thing as idea and
The idea as thing. She is half who made her.
This is the final Projection, C.

The arrangement contains the desire of
The artist. But one confides in what has no
Concealed creator. One walks easily

The unpainted shore, accepts the world
As anything but sculpture. Good-bye,
Mrs. Pappadopoulos, and thanks.   *Wallace Stevens*

Oh, Stop Being Thankful All over the Place

In the glittering collection of paste diamonds one in particular
    ranks very high,
And that is the often-quoted remark of the prominent and
    respectable dignitary who on seeing a condemned man on
    his way to the scaffold crashed into a thousand antholo-
    gies by remarking, There but for the grace of God go I.

Here is a deplorable illustration
Of sloppy ratiocination;
Here is a notable feat
Of one-way thinking on a two-way street.
It must certainly have been the speaker's lucky day,
Or otherwise he would have been run over by his speech turning around and coming back the other way,
Because did he stop to work out his premise to its logical conclusion? Ah no,
He just got it off and let it go,
And now whenever people are with people they want to impress with their combined greatheartedness and book-learning they cry
Oh look at that condemned man on his way to the scaffold, there but for the grace of God go I.
Which is so far so good, but they neglect to continue with the heretofore unspoken balance of the theme, which is equally true,
That there but for the grace of God goes Jimmy Durante or the Prince of Wales or Aimee Semple McPherson or Dr. Wellington Koo,
Or Moses or Napoleon or Cleopatra or King Midas,
Or a man named Harris who is just getting over an attack of tonsilidas.
So away with you, all you parrot-like repeaters of high-sounding phrases that you never stop to consider what they actually mean,
I wouldn't allow you to stay in any college of which I was the Dean.
I can never listen to you without thinking Oh my,
There but for the grace of God speak I.

Ogden Nash

The Terrible People

People who have what they want are very fond of telling people
who haven't what they want that they really don't want it,
And I wish I could afford to gather all such people into a
gloomy castle on the Danube and hire half a dozen capa-
ble Draculas to haunt it.
I don't mind their having a lot of money, and I don't care how
they employ it,
But I do think that they damn well ought to admit they enjoy it.
But no, they insist on being stealthy
About the pleasures of being wealthy,
And the possession of a handsome annuity
Makes them think that to say how hard it is to make both ends
meet is their bounden duity.
You cannot conceive of an occasion
Which will find them without some suitable evasion.
Yes indeed, with arguments they are very fecund;
Their first point is that money isn't everything, and that they
have no money anyhow is their second.
Some people's money is merited,
And other people's is inherited,
But wherever it comes from,
They talk about it as if it were something you got pink gums
from.
This may well be,
But if so, why do they not relieve themselves of the burden by
transferring it to the deserving poor or to me?
Perhaps indeed the possession of wealth is constantly dis-
tressing,
But I should be quite willing to assume every curse of wealth
if I could at the same time assume every blessing.
The only incurable troubles of the rich are the troubles that
money can't cure,
Which is a kind of trouble that is even more troublesome if
you are poor.
Certainly there are lots of things in life that money won't buy,
but it's very funny—
Have you ever tried to buy them without money?

Ogden Nash

To a Lady on Her Passion for Old China

What ecstasies her bosom fire!
How her eyes languish with desire!
How blest, how happy should I be,
Were that fond glance bestow'd on me!
New doubts and fears within me war:
What rival's near? a china jar.

China's the passion of her soul;
A cup, a plate, a dish, a bowl,
Can kindle wishes in her breast,
Inflame with joy, or break her rest.

Some gems collect; some medals prize,
And view the rust with lover's eyes;
Some court the stars at midnight hours;
Some dote on Nature's charms in flowers!
But ev'ry beauty I can trace
In Laura's mind, in Laura's face;
My stars are in this brighter sphere,
My lily and my rose is here.

Philosophers more grave than wise
Hunt science down in butterflies;
Or fondly poring on a spider
Stretch human contemplation wider;
Fossils give joy to Galen's soul,
He digs for knowledge, like a mole;
In shells so learn'd, that all agree
No fish that swims knows more than he!
In such pursuits if wisdom lies,
Who, Laura, shall thy taste despise?

When I some antique jar behold,
Or white, or blue, or speck'd with gold,
Vessels so pure, and so refined,
Appear the types of woman-kind:
Are they not valued for their beauty,
Too fair, too fine, for household duty?
With flowers and gold and azure dyed,
Of ev'ry house the grace and pride?
How white, how polish'd is their skin,
And valued most when only seen!
She who before was highest prized,
Is for a crack or flaw despised;
I grant they're frail, yet they're so rare,
The treasure cannot cost too dear!
But man is made of coarser stuff,
And serves convenience well enough;
He's a strong earthen vessel made,

For drudging, labor, toil, and trade;
And when wives lose their other self,
With ease they bear the loss of delf.
  Husbands more covetous than sage
Condemn this china-buying rage;
They count that woman's prudence little,
Who sets her heart on things so brittle.
But are those wise men's inclinations
Fixt on more strong, more sure foundations?
If all that's frail we must despise,
No human view or scheme is wise.
Are not ambition's hopes as weak?
They swell like bubbles, shine and break.
A courtier's promise is so slight,
'Tis made at noon, and broke at night.
What pleasure's sure? The miss you keep
Breaks both your fortune and your sleep,
The man who loves a country life,
Breaks all the comforts of his wife;
And if he quit his farm and plow,
His wife in town may break her vow.
Love, Laura, love, while youth is warm,
For each new winter breaks a charm,
And woman's not like china sold,
But cheaper grows in growing old;
Then quickly choose the prudent part,
Or else you break a faithful heart.   *John Gay*

Beauty

Beauty, thou wild fantastic ape,
Who dost in ev'ry country change thy shape!
Here black, there brown, here tawny, and there white;
Thou flatt'rer which compli'st with every sight!
  Thou babel which confound'st the eye
With unintelligible variety!
Who hast no certain what, nor where,
But vary'st still, and dost thy self declare
  Inconstant, as thy she-professors are.

Beauty, love's scene and masquerade,
So gay by well-plac'd lights, and distance made;
False coin, with which th' impostor cheats us still;
The stamp and color good, but metal ill!
  Which light, or base we find, when we
Weigh by enjoyment, and examine thee!
  For though thy being be but show,

'Tis chiefly night which men to thee allow:
And choose t'enjoy thee, when thou least art thou.

    Beauty, thou active, passive ill!
Which diest thy self as fast as thou dost kill!
Thou tulip, who thy stock in paint dost waste,
Neither for physic good, nor smell, nor taste.
    Beauty, whose flames but meteors are,
Short-liv'd and low, though thou wouldst seem a star,
    Who dar'st not thine own home descry,
Pretending to dwell richly in the eye,
When thou, alas, dost in the fancy lie.

    Beauty, whose conquests still are made
O'er hearts by cowards kept, or else betray'd!
Weak victor! who thy self destroy'd must be
When sickness storms, or time besieges thee!
    Thou unwholesome thaw to frozen age!
Thou strong wine, which youth's fever dost enrage,
    Thou tyrant which leav'st no man free!
Thou subtle thief, from whom nought safe can be!
Thou murth'rer which hast kill'd, and devil which
        wouldst damn me.

Abraham Cowley

Thoughts Thought While Waiting for a Pronouncement from a Doctor, a Big Executive, the Department of Internal Revenue, or Any Other Momentous Pronouncer

Is Time on my hands? Yes, it is; it is on my hands and my face
        and my torso and my tendons of Achilles,
And, frankly, it gives me the willies.
The quarter-hour grows to the half-hour as chime clings to the
        tail of the preceding chime,
And I am tarred and feathered with Time.
No matter how frantically I shake my hands, the hours will not
        drop off or evaporate,
Nor will even the once insignificant minutes coöperate.
The clock has stopped at Now; there is no Past, no Future,
        and, oddly enough, also no Now;
Only the hot, moist, beaded seconds on the brow,
Only the days and nights in a gluey lump,
And the smothering weeks that stick like a swarm of bees to
        a stump.
Time stands still, or it moves forward or backward, or at least
        it exists for ex-Senator Rush Holt, for Dr. Dafoe, for
        Simon & Schuster, yes, and for Schiaparelli,

But for me it is limbo akimbo, an inverted void, a mouse with
    its tail pulled out of its mouth through its belly.
O, The World's Most Honored Watch, I haven't been there,
    I've been here,
For how long—for one small seventeen-jeweled tick, or have I
    been sitting a year?
I'm a speck in infinite space,
Entombed behind my face.
Shall I suddenly start to gyrate, to rotate, to spiral, to expand
    through a nebular process to a new universe, maybe, or
    maybe only a galaxy?
But such a Goldbergian scheme to extinguish one lonely iden-
    tity seems, well, under-simplified and, if I may say so,
    smart-alexy.
Oh, I shall arise and go now, preferably in a purple-and-gold
    palanquin
Borne on the copper shoulders of a Seminole, an Apache, a
    Crow, and an Algonquin,
And whatever be my heart's desire, be it a new understanding
    of Time or a cup of dew gathered from the spring's
    first jonquil.
Why, if none of the other three will bring it to me, why, per-
    haps the Algonquil.

Ogden Nash

Fire and Ice

Some say the world will end in fire,
Some say in ice.
From what I've tasted of desire
I hold with those who favor fire.
But if it had to perish twice,
I think I know enough of hate
To say that for destruction ice
Is also great
And would suffice.

Robert Frost

The Jung Idea

The young things who frequent picture-palaces
Have no use for this psycho-analysis;
    And although Doctor Freud
    Would be distinctly annoyed
They cling to their long-standing fallacies.

P. H.

Sestina of the Tramp-Royal

Speakin' in general, I 'ave tried 'em all—
The 'appy roads that take you o'er the world.
Speakin' in general, I 'ave found them good
For such as cannot use one bed too long,
But must get 'ence, the same as I 'ave done,
An' go observin' matters till they die.

What do it matter where or 'ow we die,
So long as we've our 'ealth to watch it all—
The different ways that different things are done,
An' men an' women lovin' in this world;
Takin' our chances as they come along,
An' when they ain't, pretendin' they are good?

In cash or credit—no, it aren't no good;
You 'ave to 'ave the 'abit or you'd die,
Unless you lived your life but one day long,
Nor didn't prophesy nor fret at all,
But drew your tucker some'ow from the world,
An' never bothered what you might ha' done.

But, Gawd, what things are they I 'aven't done!
I've turned my 'and to most, an' turned it good,
In various situations round the world—
For 'im that doth not work must surely die;
But that's no reason man should labor all
'Is life on one same shift—life's none so long.

Therefore, from job to job I've moved along.
Pay couldn't 'old me when my time was done,
For something in my 'ead upset it all,
Till I 'ad dropped whatever 't was for good,
An' out at sea, be'eld the dock-lights die,
An' met my mate—the wind that tramps the world!

It's like a book, I think, this bloomin' world,
Which you can read and care for just so long,
But presently you feel that you will die
Unless you get the page you're readin' done,
An' turn another—likely not so good;
But what you're after is to turn 'em all.

Gawd bless this world! Whatever she 'ath done—
Excep' when awful long—I've found it good.
So write, before I die, " 'E liked it all!"

Rudyard Kipling

The Last Leaf

I saw him once before,
As he passed by the door,
   And again
The pavement stones
  resound,
As he totters o'er the ground
   With his cane.

They say that in his prime,
Ere the pruning-knife of
  Time
   Cut him down,
Not a better man was found
By the Crier on his round
   Through the town.

But now he walks the streets,
And he looks at all he meets
   Sad and wan,
And he shakes his feeble
  head,
That it seems as if he said,
   "They are gone."

The mossy marbles rest
On the lips that he has pressed
   In their bloom,
And the names he loved to
  hear
Have been carved for many
  a year
   On the tomb.

My grandmamma has said—
Poor old lady, she is dead
   Long ago—
That he had a Roman nose,
And his cheek was like a rose
   In the snow;

But now his nose is thin,
And it rests upon his chin
   Like a staff,
And a crook is in his back,
And a melancholy crack
   In his laugh.

I know it is a sin
For me to sit and grin
   At him here;
But the old three-cornered
  hat,
And the breeches, and all
  that,
   Are so queer!

And if I should live to be
The last leaf upon the tree
   In the spring,
Let them smile, as I do now,
At the old forsaken bough
   Where I cling.

O. W. Holmes

The Labyrinth

Anthropos apteros for days
Walked whistling round and round the Maze,
Relying happily upon
His temperament for getting on.

The hundredth time he sighted, though,
A bush he left an hour ago,
He halted where four alleys crossed,
And recognized that he was lost.

"Where am I? Metaphysics says
No question can be asked unless
It has an answer, so I can
Assume this maze has got a plan.

If theologians are correct,
A Plan implies an Architect:
A God-built maze would be, I'm sure,
The Universe in miniature.

Are data from the world of Sense,
In that case, valid evidence?
What in the universe I know
Can give directions how to go?

All Mathematics would suggest
A steady straight line as the best,
But left and right alternately
Is consonant with History.

Aesthetics, though, believes all Art
Intends to gratify the Heart:
Rejecting disciplines like these,
Must I, then, go which way I please?

Such reasoning is only true
If we accept the classic view,
Which we have no right to assert,
According to the Introvert.

His absolute presupposition
Is—Man creates his own condition:
This maze was not divinely built,
But is secreted by my guilt.

The center that I cannot find
Is known to my Unconscious Mind;
I have no reason to despair
Because I am already there.

My problem is how *not* to will;
They move most quickly who stand still;
I'm only lost until I see
I'm lost because I want to be.

If this should fail, perhaps I should,
As certain educators would,
Content myself with the conclusion;
In theory there is no solution.

All statements about what I feel,
Like I-am-lost, are quite unreal:
My knowledge ends where it began;
A hedge is taller than a man."

Anthropos apteros, perplexed
To know which turning to take next,
Looked up and wished he were the bird
To whom such doubts must seem absurd.

W. H. Auden

I Never Even Suggested It

I know lots of men who are in love and lots of men who are
    married and lots of men who are both,
And to fall out with their loved ones is what all of them are
    most loth.
They are conciliatory at every opportunity.
Because all they want is serenity and a certain amount of im-
    punity.
Yes, many the swain who has finally admitted that the earth
    is flat
Simply to sidestep a spat,
Many the masculine Positively or Absolutely which has been
    diluted to an If

Simply to avert a tiff,
Many the two-fisted executive whose domestic conversation is
limited to a tactfully interpolated Yes,
And then he is amazed to find that he is being raked backwards
over a bed of coals nevertheless.
These misguided fellows are under the impression that it takes
two to make a quarrel, that you can sidestep a crisis by non-
aggression and nonresistance,
Instead of removing yourself to a discreet distance.
Passivity can be a provoking *modus operandi;*
Consider the Empire and Gandhi.
Silence is golden, but sometimes invisibility is golder.
Because loved ones may not be able to make bricks without
straw but often they don't need any straw to manufacture a
bone to pick or blood in their eye or a chip for their soft
white shoulder.
It is my duty, gentlemen, to inform you that women are dicta-
tors all, and I recommend to you this moral:
In real life it takes only one to make a quarrel.

Ogden Nash

Three Links of Light Armour

I. LADY SHOPPERS, BEWARE

Show-window manikins
Have slenderer fannykins.

II. MIDDLE AGE

Middle age is a time of life
That a man first notices in his wife.

III. OFF-THE-CUFF REMARK ON OFF-THE-SHOULDER DRESSES

Here's one conviction that I hold
I've never been in error:
If low-cut dresses leave you cold,
You're probably the wearer.

Richard Armour

Unquestionable Questions

Why are doors brass,
Or blocks square,
Or why do mothers
Braid their daughters' hair?

Hy Sobiloff

Thoughts on Progress

In days of old when knights caught cold,
They were not quickly cured;
No aspirin pill would check the ill,
Which had to be endured.
You sat it out if toothache hurt you;
Patience was esteemed a virtue.

The dentist's way in Hogarth's day
Was pretty rough and ready;
His foot he'd rest an patient's breast
To keep his pincers steady,
And if the dentist's patient screamed,
The dentist was the more esteemed.

De Quincey's age could well assuage
Some kinds of pain and grief;
To bard in bed with aching head
Laudanum gave relief,
And sometimes in the process brought
A quickening of poetic thought.

When chloroform became the norm
For those who faced the surgeon,
A man or wife would meet the knife
Without excessive urgin',
And dentists learned to stop the pain
With useful things like novocain.

The anesthetic's with us yet,
And so's the analgesic,
And dramamine relieves the keen
Afflictions of the seasick.
And we've new blessings for the ill in
Sulfa drugs and penicillin.

When modern wight retires at night
With streptomycin handy,
He finds repose at once; he knows
That everything is dandy.
No fear of sudden plague will keep
The trustful modern from his sleep.

Yet pharmacists have got long lists
Of pills that hasten slumber,
And they report that of that sort

They sell a shocking number,
For somehow still we cannot find,
It seems, a settled peace of mind.

Try, try again, you medicine men!
The riddle's tough and bitter;
We've got the drugs that kill the bugs
But still we tense and jitter.
Ancestral terrors haunt us still—
Anxiety, where is thy pill?   *David Daiches*

To Be or Not to Be

I sometimes think I'd rather crow
And be a rooster than to roost
And be a crow. But I dunno.

A rooster he can roost also,
Which don't seem fair when crows can't crow.
Which may help, some. Still I dunno.

Crows should be glad of one thing, though;
Nobody thinks of eating crow,
While roosters they are good enough
For anyone unless they're tough.

There are lots of tough old roosters though,
And anyway a crow can't crow,
So mebby roosters stand more show.
It looks that way. But I dunno.   *Anonymous*

What Are Folks Made Of?

What are little boys made of, made of?
What are little boys made of?
Piggins and pails and little puppy tails,
That's what little boys are made of.
What are little girls made of? etc.
Sugar and spice and all things nice
And that's what little girls are made of.
What are young men made of? etc.
Thorns and briars, they're all bad liars,
And that's what young men are made of.
What's young women made of? etc.
Rings and jings and all fine things
And that's what young women's made of.
What are old men made of? etc.
Whiskey and brandy and sugar and candy,
And that's what old men are made of.   *Anonymous*

Upon Differences of Opinion

My cousin's wife, the diabetic,
And me, the asthmatic:
So you go to your church,
And I'll go to mine.   *Hy Sobiloff*

Fruits of Experience

Pomegranates come from red hot pearls.
Cherries are the hearts of baby girls.
Persimmons come up on the bosom of dawn.
Plums fill the sky when the day is gone.
Pineapples grow on the heads of kings.
Bananas are nothing but naughty things.

A serious person is a serious business
and serious business is a serious thing
and serious things are very serious
and taken seriously are dead serious
and nothing is as serious as a serious person
and a serious person is seriously dead.
                    James Broughton

Fable

The mountain and the squirrel
Had a quarrel;
And the former called the latter "Little Prig."
Bun replied,
"You are doubtless very big;
But all sorts of things and weather
Must be taken in together
To make up a year
And a sphere.
And I think it's no disgrace
To occupy my place.
If I'm not so large as you,
You are not so small as I,
And not half so spry.
I'll not deny you make
A very pretty squirrel track;
Talents differ: all is well and wisely put;
If I cannot carry forests on my back,
Neither can you crack a nut."   *R. W. Emerson*

PART THREE

Rigmaroles, Burlesques, and Tours de Force

What's the Matter, Haven't You Got Any Sense of Humor?

There is at least one thing I would less rather have in the neigh-
borhood than a gangster,
And that one thing is a practical prankster.
I feel that we should differ more sharply than Montagues and
Capulets or York and Lancaster,
Me and a practical prancaster.
If there is a concentration camp in limbo, that is the spot for
which I nominate them,
Not because I don't like them, but simply because I abominate
them.
The born practical prankster starts out in early youth by offer-
ing people a chair,
And when they sit down it isn't there,
And he is delighted and proceeds to more complicated wheezes,

67

Such as ten cent X-rays to see through people's clothes with
    and powders to give them itches and sneezes,
And his boutonniere is something that people get squirted in
    the eye out of,
And their beds are what he makes apple pie out of.
Then as he matures he widens his scope,
And he is no longer content to present people with exploding
    cigars and chocolate creams with centers of soap,
So he dresses up as an Oriental potentate and reviews the
    British fleet,
Or collects a little group of kinsprits and a few pickaxes and a
    STREET CLOSED sign and digs up a busy street,
And if people are jumpy about their past or present private
    lives he hints that he is writing his memoirs and is devoting
    an entire chapter to their particular skeleton,
And finally he reaches the apex of his career when he slips into
    somebody's bathroom and fills up all the modern conven-
    iences with water and then adds raspberry gelatin.
I have recently read with complete satisfaction of a practical
    prankster two of whose friends had just been married,
Which was of course in itself simply a challenge to be harried,
And it was a challenge he was eager to meet,
And he went to the roof of their hotel and tied a rope around
    his waist and a colleague lowered him to where he could
    clash a pair of cymbals outside the window of the nuptial
    suite,
And he weighed two hundred and eighty pounds and the rope
    broke,
And that to my mind is the perfect practical joke. *Ogden Nash*

I Am Rose

I am Rose my eyes are blue
I am Rose and who are you
I am Rose and when I sing
I am Rose like anything   *Gertrude Stein*

This Is the Key

This is the key of the kingdom:
In that kingdom there is a city.
In that city there is a town.
In that town there is a street.
In that street there is a lane.
In that lane there is a yard.
In that yard there is a house.
In that house there is a room.
In that room there is a bed.
On that bed there is a basket.
In that basket there are some flowers.

Flowers in a basket.
Basket in the bed.
Bed in the room.
Room in the house.
House in the yard.
Yard in the lane.
Lane in the street.
Street in the town.
Town in the city.
City in the kingdom.
Of the kingdom this is the key.

Anonymous

Peanuts

The boy stood on the burning deck
Eating peanuts by the peck;
His father called him, he wouldn't go,
Because he loved the peanuts so.

Anonymous

The Purple Cow

I never saw a Purple Cow,
  I never hope to see one;
But I can tell you, anyhow,
  I'd rather see than be one.

Gelett Burgess

Ah, yes, I wrote the "Purple Cow"—
  I'm sorry, now, I wrote it!
But I can tell you, anyhow,
  I'll kill you if you quote it.

Gelett Burgess

Who Wants to Travel All Over Europe and See Nothing but a Lot of American Tourists? I Do

This is the season when I long for a pen as sadly eloquent as
    Verlaine's,
The season of teeming sea lanes and air lanes,
When life is a round of farewell parties for friends departing
    toward Venice and Paris
And the Greek islands and the Edinburgh Festival and the Vale
    of Kashmir, with side trips on the Kungsholm and the
    Stella Polaris.
Everybody else is boarding a plane or a liner or a sailing vessel
    with a real kitchen and baths, and cabins with eight-foot
    headroom,
And you are pricing air-conditioners for your bedroom,
Which you never get to get, because the economic reasons ad-
    vanced for staying at home turn out to be a fraud,
Because the going-away presents cost you more than the air-
    conditioner, and, indeed, as much as a trip abroad.
Here is one Odysseus who is tired of fretting over the cost of a
    bus trip to Ashtabula,
Who is tired of being an island of indigence in a sea of moola.
Would I were one of that foursome of Texans who wished to
    play golf at St. Andrews, far from the land of their birth,
And the caddie master said he was out of caddies and they said,
    Well, just this once we'll go around in Chevvies, but
    don't let it get back to Fort Worth.   *Ogden Nash*

Pointillism

The Duke di Broccoli and the Countess of Points,
Entertained at the home of Demijohn J. Pavilion.
At Antibes, a twelvemonth of deluxe.

Duchess was not till Irma came;
Points fell, and deluxe was the issue;
The Broccoli bed a field in dispute.

These nobles dined on filigree of potassium;
Permanganate their purple drink.
This vintage bubbled in the cup.
Mr. Pavilion was astonished.

The Countess wore a long black gown,
A candle in her lampblack hair.
The Duchess whirled in motorcars,
Came and went in pale peach dresses.
Pavilion's cobblestones beheld the Duke.

He Broccoli now held a pipe
And gazed upon the sunset of
The western sea. His vegetables
Were ruminant; his women shrieked.

Peach Irma ran upon the cliff.
Her sails were pale, and potash Points
Pursued with cruel diamonds.
Her jealousy in jagged points
Went black and darting, fixing in
The sails. A baleful card! (The Queen
Of Spades) But Broccoli waits beneath
The cliff with skiff; deluxe will save.   *Joseph Bennett*

Mr. Walter de la Mare Makes the Little Ones Dizzy

Speckled with glints of star and moonshine,
The house is dark and still as stone,
And Fido sleeps in the dogwood kennel
With forelegs over his mutton bone.

Then out of the walnut wood, the squirrels
Peep, with their bushy tails upreared,
And the oak on the wood's-edge stretches his branches,
And combs with his roots his mossy beard.

Then ninnies and oafs and hook-nosed zanies,
And rabbits bred in the realm of Wales,
Dance and scream in the frosty starlight,
Swinging the squirrels by the tails.

Till out of the wood, Grandfather Nightmare
Rides in a chariot of Stilton cheese,
And eats the ninnies, the oafs and zanies,
The rabbits, the oak and the walnut trees.
    Samuel Hoffenstein

The March to Moscow

The Emperor Nap he would set off
On a summer excursion to Moscow;
The fields were green and the sky was blue,
Morbleu! Parbleu!
What a splendid excursion to Moscow!

The Emperor Nap he talk'd so big
That he frighten'd Mr. Roscoe.
And Counsellor Brougham was all in a fume
At the thought of the march to Moscow:
The Russians, he said, they were undone,
And the great Fee-Faw-Fum
Would presently come.
With a hop, step, and jump, unto London,
For, as for his conquering Russia,
However some persons might scoff it,
Do it he could, do it he would,
And from doing it nothing would come but good,
And nothing would call him off it.

But the Russians stoutly they turned to
Upon the road to Moscow.
Nap had to fight his way all through;
They could fight, though they could not parlez-vous;
But the fields were green, and the sky was blue,
Morbleu! Parbleu!
But to march back again from Moscow.

The Russians they stuck close to him
All on the road from Moscow—
And Shouvaloff he shovell'd them off,
And Markoff he mark'd them off,
And Krosnoff he cross'd them off,
And Touchkoff he touch'd them off,
And Boroskoff he bored them off,
And Kutousoff he cut them off,
And Parenzoff he pared them off,
And Worronzoff he worried them off,
And Doctoroff he doctor'd them off,
And Rodinoff he flogg'd them off.
And, last of all, an Admiral came,
A terrible man with a terrible name,
A name which you all know by sight very well,
But which no one can speak, and no one can spell.

And then came on the frost and snow
    All on the road from Moscow.
Worse and worse every day the elements grew,
The fields were so white and the sky was so blue,
        Sacrebleu! Ventrebleu!
What a horrible journey from Moscow.

Too cold upon the road was he;
Too hot he had been at Moscow;
But colder and hotter he may be,
For the grave is colder than Muscovy;
And a place there is to be kept in view,
Where the fire is red, and the brimstone blue,
        Morbleu! Parbleu!
But there he must stay for a very long day,
For from thence there is no stealing away,
    As there was on the road from Moscow.

Robert Southey

The Cutty Wren

O where are you going, says Milder to Malder,
O, I cannot tell, says Festel to Fose,
We're going to the woods, says John the Red Nose,
We're going to the woods, says John the Red Nose.

O, what will you do there, says Milder to Malder,
O, I cannot tell, says Festel to Fose,
We'll shoot the Cutty Wren, says John the Red Nose,
We'll shoot the Cutty Wren, says John the Red Nose.

O, how will you shoot her, says Milder to Malder,
O, I cannot tell, says Festel to Fose,
With arrows and bows, says John the Red Nose,
With arrows and bows, says John the Red Nose.

O, that will not do, says Milder to Malder,
O, what will do then, says Festel to Fose,
Big guns and cannons, says John the Red Nose,
Big guns and cannons, says John the Red Nose.

O, how will you bring her home, says Milder to Malder,
O, I cannot tell, says Festel to Fose,
On four strong men's shoulders, says John the Red Nose,
On four strong men's shoulders, says John the Red Nose.

O, that will not do, says Milder to Malder,
O, what will do then, says Festel to Fose,

Big carts and waggons, says John the Red Nose,
Big carts and waggons, says John the Red Nose.

O, what will you cut her up with, says Milder to Malder,
O, I cannot tell, says Festel to Fose,
With knives and with forks, says John the Red Nose,
With knives and with forks, says John the Red Nose.

O, that will not do, says Milder to Malder,
O, what will do then, says Festel to Fose,
Hatchets and cleavers, says John the Red Nose,
Hatchets and cleavers, says John the Red Nose.

O, how will you boil her, says Milder to Malder,
O, I cannot tell, says Festel to Fose,
In pots and in kettles, says John the Red Nose,
In pots and in kettles, says John the Red Nose.

O, that will not do, says Milder to Malder,
O, what will do then, says Festel to Fose,
Brass pans and cauldrons, says John the Red Nose,
Brass pans and cauldrons, says John the Red Nose.

O, who'll have the spare ribs, says Milder to Malder,
O, I cannot tell, says Festel to Fose,
We'll give them to the poor, says John the Red Nose,
We'll give them to the poor, says John the Red Nose.

Anonymous

Epilogue

"O where are you going?" said reader to rider,
"That valley is fatal when furnaces burn,
Yonder's the midden whose odors will madden,
That gap is the grave where the tall return."

"O do you imagine," said fearer to farer,
"That dusk will delay on your path to the pass,
Your diligent looking discover the lacking
Your footsteps feel from granite to grass?"

"O what was that bird," said horror to hearer,
"Did you see that shape in the twisted trees?
Behind you swiftly the figure comes softly,
The spot on your skin is a shocking disease."

"Out of this house"—said rider to reader
"Yours never will"—said farer to fearer
"They're looking for you"—said hearer to horror
As he left them there, as he left them there.

W. H. Auden

The Poet's Welcome to His Love-begotten Daughter

Thou's welcome, wean! mishanter fa' me,
If ought of thee, or of thy mammy,
Shall ever daunton me, or awe me,
    My sweet wee lady,
Or if I blush when thou shalt ca' me
    Tit-ta or daddy.

Wee image of my bonnie Betty,
I fatherly will kiss and daut thee,
As dear an' near my heart I set thee
    Wi' as guid will,
As a' the priests had seen me get thee
    That's out o' hell.

What tho' they ca' me fornicator,
An' tease my name in kintra clatter:
The mair they talk I'm kent the better,
    E'en let them clash;
An auld wife's tongue's a feckless matter
    To gie ane fash.

Welcome, my bonnie, sweet wee dochter—
Tho' ye come here a wee unsought for,
An' tho' your comin' I hae fought for
    Baith kirk an' queir;
Yet, by my faith, ye're no unwrought for!
    That I shall swear!

Sweet fruit o' mony a merry dint,
My funny toil is now a' tint,
Sin' thou came to the warl asklent,
    Which fools may scoff at;
In my last plack thy part's be in't—
    The better half o't.

An' if thou be what I wad hae thee,
An' tak the counsel I shall gie thee,
A lovin' father I'll be to thee,
      If thou be spar'd;
Thro' a' thy childish years I'll ee thee,
      An' think't weel war'd.

Tho' I should be the waur bested,
Thou's be as braw an' bienly clad,
An' thy young years as nicely bred
      Wi' education,
As ony brat o' wedlock's bed
      In a' thy station.

Gude grant that thou may aye inherit
Thy mither's person, grace, an' merit,
An' thy poor worthless daddy's spirit,
      Without his failins;
'Twill please me mair to see and hear o't,
      Than stockit mailins.   *Robert Burns*

John Henry

John Henry was a lil baby,
Sittin' on his mama's knee,
Said: "De Big Bend Tunnel on de C. & O. road
Gonna cause de death of me,
Lawd, lawd, gonna cause de death of me."

Cap'n says to John Henry,
"Gonna bring me a steam drill 'round,
Gonna take dat steam drill out on de job,
Gonna whop dat steel on down,
Lawd, Lawd, gonna whop dat steel on down."

John Henry tol' his cap'n,
Lightnin' was in his eye:
"Cap'n, bet yo' las' red cent on me,
Fo' I'll beat it to de bottom or I'll die,
Lawd, Lawd, I'll beat it to de bottom or I'll die."

Sun shine hot an' burnin',
Wer'n't no breeze a-tall,
Sweat ran down like water down a hill,
Dat day John Henry let his hammer fall,
Lawd, Lawd, dat day John Henry let his hammer fall.

John Henry went to de tunnel,
An' dey put him in de lead to drive,

De rock so tall an' John Henry so small,
Dat he lied down his hammer an' he cried,
Lawd, Lawd, dat he lied down his hammer an' he cried.

John Henry started on de right hand,
De steam drill started on de lef'—
"Before I'd let dis steam drill beat me down,
I'd hammer my fool self to death,
Lawd, Lawd, I'd hammer my fool self to death."

White man tol' John Henry,
"Nigger, damn yo' soul,
You might beat dis steam an' drill of mine,
When de rocks in dis mountain turn to gol',
Lawd, Lawd, when de rocks in dis mountain turn to gol'."

John Henry said to his shaker,
"Nigger, why don' you sing?
I'm throwin' twelve poun's from my hips on down,
Jes' listen to de col' steel ring,
Lawd, Lawd, jes' listen to de col' steel ring."

Oh, de captain said to John Henry,
"I b'lieve this mountain's sinkin' in."
John Henry said to his captain, oh my!
"Ain' nothin' but my hammer suckin' win',
Lawd, Lawd, ain' nothin' but my hammer suckin' win'."

John Henry tol' his shaker,
"Shaker, you better pray,
For, if I miss dis six-foot steel,
Tomorrow'll be yo' buryin' day,
Lawd, Lawd, tomorrow'll be yo' buryin' day."

John Henry tol' his captain,
"Look yonder what I see—
Yo' drill's done broke an' yo' hole's done choke,
An' you cain' drive steel like me,
Lawd, Lawd, an' you cain' drive steel like me."

De man dat invented de steam drill,
Thought he was mighty fine.
John Henry drove his fifteen feet,
An' de steam drill only made nine,
Lawd, Lawd, an' de steam drill only made nine.

De hammer dat John Henry swung,
It weighed over nine pound;

He broke a rib in his lef'-han' side,
An' his intrels fell on de groun',
Lawd, Lawd, an' his intrels fell on de groun'.

All de womens in de Wes',
When dey heared of John Henry's death,
Stood in de rain, flagged de eas'-boun' train,
Goin' where John Henry fell dead,
Lawd, Lawd, goin' where John Henry fell dead.

John Henry's lil mother,
She was all dressed in red,
She jumped in bed, covered up her head,
Said she didn' know her son was dead,
Lawd, Lawd, didn' know her son was dead.

Dey took John Henry to de graveyard,
An' dey buried him in de san',
An' every locomotive come roarin' by,
Says, "Dere lays a steel-drivin' man,
Lawd, Lawd, dere lays a steel-drivin' man."

Anonymous

To a Lady

Of the Characters of Women

Nothing so true as what you once let fall,
"Most women have no characters at all."
    How many pictures of one nymph we view,
All how unlike each other, all how true!
Arcadia's Countess, here, in ermined pride,
Is, there, Pastora by a fountain side.
Here Fannia, leering on her own good man,
And there, a naked Leda with a swan.
Let then the fair one beautifully cry,
In Magdalen's loose hair, and lifted eye,
Or dressed in smiles of sweet Cecilia shine,
With simp'ring angels, palms, and harps divine;
Whether the charmer sinner it, or saint it,
If folly grow romantic, I must paint it.
    Come then, the colors and the ground prepare!
Dip in the rainbow, trick her off in air;
Choose a firm cloud, before it fall, and in it
Catch, ere she change, the Cynthia of this minute,
    Rufa, whose eye quick-glancing o'er the park,
Attracts each light gay meteor of a spark,

Agrees as ill with Rufa studying Locke,
As Sappho's diamonds with her dirty smock;
Or Sappho at her toilet's greasy task,
With Sappho fragrant at an evening masque:
So morning insects that in muck begun,
Shine, buzz, and fly-blow in the setting sun.

How soft is Silia! fearful to offend;
The frail one's advocate, the weak one's friend:
To her, Calista proved her conduct nice;
And good Simplicius asks of her advice.
Sudden, she storms! she raves! You tip the wink,
But spare your censure; Silia does not drink.
All eyes may see from what the change arose,
All eyes may see—a pimple on her nose.

Papillia, wedded to her am'rous spark,
Sighs for the shades—"How charming is a park!"
A park is purchased, but the fair he sees
All bathed in tears—"Oh, odious, odious trees!"

Ladies, like variegated tulips, show;
'Tis to their changes half their charms we owe;
Fine by defect, and delicately weak,
Their happy spots the nice admirer take,
'Twas thus Calypso once each heart alarmed,
Awed without virtue, without beauty charmed;
Her tongue bewitched as oddly as her eyes,
Less wit than mimic, more a wit than wise;
Strange graces still, and stranger flights she had,
Was just not ugly, and was just not mad;
Yet ne'er so sure our passion to create,
As when she touched the brink of all we hate.

Narcissa's nature, tolerably mild,
To make a wash, would hardly stew a child;
Has even been proved to grant a lover's prayer,
And paid a tradesman once to make him stare;
Gave alms at Easter, in a Christian trim,
And made a widow happy, for a whim.
Why then declare good-nature is her scorn,
When 'tis by that alone she ban be borne?
Why pique all mortals, yet affect a name?
A fool to pleasure, yet a slave to fame:
Now deep in Taylor and the Book of Martyrs,
Now drinking citron with his Grace and Chartres:
Now conscience chills her, and now passion burns;
And atheism and religion take their turns;
A very heathen in the carnal part,
Yet still a sad, good Christian at her heart.

See sin in state, majestically drunk;
Proud as a peeress, prouder as a punk;
Chaste to her husband, frank to all beside,
A teeming mistress, but a barren bride.
What then? let blood and body bear the fault,
Her head's untouched, that noble seat of thought:
Such this day's doctrine—in another fit
She sins with poets through pure love of wit.
What has not fired her bosom or her brain?
Cæsar and Tall-boy, Charles and Charlemagne.
As Helluo, late Dictator of the Feast,
The nose of Hautgout, and the tip of taste,
Critic'd your wine, and analyzed your meat,
Yet on plain pudding deigned at home to eat;
So Philomedé, lect'ring all mankind
On the soft passion, and the taste refined,
Th' address, the delicacy—stoops at once,
And makes her hearty meal upon a dunce.

Flavia's a wit, has too much sense to pray;
To toast our wants and wishes, is her way;
Nor asks of God, but of her stars, to give
The mighty blessing, "while we live, to live."
Then all for death, that opiate of the soul!
Lucretia's dagger, Rosamonda's bowl.
Say, what can cause such impotence of mind?
A spark too fickle, or a spouse too kind.
Wise wretch! with pleasures too refined to please;
With too much spirit to be e'er at ease;
With too much quickness ever to be taught;
With too much thinking to have common thought:
You purchase pain with all that joy can give,
And die of nothing but a rage to live.

Turn then from wits; and look on Simo's mate,
No ass so meek, no ass so obstinate.
Or her, that owns her faults, but never mends,
Because she's honest, and the best of friends.
Or her, whose life the Church and scandal share,
For ever in a passion, or a prayer.
Or her, who laughs at Hell, but (like her Grace)
Cries, "Ah! how charming, if there's no such place!"
Or who in sweet vicissitude appears
Of mirth and opium, ratafie and tears,
The daily anodyne, and nightly draught,
To kill those foes to fair ones, time and thought.
Woman and fool are two hard things to hit;
For true no-meaning puzzles more than wit.

But what are these to great Atossa's mind?
Scarce once herself, by turns all womankind!
Who, with herself, or others, from her birth
Finds all her life one warfare upon earth:
Shines in exposing knaves, and painting fools,
Yet is, whate'er she hates and ridicules.
No thought advances, but her eddy brain
Whisks it about, and down it goes again.
Full sixty years the world has been her trade,
The wisest fool much time has ever made.
From loveless youth to unrespected age,
No passion gratified except her rage.
So much the fury still out-ran the wit,
The pleasure missed her, and the scandal hit.
Who breaks with her, provokes revenge from Hell,
But he's a bolder man who dares be well.
Her every turn with violence pursued,
Nor more a storm her hate than gratitude:
To that each passion turns, or soon or late;
Love, if it makes her yield, must make her hate:
Superiors? death! and equals? what a curse!
But an inferior not dependent? worse.
Offend her, and she knows not to forgive;
Oblige her, and she'll hate you while you live:
But die, and she'll adore you—then the bust
And temple rise—then fall again to dust.
Last night, her lord was all that 's good and great;
A knave this morning, and his will a cheat.
Strange! by the means defeated of the ends,
By spirit robbed of power, by warmth of friends,
By wealth of followers! without one distress
Sick of herself through very selfishness!
Atossa, cursed with every granted prayer,
Childless with all her children, wants an heir.
To heirs unknown descends th' unguarded store,
Or wanders, Heaven-directed, to the poor.

Pictures like these, dear Madam, to design,
Asks no firm hand, and no unerring line;
Some wand'ring touches, some reflected light,
Some flying stroke alone can hit 'em right:
For how should equal colors do the knack?
Chameleons who can paint in white and black?

"Yet Chloe sure was formed without a spot"—
Nature in her then erred not, but forgot.
"With every pleasing, every prudent part,
Say, what can Chloe want?"—She wants a heart.

She speaks, behaves, and acts just as she ought;
But never, never, reached one gen'rous thought.
Virtue she finds too painful an endeavor,
Content to dwell in decencies for ever.
So very reasonable, so unmoved,
As never yet to love, or to be loved.
She, while her lover pants upon her breast,
Can mark the figures on an Indian chest;
And when she sees her friend in deep despair,
Observes how much a chintz exceeds mohair.
Forbid it Heaven, a favor or a debt
She e'er should cancel—but she may forget.
Safe is your secret still in Chloe's ear;
But none of Chloe's shall you ever hear.
Of all her dears she never slandered one,
But cares not if a thousand are undone.
Would Chloe know if you're alive or dead?
She bids her footman put it in her head.
Chloe is prudent—Would you too be wise?
Then never break your heart when Chloe dies.

Alexander Pope

In Montana: A Land of Contrasts

Oh, mountains loom the grandest in Montana
And summer air feels blandest in Montana
Moonshine kicks the strongest
Highways curve the wrongest
Winters last the longest   *in Montana.*

Women smile the fairest in Montana
Though busted hearts are rarest in Montana
Copper mines grow deepest
Forest trails the steepest
Leap-years come the leapest   *in Montana.*

Broncos ride the roughest in Montana
Cowhands are the toughest in Montana
Bunco games are bunker
Tires sink much sunker
Injuns get heap drunker   *in Montana.*

Christmases dawn whitest in Montana
Children's hearts beat lightest in Montana
Sugar beets grow sweetest
Lamb crops sound the bleatest
Meadowlarks twect-tweetest   *in Montana.*

Biscuits bake the hardest in Montana
Hot meat comest the lardest in Montana
Bronchial tubes are wheezier
Orators sound breezier
Bankers are some easier   *in Montana.*

Chipmunks are the chippiest in Montana
Waitresses are flippiest in Montana
Handshakes are less clammy
Hotels not so crammy
Life flows freer, damme!   *in Montana.*

Bad men act the baddest in Montana
Pedagogues go maddest in Montana
Beefsteaks there are "juicer"
Papooses are papooser
Women run less looser   *in Montana.*

Wildlife roams the wildest in Montana
Flu bugs bite the mildest in Montana
Woodticks are the tickest
Politicians slickest
Cardsharps shuffle quickest   *in Montana.*

Fellowship is stronger in Montana
Funerals take longer in Montana
Grub-stakes are the surest
Latch-strings the securest
Pawn-shops grow the poorest   *in Montana.*

                              Washington Jay McCormick

Unearned Increment

The Old Mandarin
Always perplexes his friend the Adjuster
At the Prune Exchange Bank
By adding his balances together
In the Chinese fashion.
For example: he once had $5000 in the bank
And drew various checks against it.
He drew $2000; thus leaving a balance of $3000.
He drew $1500; thus leaving a balance of $1500.
He drew $900; thus leaving a balance of $600.
He drew $600; thus leaving a balance of   000.

$5000. $5100.

Yet, as you see, when he adds his various balances
He finds that they total $5100
And the Old Mandarin therefore maintains
There should still be $100 to his credit.
They had to engage the Governor of the Federal Reserve
To explain the fallacy to him.   *Christopher Morley*

The Humane Mikado

A more humane Mikado never
    Did in Japan exist;
        To nobody second,
        I'm certainly reckoned
    A true philanthropist.
It is my very humane endeavor
    To make, to some extent,
        Each evil liver
        A running river
    Of harmless merriment.

*Chorus: My object all sublime
        I shall achieve in time—
    To let the punishment fit the crime—
        The punishment fit the crime;
        And make each prisoner pent
        Unwillingly represent
    A source of innocent merriment—
        Of innocent merriment!*

All prosy dull society sinners,
    Who chatter and bleat and bore,
        Are sent to hear sermons
        From mystical Germans

Who preach from ten to four:
The amateur tenor, whose vocal villainies
 All desire to shirk,
  Shall, during off-hours,
  Exhibit his powers
To Madame Tussaud's waxwork:
The lady who dyes a chemical yellow,
 Or stains her grey hair puce,
  Or pinches her figger,
  Is blacked like a nigger
With permanent walnut juice:
The idiot who, in railway carriages,
 Scribbles on window panes,
  We only suffer
  To ride on a buffer
In Parliamentary trains.

   (Chorus)

The advertising quack who wearies
 With tales of countless cures,
  His teeth, I've enacted,
  Shall all be extracted
By terrified amateurs:
The music-hall singer attends a series
 Of masses and fugues and "ops"
  By Bach, interwoven
  With Spohr and Beethoven,
   At classical Monday Pops:
The billiard sharp whom any one catches
 His doom's extremely hard—
  He's made to dwell
  In a dungeon cell
On a spot that's always barred;
And there he plays extravagant matches
 In fitless finger-stalls,
  On a cloth untrue
  With a twisted cue,
And elliptical billiard balls!

   (Chorus)

       Sir W. S. Gilbert

The Akond of Swat

Who or why, or which, or *what*,
                    Is the Akond of SWAT?

Is he tall or short, or dark or fair?
Does he sit on a stool or a sofa or chair,   or SQUAT,
                   The Akond of Swat?

Is he wise or foolish, young or old?
Does he drink his soup and his coffee cold,   or HOT,
                   The Akond of Swat?

Does he sing or whistle, jabber or talk,
And when riding abroad does he gallop or walk,   or TROT,
                   The Akond of Swat?

Does he wear a turban, a fez, or a hat?
Does he sleep on a mattress, a bed, or a mat,   or a COT,
                   The Akond of Swat?

When he writes a copy in round-hand size,
Does he cross his T's and finish his I's   with a DOT,
                   The Akond of Swat?

Can he write a letter concisely clear
Without a speck or a smudge or smear   or BLOT,
                   The Akond of Swat?

Do his people like him extremely well?
Or do they, whenever they can, rebel,   or PLOT,
                   At the Akond of Swat?

If he catches them then, either old or young,
Does he have them chopped in pieces or hung,   or SHOT,
                   The Akond of Swat?

Do his people prig in the lanes or park?
Or even at times, when days are dark,   GAROTTE?
                   O the Akond of Swat?

Does he study the wants of his own dominion?
Or doesn't he care for public opinion　a JOT,
　　　　　　　　　The Akond of Swat?

To amuse his mind do his people show him
Pictures, or any one's last new poem,　or WHAT,
　　　　　　　　　For the Akond of Swat?

At night if he suddenly screams and wakes,
Do they bring him only a few small cakes,　or a LOT,
　　　　　　　　　For the Akond of Swat?

Does he live on turnips, tea, or tripe?
Does he like his shawl to be marked with a stripe,　or a DOT,
　　　　　　　　　The Akond of Swat?

Does he like to lie on his back in a boat
Like the lady who lived in that isle remote,　SHALLOTT,
　　　　　　　　　The Akond of Swat?

Is he quiet, or always making a fuss?
Is his steward a Swiss or a Swede or a Russ,　or a SCOT,
　　　　　　　　　The Akond of Swat?

Does he like to sit by the calm blue wave?
Or to sleep and snore in a dark green cave,　or a GROTT,
　　　　　　　　　The Akond of Swat?

Does he drink small beer from a silver jug?
Or a bowl? or a glass? or a cup? or a mug?　or a POT,
　　　　　　　　　The Akond of Swat?

Does he beat his wife with a gold-topped pipe,
When she lets the gooseberries grow too ripe,　or ROT,
　　　　　　　　　The Akond of Swat?

Does he wear a white tie when he dines with friends,
And tie it neat in a bow with ends,　or a KNOT,
　　　　　　　　　The Akond of Swat?

Does he like new cream, and hate mince pies?
When he looks at the sun does he wink his eyes,　or NOT,
　　　　　　　　　The Akond of Swat?

Does he teach his subjects to roast and bake?
Does he sail about on an inland lake,　in a YACHT,
　　　　　　　　　The Akond of Swat?

Some one, or nobody, knows I wot
Who or which or why or what
　　　　　　　　　Is the Akond of Swat!
　　　　　　　　　　　　　　Edward Lear

The Higher Pantheism in a Nutshell

One, who is not, we see; but one, whom we see not, is;
Surely, this is not that; but that is assuredly this.

What, and wherefore, and whence: for under is over and
    under;
If thunder could be without lightning, lightning could be with-
    out thunder.

Doubt is faith in the main; but faith, on the whole, is doubt;
We cannot believe by proof; but could we believe without?

Why, and whither, and how? for barley and rye are not clover;
Neither are straight lines curves; yet over is under and over.

One and two are not one; but one and nothing is two;
Truth can hardly be false, if falsehood cannot be true.

Parallels all things are; yet many of these are askew;
You are certainly I; but certainly I am not you.

One, whom we see not, is; and one, who is not, we see;
Fiddle, we know, is diddle; and diddle, we take it, is dee.

Algernon Charles Swinburne

A Baker's Dozen of Captious Couplets

I. THE SPAN OF LIFE

The old dog barks backward without getting up.
I can remember when he was a pup.

Robert Frost

II. A POLITICIAN IS AN ARSE UPON

a politician is an arse upon
which everyone has sat except a man

e. e. cummings

III. THE HORSE

I know two things about the horse,
And one of them is rather coarse.

Naomi Royde Smith

IV. A TAIL FOR THE HORSE

And that's what sits upon its torse
And says, "Giddyap!" to the poor horse.

Anonymous

V. UP IN THE NORTH

Up in the North, a long way off,
The donkey's got the whooping-cough.

Anonymous

VI. WINTER IS GONE

Winter is gone, and spring is over,
The cuckoo-flowers grow mauver and mauver.

Alfred Austin

VII. ENGRAVED ON THE COLLAR OF A DOG, WHICH I GAVE TO HIS ROYAL HIGHNESS

I am his Highness' dog at Kew;
Pray tell me, sir, whose dog are you?

Alexander Pope

VIII. ALL THINGS HAVE SAVOR

All things have savor, though some very small,
Nay, a box on the ear hath no smell at all.

Anonymous

IX. TREASON

Treason doth never prosper—What's the reason?
If it doth prosper, none dare call it treason.

Sir John Harington

X. ON JOE

Joe hates a sycophant. It shows
Self love is not a fault of Joe's.

P. Dodd

XI. A NOTE ON THE LATIN GERUNDS

When Dido found Aeneas would not come,
She mourned in silence, and was Di-do-dum.

Richard Porson

XII. EPIGRAM

You beat your pate, and fancy wit will come:
Knock as you please, there's nobody at home.

Alexander Pope

XIII. WHEN A MAN HAS MARRIED A WIFE

When a Man has Married a Wife, he finds out whether
her knees & elbows are only glewed together.

William Blake

The Modern Hiawatha

When he killed the Mudjokivis,
Of the skin he made him mittens,
Made them with the fur side inside,
Made them with the skin side outside,
He, to get the warm side inside,
Put the inside skin side outside;
He, to get the cold side outside,
Put the warm side fur side inside.
That's why he put the fur side inside,
Why he put the skin side outside,
Why he turned them inside outside.

Anonymous

A Man of Words

A man of words and not of deeds,
Is like a garden full of weeds;
And when the weeds begin to grow,
It's like a garden full of snow;
And when the snow begins to fall,
It's like a bird upon the wall;
And when the bird away does fly,
It's like an eagle in the sky;
And when the sky begins to roar,
It's like a lion at the door;
And when the door begins to crack,
It's like a stick across your back;
And when your back begins to smart,
It's like a penknife in your heart;
And when your heart begins to bleed,
You're dead, and dead, and dead indeed.

Anonymous

Headline History

Grave Charge in Mayfair Bathroom Case;
Roman Remains for Middle West;
Golfing Bishop Calls for Prayers;
How Murdered Bride was Dressed;

Boxer Insures his Joie-de-Vivre;
Duchess Denies that Vamps are Vain;
Do Women make Good Wives?
Giant Airship over Spain;

Soprano Sings for Forty Hours;
Cocktail Bar on Mooring Mast;

"Noise, more Noise!" Poet's Last Words;
Compulsory Wireless Bill is Passed;

Alleged Last Trump Blown Yesterday;
Traffic Drowns Call to Quick and Dead;
Cup Tie Crowd sees Heavens Ope;
"Not End of World," says Well-Known Red.

William Plomer

A Gentle Echo on Woman
(In the Doric Manner)

SHEPHERD: Echo, I ween, will in the wood reply,
And quaintly answer questions: shall I try?
ECHO: Try.
What must we do our passion to express?
Press.
How shall I please her, who ne'er loved before?
Be Fore.
What most moves women when we them address?
A dress.
Say, what can keep her chaste whom I adore?
A door.
If music softens rocks, love tunes my lyre.
Liar.
Then teach me, Echo, how shall I come by her?
Buy her.
When bought, no question I shall be her dear?
Her deer.
But deer have horns: how must I keep her under?
Keep her under.
But what can glad me when she's laid on bier?
Beer.
What must I do when women will be kind?
Be kind.
What must I do when women will be cross?
Be cross.
Lord, what is she that can so turn and wind?
Wind.
If she be wind, what stills her when she blows?
Blows.
But if she bang again, still should I bang her?
Bang her.
Is there no way to moderate her anger?
Hang her.
Thanks, gentle Echo! right thy answers tell
What woman is and how to guard her well.
Guard her well.

Jonathan Swift

The Death of Polybius Jubb

He died in attempting to swallow,
Which proves that, though fat, he was hollow—
For in gasping for space
He swallowed his face,
And hadn't the courage to follow.

Roy Campbell

To Sit in Solemn Silence

To sit in solemn silence in a dull, dark dock,
In a pestilential prison, with a life-long lock,
Awaiting the sensation of a short, sharp shock,
From a cheap and chippy chopper on a big black block!

Sir W. S. Gilbert

Dash Back

Dash back that ocean with a pier,
    Strow yonder mountain flat,
A railway here, a tunnel there,
    Mix me this zone with that.

Alfred, Lord Tennyson

The Platitude

Does the duckbilled Platitude
Give you Social Latitude?
If so, knock that Attitude
Into a cocked Hattitude!

Enid Williams

A Nocturnal Sketch

Even is come; and from the dark Park, hark
The signal of the setting sun—one gun!
And six is sounding from the chime, prime time
To go and see the Drury-Lane Dane slain,—
Or hear Othello's jealous doubt spout out,—
Or Macbeth raving at that shade-made blade,
Denying to his frantic clutch much touch;—
Or else to see Ducrow with wide stride ride
Four horses as no other man can span;
Or in the small Olympic Pit, sit split
Laughing at Liston, while you quiz his phiz.

Anon Night comes, and with her wings brings things
Such as, with his poetic tongue, Young sung;
The gas up-blazes with its bright white light,

And paralytic watchmen prowl, howl, growl,
About the streets and take up Pall-Mall Sal,
Who, hasting to her nightly jobs, robs fobs.

Now thieves to enter for your cash, smash, crash,
Past drowsy Charley, in a deep sleep, creep,
But frightened by Policeman B.3, flee,
And while they're going, whisper low, "No go!"
Now puss, while folks are in their beds, treads leads
And sleepers waking, grumble—"Drat that cat!"
Who in the gutter caterwauls, squalls, mauls
Some feline foe, and screams in shrill ill-will.

Now Bulls of Bashan, of a prize size, rise
In childish dreams, and with a roar gore poor
Georgy, or Charley, or Billy, willy-nilly;—
But Nursemaid, in a nightmare rest, chest-pressed,
Dreameth of one of her old flames, James Games,
And that she hears—what faith is man's!—Ann's banns
And his, from Reverend Mr. Rice, twice, thrice:
White ribbons flourish, and a stout shout out,
That upward goes, shows Rose knows those bows' woes!

Thomas Hood

Cubism

Dinosaurs and violins played in the sky,
Their music disappearing over the city;
Ill-tuned strings screeched bumpy sounds
Of age, anger and broken pitchers.

The music disappeared deep in the city
Whistling empty sounds;
A violin lay against a building,
A cubist painting hiding sound in a basket.

Hy Sobiloff

He Lived Amidst th' Untrodden Ways

He lived amidst th' untrodden ways
    To Rydal Lake that lead;
A bard whom there were none to praise,
    And very few to read.

Behind a cloud his mystic sense,
    Deep hidden, who can spy?
Bright as the night when not a star
    Is shining in the sky.

Unread his works—his "Milk White Doe"
    With dust is dark and dim;
It's still in Longman's shop, and oh!
    The difference to him!

Hartley Coleridge

Father William

"You are old, Father William," the young man said,
    "And your hair has become very white;
And yet you incessantly stand on your head—
    Do you think, at your age, it is right?"

"In my youth," Father William replied to his son,
    "I feared it might injure the brain;
But, now that I'm perfectly sure I have none,
    Why, I do it again and again."

"You are old," said the youth, "as I mentioned before,
    And have grown most uncommonly fat;
Yet you turned a back-somersault in at the door—
    Pray, what is the reason of that?"

"In my youth," said the sage, as he shook his gray locks,
    "I kept all my limbs very supple
By the use of this ointment—one shilling the box—
    Allow me to sell you a couple?"

"You are old," said the youth, "and your jaws are too weak
    For anything tougher than suet;
Yet you finished the goose, with the bones and the beak—
    Pray, how did you manage to do it?"

"In my youth," said his father, "I took to the law,
    And argued each case with my wife;
And the muscular strength which it gave to my jaw,
    Has lasted the rest of my life."

"You are old," said the youth, "one would hardly suppose
  That your eye was as steady as ever;
Yet you balanced an eel on the end of your nose—
  What made you so awfully clever?"

"I have answered three questions, and that is enough,"
  Said his father; "don't give yourself airs!
Do you think I can listen all day to such stuff?
  Be off, or I'll kick you downstairs."

Lewis Carroll

Father William

"You are old, Father William," the young man said,
  "And your nose has a look of surprise;
Your eyes have turned round to the back of your head,
  And you live upon cucumber pies."
"I know it, I know it," the old man replied,
  "And it comes from employing a quack,
Who said if I laughed when the crocodile died
  I should never have pains in my back."

"You are old, Father William," the young man said,
  "And your legs always get in your way;
You use too much mortar in mixing your bread,
  And you try to drink timothy hay."
"Very true, very true," said the wretched old man,
  "Every word that you tell me is true;
And it's caused by my having my kerosene can
  Painted red where it ought to be blue."

"You are old, Father William," the young man said,
  "And your teeth are beginning to freeze,
Your favorite daughter has wheels in her head,
  And the chickens are eating your knees."
"You are right," said the old man, "I cannot deny,
  That my troubles are many and great,
But I'll butter my ears on the Fourth of July,
  And then I'll be able to skate."

Anonymous

Investor's Soliloquy

To buy, or not to buy; that is the question:
Whether 'tis nobler in the mind to suffer
The slings and arrows of an outrageous market,
Or to take cash against a sea of troubles,
And by selling, end them. To buy, to keep—
No more; and by this keeping, to say we end

The bear trend and the thousand natural shocks
That stocks are heir to—'tis a consummation
Devoutly to be wish'd—To buy, to keep—
To keep? Perchance on margin! Ay, there's the rub!
For in that margining what dreams may come,
When we have shuffled off our buying power,
Must give us pause. There's the respect
That makes calamity of so long a position.
For who would bear the whips and scorns of debit balances,
The broker's interest, the shorts' contumely,
The pangs of dispriz'd appreciation, the market's delay,
The insolence of bankers, and the spurns
That patient merit of the unworthy takes,
When he himself might the quietus make
With a bare short sale? Who would losses bear
To grunt and sweat under a falling market,
But that the dread of something after selling,
The undiscover'd rally—from whose bourn
No short seller returns, puzzles the will
And makes us rather bear those losses we have
Than fly to others that we know not of?
Thus ambivalence does make cowards of us all.
And thus the native hue of resolution
Is sicklied o'er with the pale cast of doubt
And enterprises of great pith and moment,
With this regard, their current turn awry,
And lose the name of profits.   *Kenneth Ward*

Hamlet's Soliloquy Imitated

To print, or not to print—that is the question.
Whether 'tis better in a trunk to bury
The quirks and crotchets of outrageous fancy,
Or send a well-wrote copy to the press,
And by disclosing, end them? To print, to doubt
No more; and by one act to say we end
The headache, and a thousand natural shocks
Of scribbling frenzy—'tis a consummation
Devoutly to be wish'd. To print—to beam
From the same shelf with Pope, in calf well bound!
To sleep, perchance, with Quarles—Ay, there's the rub—
For to what class a writer may be doom'd,
When he hath shuffled off some paltry stuff,
Must give us pause.—There's the respect that makes
Th' unwilling poet keep his piece nine years.
For who would bear th' impatient thirst of fame,
The pride of conscious merit, and 'bove all,

The tedious importunity of friends,
When as himself might his quietus make
With a bare inkhorn? Who would fardles bear?
To groan and sweat under a load of wit?
But that the tread of steep Parnassus' hill,
That undiscover'd country, with whose bays
Few travellers return, puzzles the will,
And makes us rather bear to live unknown,
Than run the hazard to be known, and damn'd.
Thus critics do make cowards of us all.
And thus the healthful face of many a poem
Is sickly'd o'er with a pale manuscript;
And enterprisers of great fire, and spirit,
With this regard from Dodsley turn away,
And lose the name of authors.

Richard Jago

A, B, C

A is an Angel of blushing eighteen:
B is the Ball where the Angel was seen:
C is the Chaperon, who cheated at cards:
D is the Deuxtemps, with Frank of the Guards:
E is the Eye, which those dark lashes cover:
F is the Fan, it peeped wickedly over:
G is the Glove of superlative kid:
H is the Hand which it spitefully hid;
I is the Ice which the fair one demanded:
J is the Juvenile, who hurried to hand it:
K is the Kerchief, a rare work of art:
L is the Lace which composed the chief part:
M is the old Maid who watched the girls dance:
N is the Nose she turned up at each glance:
O is the Olga (just then in its prime):
P is the Partner who wouldn't keep time:
Q 's a Quadrille, put instead of the Lancers:
R the Remonstrances made by the dancers:
S is the Supper, where all went in pairs:
T is the Twaddle they talked on the stairs:
U is the Uncle who "thought we'd be going":
V is the Voice which his niece replied "No" in:
W is the Waiter, who sat up till eight:
X is his Exit, not rigidly straight:
Y is a Yawning fit caused by the Ball:
Z stands for Zero, or nothing at all.

C. S. Calverley

PART FOUR

Literary Cocktail Party

Survey of Literature

In all good Greek of Plato
I lack my roastbeef and potato.

A better man was Aristotle,
Pulling steady on the bottle.

I dip my hat to Chaucer,
Swilling soup from his saucer,

98

And to Master Shakespeare
Who wrote big on small beer.

The abstemious Wordsworth
Subsisted on a curd's-worth,

But a slick one was Tennyson,
Putting gravy on his venison.

What these men had to eat and drink
Is what we say and what we think.

The influence of Milton
Came wry out of Stilton.

Sing a song for Percy Shelley,
Drowned in pale lemon jelly,

And for precious John Keats,
Dripping blood of pickled beets.

Then there was poor Willie Blake,
He foundered on sweet cake.

God have mercy on the sinner
Who must write with no dinner,

No gravy and no grub,
No pewter and no pub,

No belly and no bowels,
Only consonants and vowels.

John Crowe Ransom

A Fistful of Writer's Cramps

I. THE WRITER

Titus reads neither prose nor rhyme;
He writes himself; he has no time.

Hildebrand Jacob

II

Another writes because his father writ,
And proves himself a bastard by his wit.

Edward Young

III

What frenzy has of late possess'd the brain!
Though few can write, yet fewer can refrain.

Samuel Garth

IV. ON PETER ROBERTSON

Here lies the peerless paper lord, Lord Peter,
Who broke the laws of God, and man, and meter.

John Gibson Lockhart

V. ON HIS BOOKS

When I am dead, I hope it may be said:
"His sins were scarlet, but his books were read."

Hilaire Belloc

VI. ON A CERTAIN SCHOLAR

He never completed his History of Ephesus,
But his name got mentioned in numerous prefaces.

W. Craddle

VII. ON SOME SOUTH AFRICAN NOVELISTS

You praise the firm restraint with which they write—
I'm with you there, of course.
They use the snaffle and the curb all right;
But where's the bloody horse?

Roy Campbell

VIII. THIS LATEST POET

This latest poet is one of those gents
Who dines astraddle, but finding that hurts,
He takes his meals on one side of the fence
And on the other his just desserts.

Anonymous

IX. EPIGRAM

Sir, I admit your general rule,
That every poet is a fool:
But you yourself may serve to show it,
That every fool is not a poet.

Matthew Prior

X. A CURE FOR POETRY

Seven wealthy towns contend for Homer dead
Thro' which the living Homer beg'd his bread.

Anonymous

XI. PIPLING

Behold a critic, pitched like the *castrati*,
Imperious youngling, though approaching forty:
He heaps few honors on a living head,
He loves himself, and the illustrious dead;
He pipes, he squeaks, he quivers through his nose,—
Some cannot praise him: *I* am one of those.

Theodore Roethke

XII. WHAT I HAVE WROTE

And now, kind friends, what I have wrote,
     I hope you will pass o'er,
And not criticize as some have done
     Hitherto herebefore.
     Julia Moore, "The Sweet Singer of Michigan"

XIII. THE LIMERICK

There was a young man from Japan
Whose limericks never would scan;
     When they said it was so,
     He replied, "Yes, I know,
But I always try to get as many words into the last line as ever
     I possibly can."

Anonymous

XIV. MALCOLM BRYLER

What could be viler
Than the verse of Malcolm Bryler?
God knows,
Unless it's his prose!

Anonymous

XV. TO A LIVING AUTHOR

Your comedy I've read, my friend,
     And like the half you pilfered best;
Be sure the piece you yet may mend—
     Take courage, man, and steal the rest.

Anonymous

XVI

As I was laying on the green,
A small English book I seen.
Carlyle's *Essay on Burns* was the edition,
So I left it laying in the same position.

Anonymous

XVII. ON A MAGAZINE SONNET

"Scorn not the sonnet," though its strength be sapped,
     Nor say malignant its inventor blundered;
The corpse that here in fourteen lines is wrapped
     Had otherwise been covered with a hundred.

R. H. Loines

XVIII. FATIGUE

I'm tired of Love: I'm still more tired of Rhyme.
But Money gives me pleasure all the time.

Hilaire Belloc

XIX. FORM 1040A

A poet seldom finds the way
To sign on form 1040A!

Phyllis Eleanor Armstrong

XX

Who killed John Keats?
I says the Quarterly,
So savage & Tartarly;
'Twas one of my feats.   *Anonymous*

The Height of the Ridiculous

I wrote some lines once on a time
   In wondrous merry mood,
And thought, as usual, men would say
   They were exceeding good.

They were so queer, so very queer,
   I laughed as I would die;
Albeit, in the general way,
   A sober man am I.

I called my servant, and he came;
   How kind it was of him
To mind a slender man like me,
   He of the mighty limb!

"These to the printer," I exclaimed,
   And, in my humorous way,
I added (as a trifling jest),
   "There'll be the devil to pay."

He took the paper, and I watched,
   And saw him peep within;
At the first line he read, his face
   Was all upon the grin.

He read the next; the grin grew broad,
   And shot from ear to ear;
He read the third; a chuckling noise
   I now began to hear.

The fourth; he broke into a roar;
   The fifth; his waistband split;
The sixth; he burst five buttons off,
   And tumbled in a fit.

Ten days and nights, with sleepless eye,
   I watched that wretched man,
And since, I never dare to write
   As funny as I can.   *O. W. Holmes*

Two Morsels of Profundity from the Minor Pre-Socratics

Or, How to Make Few or No Words Go Far

II. CRATYLUS

The relativity that cloaks the Word
Made Cratylus reject it as absurd,
And turn to suchlike vocal absolutes
As hisses, grunts, moans, bellowings, and hoots.
And thus of all the Ancients, be it noted,
Cratylus is the most frequently quoted.

III. AMEINIAS

Of Ameinias nothing more is known for sure
Except: he was most worthy, though quite poor.
Which may explain why he remains obscure.

John Simon

Epitaph on Robert Southey

Beneath these poppies buried deep,
    The bones of Bob the bard lie hid;
Peace to his manes; and may he sleep
    As soundly as his readers did!

Through every sort of verse meandering,
    Bob went without a hitch or fall,
Through epic, Sapphic, Alexandrine,
    To verse that was no verse at all;

Till fiction having done enough,
    To make a bard at least absurd,
And give his readers *quantum suff.*,
    He took to praising George the Third.

And now, in virtue of his crown,
    Dooms us, poor whigs, at once to slaughter;
Like Donellan of bad renown,
    Poisoning us all with laurel-water.

And yet at times some awful qualms he
    Felt about leaving honor's track;
And though he's got a butt of Malmsey,
    It may not save him from a sack.

Death, weary of so dull a writer,
    Put to his books a *finis* thus.
Oh! may the earth on him lie lighter
    Than did his quartos upon us!   *Thomas Moore*

On Thomas Moore's Poems

Lalla Rookh
Is a naughty book
By Tommy Moore,
Who has written four;

Each warmer
Than the former,
So the most recent
Is the least decent.

Anonymous

To Minerva

My temples throb, my pulses boil,
    I'm sick of Song, and Ode, and Ballad—
So, Thyrsis, take the Midnight Oil,
    And pour it on a lobster salad.

My brain is dull, my sight is foul,
    I cannot write a verse, or read,—
Then, Pallas, take away thine Owl,
    And let us have a lark instead.   *Thomas Hood*

The Lake Isle

O God, O Venus, O Mercury, patron of thieves,
Give me in due time, I beseech you, a little tobacco shop,
With the little bright boxes
        piled up neatly upon the shelves
And the loose fragrant cavendish
        and the shag,
And the bright Virginia
        loose under the bright glass cases,
And a pair of scales not too greasy,
And the whores dropping in for a word or two in passing,
For a flip word, and to tidy their hair a bit.

O God, O Venus, O Mercury, patron of thieves,
Lend me a little tobacco shop,
        or install me in any profession
Save this damn'd profession of writing,
        where one needs one's brains all the time.

Ezra Pound

Prologue to "Aureng-Zebe"

Our author by experience finds it true,
'Tis much more hard to please himself than you;
And out of no feign'd modesty, this day,
Damns his laborious trifle of a play;
Not that it's worse than what before he writ,
But he has now another taste of Wit;
And, to confess a truth (though out of time,)
Grows weary of his long-loved mistress Rhyme.
Passion 's too fierce to be in fetters bound,
And Nature flies him like enchanted ground:
What verse can do he has perform'd in this,
Which he presumes the most correct of his;
But spite of all his pride, a secret shame
Invades his breast at Shakespeare's sacred name:
Aw'd when he hears his godlike Romans rage,
He in a just despair would quit the stage;
And to an age less polished, more unskilled,
Does with disdain the foremost honors yield.
As with the greater dead he dares not strive,
He would not match his verse with those who live:
Let him retire, betwixt two ages cast,
The first of this, and hindmost of the last.
A losing gamester, let him sneak away;
He bears no ready money from the play.
The fate which governs poets, thought it fit,
He should not raise his fortunes by his Wit.
The clergy thrive, and the litigious bar;
Dull heroes fatten with the spoils of war:
All southern vices, Heaven be praised, are here;
But Wit's a luxury you think too dear.
When you to cultivate the plant are loth,
'Tis a shrewd sign 'twas never of your growth:
And Wit in northern climates will not blow,
Except, like orange-trees, 'tis hous'd from snow.
There needs no care to put a playhouse down,
'Tis the most desert place of all the town:
We and our neighbors, to speak proudly, are
Like monarchs, ruined with expensive war;
While, like wise English, unconcerned you sit,
And see us play the tragedy of Wit.

John Dryden

Prologue to "Love Triumphant"

So now, this poet, who forsakes the stage
Intends to gratify the present age.
One warrant shall be signed for every man;
All shall be wits that will; and beaux that can:
He dies, at least to us, and to the stage,
And what he has he leaves this noble age.
He leaves you, first, all plays of his inditing,
The whole estate which he has got by writing.
The beaux may think this nothing but vain praise;
They'll find it something, the testator says;
For half their love is made from scraps of plays.
To his worst foes, he leaves his honesty,
That they may thrive upon't as much as he.
He leaves his manners to the roaring boys,
Who come in drunk, and fill the house with noise.
He leaves to the dire critics of his wit
His silence and contempt of all they writ.
To Shakespeare's critic, he bequeaths the curse,
To find his faults, and yet himself make worse;
Last, for the fair, he wishes you may be
From your dull critics, the lampooners free.
Tho' he pretends no legacy to leave you,
An old man may at least good wishes give you.

John Dryden

A Memory

When I was as high as that
I saw a poet in his hat.
I think the poet must have smiled
At such a solemn gazing child.

Now wasn't it a funny thing
To get a sight of J. M. Synge,
And notices nothing but his hat?
Yet life is often queer like that.

L. A. G. Strong

A Strike among the Poets

In his chamber, weak and dying,
    While the Norman Baron lay,
Loud, without, his men were crying,
    "Shorter hours and better pay."

Know you why the plowman, fretting,
    Homeward plods his weary way

Ere his time? He's after getting
   Shorter hours and better pay.

See! the Hesperus is swinging
   Idle in the wintry bay,
And the skipper's daughter's singing,
   "Shorter hours and better pay."

Where's the minstrel boy? I've found him
   Joining in the labor fray
With his placards slung around him,
   "Shorter hours and better pay."

Oh, young Lochinvar is coming;
   Though his hair is getting gray,
Yet I'm glad to hear him humming,
   "Shorter hours and better pay."

E'en the boy upon the burning
   Deck has got a word to say,
Something rather cross concerning
   Shorter hours and better pay.

Lives of great men all remind us
   We can make as much as they,
Work no more, until they find us
   Shorter hours and better pay.

Hail to thee, blithe spirit! (Shelley)
   Wilt thou be a blackleg? Nay.
Soaring, sing above the mêlée,
   "Shorter hours and better pay."

Anonymous

The Monster

Through a wild midnight all my mountainous past
Labored and heaved with all I had forgotten
Until a poem no bigger than a mouse
Came forth. And with the darkness finally passed
We faced each other, begetter and begotten:
"Monster!" I cried. And "Monster!" cried the mouse.

Henry Rago

A Poem Intended to Incite the Utmost Depression

Cervantes, Dostoievsky, Poe,
Drained the dregs and lees of woe;
Gogol, Beethoven and Keats
Got but meager share of sweets.
Milton, Homer, Dante had
Reason to be more than sad;
Caesar and Napoleon
Saw the blood upon their sun;
Martyr, hermit, saint and priest
Lingered long at Sorrow's feast:
Paid with pyre and perishing
For every feather in each wing;—
Well, if such as these could be
So foredoomed to misery,
And Fate despise her own elect—
What the deuce do you expect?

Samuel Hoffenstein

Villanelle

(How to compose a *villanelle,* which is said to require "an elaborate amount of care in production, which those who read only would hardly suspect existed.")

It's all a trick, quite easy when you know it,
As easy as reciting ABC;
You need not be an atom of a poet.

If you've a grain of wit, and want to show it,
Writing a *villanelle*—take this from me—
It's all a trick, quite easy when you know it.

You start a pair of rimes, and then you "go it"
With rapid-running pen and fancy free;
You need not be an atom of a poet.

Take any thought, write round it or below it,
Above or near it, as it liketh thee;
It's all a trick, quite easy when you know it.

Pursue your task, till, like a shrub, you grow it,
Up to the standard size it ought to be;
You need not be an atom of a poet.

Clear it of weeds and water it, and hoe it,
Then watch it blossom with triumphant glee.
It's all a trick, quite easy when you know it;
You need not be an atom of a poet. *W. W. Skeat*

Poetical Economy

What hours I spent of precious time,
   What pints of ink I used to waste,
Attempting to secure a rhyme
   To suit the public taste,
Until I found a simple plan
Which makes the lamest lyric scan!

When I've a syllable de trop,
   I cut it off, without apol.:
This verbal sacrifice, I know,
   May irritate the schol.;
But all must praise my dev'lish cunn.
Who realize that Time is Mon.

My sense remains as clear as cryst.,
   My style as pure as any Duch.
Who does not boast a bar sinist.
   Upon her fam. escutch.;
And I can treat with scornful pit.
The sneers of ev'ry captious crit.

I gladly publish to the pop.
   A scheme of which I make no myst.,
And beg my fellow scribes to cop.
   This labor-saving syst.
I offer it to the consid.
Of ev'ry thoughtful individ.

The author, working like a beav.,
   His readers' pleasure could redoub.
Did he but now and then abbrev.
   The work he gives his pub.
(This view I most partic. suggest
To A. C. Bens. and G. K. Chest.)

If Mr. Caine rewrote The Scape.,
   And Miss Corell. condensed Barabb.,
What could they save in foolscap pape.
   Did they but cult. the hab.,
Which teaches people to suppress
All syllables that are unnec.!

If playwrights would but thus dimin.
   The length of time each drama takes,
(The Second Mrs. Tanq. by Pin.

Or even Ham., by Shakes.)
We could maintain a watchful att.
When at a Mat. on Wed. or Sat.

Have done, ye bards, with dull monot.!
    Foll. my examp., O, Stephen Phill.,
O, Owen Seam., O, William Wat.,
    O, Ella Wheeler Wil.,
And share with me the grave respons.
Of writing this amazing nons.!

Harry Graham

Intermission, Please!

What poet wrote these lovely lines?
What theme is this, from what sonata?
What king invented minus signs?
What's English for *persona grata?*

The aria we now shall hear
Is sung by basso, alto, tenor—?
What actress first played "Chanticleer"?
What's *Lebensraum?* What's *Sprachenkenner?*

Whichever way I turn the dial,
Somebody's asking someone something,
Somebody's learning is on trial,
Someone is being proved a dumb thing.

Where is the Yard? The Hook of Holland?
The Taj Mahal? The Iron Lung?
What college sings the Song of Roland?
How do you tie a person's tongue?

The famous crowd the microphones
Primed with *bon mots* and information—
A movie star on postal zones,
A prince on pin-point carbonation.

Name four, name six, name three, name two.
Send the tinfoil, send in the bottle.
Send in your question; we'll send you
A full Greek text of Aristotle.

I listen as they quip and quiz
And get a joke or get an answer:

What's the pluperfect tense of *Is?*
Whose head was carried by what dancer?

And as the quizzes end I go
(Sometimes I last but halfway through them)
To study hard until I know
So much I needn't listen to them.

Irwin Edman

The Arrest of Oscar Wilde at the Cadogan Hotel

He sipped at a weak hock and seltzer
  As he gazed at the London skies
Through the Nottingham lace of the curtains
  Or was it his bees-winged eyes?

To the right and before him Pont Street
  Did tower in her new built red,
As hard as the morning gaslight
  That shone on his unmade bed.

"I want some more hock in my seltzer,
  And Robbie, please give me your hand—
Is this the end or beginning?
  How can I understand?

"So you've brought me the latest *Yellow Book:*
  And Buchan has got in it now:
Approval of what is approved of
  Is as false as a well-kept vow.

"More hock, Robbie—where is the seltzer?
  Dear boy, pull again at the bell!
They are all little better than *cretins,*
  Though this *is* the Cadogan Hotel.

"One astrakhan coat is at Willis's—
  Another one's at the Savoy:
Do fetch my morocco portmanteau,
  And bring them on later, dear boy."

A thump, and a murmur of voices—
  ("Oh why must they make such a din?")
As the door of the bedroom swung open
  And Two Plain Clothes POLICEMEN came in:

"Mr. Woilde, we 'ave come for tew take yew
    Where felons and criminals dwell:
We must ask yew tew leave with us quoietly
    For this *is* the Cadogan Hotel."

He rose, and he put down *The Yellow Book*.
    He staggered—and, terrible-eyed,
He brushed past the palms on the staircase
    And was helped to a hansom outside.

John Betjeman

Oscar Wilde

When Oscar came to join his God,
Not earth to earth, but sod to sod,
    It was for sinners such as this
    Hell was created bottomless.

Attributed to Algernon Charles Swinburne

There's a Notable Clan Yclept Stein

There's a notable clan yclept Stein:
There's Gertrude, there's Ep, and there's Ein.
    Gert's prose has no style,
    Ep's statues are vile,
And nobody understands Ein.

Anonymous

Alfred, Lord Tennyson

That is all you will ever make from poetry.
—The Rev. George Tennyson, upon giving his son
Alfred half a guinea for some early verses.

Alfred was a ninny
With his father's half
    guinea.
He didn't make more
Till he was thirty-four,
And what he got then
Was a gift from the Queen
For having a bit
Of a deficit.

But at fifty, ah,
He lived like a Shah,
And said to himself,
My name is pelf.
He took a big bite
Of the Isle of Wight,
And as his publisher failed
His fortune sailed
Up, up
With Morgan and Krupp.

So when he died
He had gratified
His heart's dear itch
To be rich, to be rich.
With considerable bother
He had shown his father
You never can tell
What will sell.

Reed Whittemore

Just a Smack at Auden

Waiting for the end, boys, waiting for the end.
What is there to be or do?
What's become of me or you?
Are we kind or are we true?
Sitting two and two, boys, waiting for the end.

Shall I build a tower, boys, knowing it will rend
Crack upon the hour, boys, waiting for the end?
Shall I pluck a flower, boys, shall I save or spend?
All turns sour, boys, waiting for the end.

Shall I send a wire, boys? Where is there to send?
All are under fire, boys, waiting for the end.
Shall I turn a sire, boys? Shall I choose a friend?
The fat is in the pyre, boys, waiting for the end.

Shall I make it clear, boys, for all to apprehend,
Those that will not hear, boys, waiting for the end,
Knowing it is near, boys, trying to pretend,
Sitting in cold fear, boys, waiting for the end?

Shall we send a cable, boys, accurately penned,
Knowing we are able, boys, waiting for the end,
Via the Tower of Babel, boys? Christ will not ascend.
He's hiding in his stable, boys, waiting for the end.

Shall we blow a bubble, boys, glittering to distend,
Hiding from our trouble, boys, waiting for the end?
When you build on rubble, boys, Nature will append
Double and redouble, boys, waiting for the end.

Shall we make a tale, boys, that things are sure to mend,
Playing bluff and hale, boys, waiting for the end?
It will be born stale, boys, stinking to offend,
Dying ere it fail, boys, waiting for the end.

Shall we go all wild, boys, waste and make them lend,
Playing at the child, boys, waiting for the end?
It has all been filed, boys, history has a trend,
Each of us enisled, boys, waiting for the end.

What was said by Marx, boys, what did he perpend?
No good being sparks, boys, waiting for the end.
Treason of the clerks, boys, curtains that descend,
Lights becoming darks, boys, waiting for the end.

Waiting for the end, boys, waiting for the end.
Not a chance to blend, boys, things have got to tend.
Think of those who vend, boys, think of how we wend,
Waiting for the end, boys, waiting for the end.

William Empson

Just a Fishing Smack at Empson

The art of lying is you cannot stand:
Trying's permitted if the lips can serve.
A mare's nest's better than no bird in hand.

To lie before one talks requires nerve:
Truth loops the loop inside an ampersand—
And Rhetoric's a boomerang maneuver.

The parts of speech can never understand
A fig leaf *cares* if it reveals a curve:
And who's solo to blow his own brass band?

The dictionary is a game preserve.
Those homonyms will eat out of your hand—
They are not carnivores: it's all reserve.

Women know best what elegance demands,
How best a cool appearance to conserve:
You keep your air in place with rubber bands.

U minus X shows the correct reserve.
Poems, like bank-clerks, should be neat and bland.
The heart of making is you must not serve.

I overlook, they say, you understand
Three cards and mirrors suffer to deceive:
We know we think we feel we understand.

George Barker

Just a Smack at Smacking

> All this smacking
> Sounds like claque-ing.   *Anonymous*

Chard Whitlow

(Mr. Eliot's Sunday Evening Postscript)

As we get older we do not get any younger.
Seasons return, and today I am fifty-five,
And this time last year I was fifty-four,
And this time next year I shall be sixty-two.
And I cannot say I should like (to speak for myself)
To see my time over again—if you can call it time:
Fidgeting uneasily under a draughty stair,
Or counting sleepless nights in the crowded tube.

There are certain precautions—though none of them very
    reliable—
Against the blast from bombs and the flying splinter,
But not against the blast from heaven, *vento dei venti,*
The wind within a wind unable to speak for wind;
And the frigid burnings of purgatory will not be touched
By any emollient.
                    I think you will find this put,
Better than I could ever hope to express it,
In the words of Kharma: "It is, we believe,
Idle to hope that the simple stirrup-pump
Will extinguish hell."
                    Oh, listeners,
And you especially who have turned off the wireless,
And sit in Stoke or Basingstoke listening appreciatively to the
    silence,
(Which is also the silence of hell) pray, not for your skins, but
    your souls.

And pray for me also under the draughty stair.
As we get older we do not get any younger.

And pray for Kharma under the holy mountain.   *Henry Reed*

Six Poets in Search of a Lawyer

Finesse be first, whose elegance deplores
All things save beauty, and the swinging doors;
Whose cleverness in writing verse is just
Exceeded by his lack of taste and lust;
Who lives off lady lovers of his verse
And thanks them by departing with their purse;
Who writes his verse in order to amaze,
To win the Pulitzer, or *Time*'s sweet praise;
Who will endure a moment, and then pass,
As hopeless as an olive in his glass.

Dullard be second, as he always will,
From lack of brains as well as lack of skill.
Expert in some, and dilettante in all
The ways of making poems gasp and fall,
He teaches at a junior college where
He's recognized as Homer's son and heir.
Respectable, brown-suited, it is he
Who represents on forums poetry,
And argues to protect the libeled Muse,
Who'd tear his flimsy tongue out, could she choose.

His opposite is anarchistic *Bomb*,
Who writes a manifesto with aplomb.
Revolt! Revolt! No matter why or when,
It's novelty, old novelty again.
Yet *Bomb* if read intently may reveal
A talent not to murder but to steal;
First from old *Gone,* whose fragmentary style
Concealed his sawdust Keats a little while;
And now from one who writes at very best
What ne'er was thought and much the less expressed.

Lucre be next, who takes to poetry
The businessman he swore he would not be.
Anthologies and lecture tours and grants
Create a solvency which disenchants.
He writes his poems now to suit his purse,
Short-lined and windy, and reserves his curse
For all the little magazines so fine
That offer only fifty cents a line.
He makes his money, certainly, to write,
But writes for money. Such is appetite.

Of *Mucker* will I tell, who tries to show
He is a kind of poet men don't know.
To shadow box at literary teas
And every girl at Bennington to seize,
To talk of baseball rather than of Yeats,
To drink straight whiskey while the bard creates—
Such is his pose, and so his poems seem
Incongruous in proving life a dream.
Some say, with Freud, that *Mucker* has a reason
For acting virile in and out of season.

Scoundrel be last. Be deaf be dumb be blind,
Who writes satiric verses on his kind.

Donald Hall

Lawyer in Search of Six Poets

And by "his kind" this *Scoundrel* means no less
Than *Mucker, Lucre, Dullard, Bomb, Finesse!*

Anonymous

mr u will not be missed

mr u will not be missed
who as an anthologist
sold the many on the few
not excluding mr u

e. e. cummings

Frostbite

Some say the world will end by Fire
And some by Frost
    By verse of ice, or vice of verser,
        (God only knows which were the worser!)
But, anyway, the world well lost.

Conrad Aiken

The Editor's Private Cocktail Party

Or, Oscar Williams Falls Forward on Many Fronts

I

Edgar Guest
Is never at his best.

II. MORE FROSTBITE

(With all due apologies)

Some say that Poesy will die by fire,
    Some say by frost;
By what I hear from Untermeyer,
    I favor either at any cost.

III

I don't like Ciardi
By the inch or by the yardi.

IV

Let us add a new word to the language of poetic rivalries:
Now wouldn't Randall Jarrell make a fine name for a literary
    disease?
So, boys, roll this over your cracker barrells:
"He himself died of the randalljarrells."

V

My life wouldn't get any darker
If I never read another line by Dorothy Parker.

VI. KILROY

Karl Shapiro
Was never here, O!

VII

London Bridge is falling down,
What ever happened to Harry Brown?

VIII

Peter Viereck
Insists he rhymes with "lyric";
But even that, I have no doubt,
In time is sure to peter out.

                                            Oscar Williams

The Blurb

Consider, please, the jacket blurb,
Which, shorn of pronoun, noun and verb,
With adjective and adverb hymns
The newborn masterpiece and limns
Its excellence, importance, justness,
Necessity, and downright mustness,
And leaves the maybes, buts, and nots
To eloquent, outspoken dots.   *Richard Armour*

One-way Song, XXIV

In any medium except that of verse
Forthwith I could enlighten you. Too terse,
And as it were compact, this form of art—
Which handles the finished product only—the hard
Master-material of selected sound.
The intellect has its workshops underground;
We cannot go back, out of this dance of words,
To become the teacher. Here we behave as birds—
The brain-that-sweats *offends,* it breaks our spell,
You do see that? we really must not *smell*
In this role: it is aristocratic but
Cudgel your brains in this case you must *not.*
So you will understand that argument,
Except in intent stylistic, or to invent
A certain pattern, is out of the question here.
I can only release, as elegant as deer,
A herd of wandering shapes, which *may* go straight,
But are just as likely to have grandly strayed,
Before we write finis out of sight and reach.
I cannot help this. It is noblesse oblige. *Wyndham Lewis*

The Shortest Poem in the World

I
Why?   *Eli Siegel*

The Next Shortest Poem in the World

You.
Boo!   *Anonymous*

The Next Next Shortest Poem in the World

We?
Whee!   *Martha Salemme*

Don't Guess, Let Me Tell You

Personally, I don't care whether a detective-story writer was
    educated in night school or day school
So long as he doesn't belong to the H.I.B.K. school,
The H.I.B.K. being a device to which too many detective-story
    writers are prone;
Namely, the Had I But Known.
Sometimes it is the Had I But Known what grim secret lurked
    behind that smiling exterior, I would never have set
    foot within the door;
Sometimes the Had I But Known then what I know now, I
    could have saved at least three lives by revealing to the
    Inspector the conversation I heard through that fortui-
    tous hole in the floor.
Had I But Known narrators are the ones who hear a stealthy
    creak at midnight in the tower where the body lies and,
    instead of locking their door or arousing the drowsy
    policeman posted outside their room, sneak off by
    themselves to the tower and suddenly they hear a breath
    exhaled behind them,
And they have no time to scream, they know nothing else till
    the men from the D.A.'s office come in next morning
    and find them.
Had I But Known-ers are quick to assume the prerogatives of
    the Deity,
For they will suppress evidence that doesn't suit their theories
    with appalling spontaneity,
And when the killer is finally trapped into a confession by some
    elaborate device of the Had I But Known-ers some
    hundred pages later than if they hadn't held their
    knowledge aloof,
Why, they say, Why, Inspector, I knew all along it was he, but
    I couldn't tell you, you would have laughed at me unless
    I had absolute proof.
Would you like for your library a nice detective story which I
    am sorry to say I didn't rent but owns?
I wouldn't have bought it had I but known it was impregnated
    with Had I But Knowns.

                         Ogden Nash

Self-portrait of the Laureate of Nonsense

How pleasant to know Mr. Lear!
    Who has written such volumes of stuff!
Some think him ill-tempered and queer,
    But a few think him pleasant enough.

His mind is concrete and fastidious,
  His nose is remarkably big;
His visage is more or less hideous,
  His beard it resembles a wig.

He has ears, and two eyes, and ten fingers,
  Leastways, if you reckon two thumbs;
Long ago he was one of the singers,
  But now he is one of the dumbs.

He sits in a beautiful parlor,
  With hundreds of books on the wall;
He drinks a great deal of Marsala,
  But never gets tipsy at all.

He has many friends, laymen and clerical;
  Old Foss is the name of his cat;
His body is perfectly spherical,
  He weareth a runcible hat.

When he walks in a waterproof white,
  The children run after him so!
Calling out, "He's come out in his night-
  Gown, that crazy old Englishman, oh!"

He weeps by the side of the ocean,
  He weeps on the top of the hill;
He purchases pancakes and lotion,
  And chocolate shrimps from the mill.

He reads but he cannot speak Spanish,
  He cannot abide ginger-beer:
Ere the days of his pilgrimage vanish,
  How pleasant to know Mr. Lear!

Edward Lear

PART FIVE

Very Much of This World

Spectator ab Extra

I

As I sat at the Café I said to myself,
They may talk as they please about what they call pelf,
They may sneer as they like about eating and drinking,
But help it I cannot, I cannot help thinking
   How pleasant it is to have money, heigh-ho!
   How pleasant it is to have money.

I sit at my table *en grand seigneur*,
And when I have done, throw a crust to the poor;
Not only the pleasure itself of good living,
But also the pleasure of now and then giving:
   So pleasant it is to have money, heigh-ho!
   So pleasant it is to have money.

They may talk as they please about what they call pelf,
And how one ought never to think of one's self,

How pleasures of thought surpass eating and drinking,—
My pleasure of thought is the pleasure of thinking
  How pleasant it is to have money, heigh-ho!
  How pleasant it is to have money.

II. LE DINER

Come along, 'tis the time, ten or more minutes past,
And he who came first had to wait for the last;
The oysters ere this had been in and been out;
Whilst I have been sitting and thinking about
  How pleasant it is to have money, heigh-ho!
  How pleasant it is to have money.

A clear soup with eggs; *voilà tout;* of the fish
The *filets de sole* are a moderate dish
A la Orly, but you're for red mullet, you say:
By the gods of good fare, who can question today
  How pleasant it is to have money, heigh-ho!
  How pleasant it is to have money.

After oysters, sauterne; then sherry; champagne,
Ere one one bottle goes, comes another again;
Fly up, thou bold cork, to the ceiling above,
And tell to our ears in the sound that they love
  How pleasant it is to have money, heigh-ho!
  How pleasant it is to have money.

I've the simplest of palates; absurd it may be,
But I almost could dine on a *poulet-au-riz,*
Fish and soup and omelette and that—but the deuce—
There were to be woodcocks, and not *Charlotte Russe!*
  So pleasant it is to have money, heigh-ho!
  So pleasant it is to have money.

Your chablis is acid, away with the hock,
Give me the pure juice of the purple médoc:
St. Peray is exquisite; but, if you please,
Some burgundy just before tasting the cheese.
  So pleasant it is to have money, heigh-ho!
  So pleasant it is to have money.

As for that, pass the bottle, and d—n the expense,
I've seen it observed by a writer of sense,
That the laboring classes could scarce live a day,
If people like us didn't eat, drink, and pay.
  So useful it is to have money, heigh-ho!
  So useful it is to have money.

One ought to be grateful, I quite apprehend,
Having dinner and supper and plenty to spend,
And so suppose now, while the things go away,
By way of a grace we all stand up and say
    How pleasant it is to have money, heigh-ho!
    How pleasant it is to have money.

III. PARVENANT

I cannot but ask, in the park and the streets
When I look at the number of persons one meets,
Whate'er in the world the poor devils can do
Whose fathers and mothers can't give them a *sou*.
    So needful it is to have money, heigh-ho!
    So needful it is to have money.

I ride, and I drive, and I care not a d—n,
The people look up and they ask who I am;
And if I should chance to run over a cad,
I can pay for the damage, if ever so bad.
    So useful it is to have money, heigh-ho!
    So useful it is to have money.

It was but this winter I came up to town,
And already I'm gaining a sort of renown;
Find my way to good houses without much ado,
Am beginning to see the nobility too.
    So useful it is to have money, heigh-ho!
    So useful it is to have money.

O dear what a pity they ever should lose it,
Since they are the people that know how to use it;
So easy, so stately, such manners, such dinners,
And yet, after all, it is we are the winners.
    So needful it is to have money, heigh-ho!
    So needful it is to have money.

It's all very well to be handsome and tall,
Which certainly makes you look well at a ball;
It's all very well to be clever and witty,
But if you are poor, why it's only a pity.
    So needful it is to have money, heigh-ho!
    So needful it is to have money.

There's something undoubtedly in a fine air,
To know how to smile and be able to stare.
High breeding is something, but well-bred or not,

In the end the one question is, what have you got.
　So needful it is to have money, heigh-ho!
　So needful it is to have money.

And the angels in pink and the angels in blue,
In muslins and moirés so lovely and new,
What is it they want, and so wish you to guess,
But if you have money, the answer is Yes.
　So needful, they tell you, is money, heigh-ho!
　So needful it is to have money.

Arthur Hugh Clough

All Saints

In a church which is furnish'd with mullion and gable,
　With altar and reredos, with gargoyle and groin,
The penitents' dresses are sealskin and sable,
　The odor of sanctity's eau-de-Cologne.
But only could Lucifer, flying from Hades,
　Gaze down on this crowd with its panniers and paints,
He would say, as he looked at the lords and the ladies,
　"Oh, where is *All Sinners*, if this is *All Saints*?"

Edmund Yates

You're So Kind

I never forget a face—
But I am willing to make an exception in your case.

Groucho Marx

A Word of Encouragement

O what a tangled web we weave
When first we practice to deceive!
But when we've practiced quite a while
How vastly we improve our style!

J. R. Pope

The Saddest Words

. . . Of all sad words of tongue or pen,
The saddest are these: "It might have been!"

J. G. Whittier

To the Terrestrial Globe

by a Miserable Wretch

Roll on, thou ball, roll on!
Through pathless realms of Space
　Roll on!
What though I'm in a sorry case?

What though I cannot meet my bills?
What though I suffer toothache's ills?
What though I swallow countless pills?
　　Never *you* mind!
　　　　Roll on!

Roll on, thou ball, roll on!
Through seas of inky air
　　Roll on!
It's true I have no shirts to wear;
It's true my butcher's bill is due;
It's true my prospects all look blue—
But don't let that unsettle you:
　　Never *you* mind!
　　　　Roll on!　　[*It rolls on.*]

Sir W. S. Gilbert

A Ballad on the Taxes

Good people, what, will you of all be bereft—
Will you never learn wit while a penny is left?
You are all like the dog in the fable betray'd,
To let go the substance and snatch at the shade;
With specious pretenses, and foreign expenses,
　　We war for Religion, and waste all our chink,
'Tis nipped, and 'tis clipped, 'tis lent, and 'tis spent,
　　Till 'tis gone, 'tis gone to the Devil I think.

We pay for our new-born, we pay for our dead,
We pay if we're single, we pay if we're wed;
To show that our merciful senate don't fail,
They begin at our head and tax down to the tail.
We pay through the nose by subjecting foes,
　　Yet for all our expenses get nothing but blows;
At home we are cheated, abroad we're defeated,
　　But the end on't, the end on't—the Lord above knows!

We parted with all our old money, to shew
We foolishly hope for a plenty of new;
But might have remember'd, when we came to the push,
That a bird in the hand is worth two in the bush:
We now like poor wretches are kept under hatches,
　　At rack and at manger like beasts in the ark,
Since our burgesses and knights make us pay for our lights—
　　Why should we, why should we be kept in the dark?

Edward Ward

Note on Intellectuals

To the man-in-the-street, who, I'm sorry to say
    Is a keen observer of life,
The word Intellectual suggests straight away
    A man who's untrue to his wife.

W. H. Auden

Woman's Will

Men dying make their wills—but wives
    Escape a work so sad;
Why should they make what all their lives
    The gentle dames have had?

John G. Saxe

Trial and Error

A lady is smarter than a gentleman, maybe.
She can sew a fine seam, she can have a baby,
She can use her intuition instead of her brain,
But she can't fold a paper on a crowded train.

Phyllis McGinley

A Baker's Duzzen uv Wize Sawz

Them ez wants, must choose.
Them ez hez, must lose.
Them ez knows, won't blab.
Them ez guesses, will gab.
Them ez borrows, sorrows.
Them ez lends, spends.
Them ez gives, lives.
Them ez keeps dark, is deep.
Them ez kin earn, kin keep.
Them ez aims, hits.
Them ez hez, gits.
Them ez waits, win.
Them ez *will, kin.*

Edward Rowland Sill

Angleworm

If we go walking on the streets
When there has been a storm
We often tread upon the feet
Of the lowly angleworm.

Herbert Cahoon

Worldly Wisdom

I. THE WISE OLD OWL

A wise old owl sat on an oak,
The more he saw the less he spoke;
The less he spoke the more he heard;
Why aren't we like that wise old bird?

Edward H. Richards

II

A promise made
Is a debt unpaid.   *Anonymous*

III

Never ask of money spent
Where the spender thinks it went.
Nobody was ever meant
To remember or invent
What he did with every cent.   *Robert Frost*

IV

From Greenland to Iceland
From Sitka to Siam,
There are so many people
More clever than I am.   *Anonymous*

V

Who does not love wine, women and song
Remains a fool his whole life long.   *J. H. Voss*

VI. FIGHT

He that is in the battle slain
Will never rise to fight again:
But he that fights and runs away
Will live to fight another day.   *Anonymous*

VII. MAN IS A FOOL

As a rule, man is a fool,
When it's hot, he wants it cool;
When it's cool, he wants it hot,
Always wanting what is not.

Anonymous

VIII

What can't be cured
Must be endured.

Anonymous

IX. EPIGRAM

To John I owed great obligation;
But John unhappily thought fit
To publish it to all nation:
So John and I are more than quit.

Matthew Prior

X. THE MERRY HEART

Jog on, jog on, the footpath way,
And merrily hent the stile-a;
A merry heart goes all the day,
Your sad tires in a mile-a.

William Shakespeare

XI. *From* THE RUBÁIYÁT

A Book of Verses underneath the Bough,
A Jug of Wine, a Loaf of Bread, and Thou
Beside me singing in the Wilderness—
Oh, Wilderness were Paradise enow!

Edward FitzGerald

XII

Reason has moons, but moons not hers,
Lie mirror'd on her sea,
Confounding her astronomers,
But, O! delighting me.

Ralph Hodgson

XIII. A CHRISTIAN

A Christian is a man who feels
Repentance on a Sunday
For what he did on Saturday
And is going to do on Monday.

Thomas Russell Ybarra

XIV. A MESSAGE FOR THE NATIONS OF THE WORLD

It's *co*-existence
Or *no* existe..ce.   *Bertrand Russell*

XV. THE LIE OF THE LAND

The same old charitable lie
Repeated as the years scoot by
Perpetually makes a hit—
"You really haven't changed a bit!"
Margaret Fishback

Hair

I'd rather have Fingers than Toes,
I'd rather have Eyes than a Nose;
And as for my Hair
I'm glad it's all there,
I'll be awfully sad when it goes. *Gelett Burgess*

More Hair

Babies haven't any hair;
Old men's heads are just as bare;—
Between the cradle and the grave
Lies a haircut and a shave. *Samuel Hoffenstein*

My Candle Burns at Both Ends

My candle burns at both ends;
It will not last the night;
But ah, my foes, and oh, my friends—
It gives a lovely light! *Edna St. Vincent Millay*

The Lesson for Today

If this uncertain age in which we dwell
Were really as dark as I hear sages tell,
And I convinced that they were really sages,
I should not curse myself with it to hell,
But leaving not the chair I long have sat in,
I should betake me back ten thousand pages
To the world's undebatably dark ages,
And getting up my medieval Latin,
Seek converse common cause and brotherhood
(By all that's liberal—I should, I should)
With poets who could calmly take the fate
Of being born at once too early and late,
And for these reasons kept from being great.
Yet singing but Dione in the wood
And *ver aspergit terram floribus*
They slowly led old Latin verse to rhyme
And to forget the ancient lengths of time,
And so began the modern world for us.

I'd say, O Master of the Palace School,
You were not Charles' nor anybody's fool:
Tell me as pedagogue to pedagogue,
You did not know that since King Charles did rule
You had no chance but to be minor, did you?
Your light was spent perhaps as in a fog
That at once kept you burning low and hid you.
The age may very well have been to blame
For your not having won to Virgil's fame.
But no one ever heard you make the claim.
You would not think you knew enough to judge
The age when full upon you. That's my point.
We have today and I could call their name
Who know exactly what is out of joint
To make their verse and their excuses lame.
They've tried to grasp with too much social fact
Too large a situation. You and I
Would be afraid if we should comprehend
And get outside of too much bad statistics
Our muscles never could again contract:
We never could recover human shape,
But must live lives out mentally agape,
Or die of philosophical distension.
That's how we feel—and we're no special mystics.

We can't appraise the time in which we act.
But for the folly of it, let's pretend
We know enough to know it for adverse.
One more millennium's about to end.
Let's celebrate the event, my distant friend,
In publicly disputing which is worse,
The present age or your age. You and I
As schoolmen of repute should qualify
To wage a fine scholastical contention
As to whose age deserves the lower mark,
Or should I say the higher one, for dark.
I can just hear the way you make it go:
There's always something to be sorry for,
A sordid peace or an outrageous war.
Yes, yes, of course. We have the same convention.
The groundwork of all faith is human woe.
It was well worth preliminary mention.
There's nothing but injustice to be had,
No choice is left a poet, you might add,
But how to take the curse, tragic or comic.
It was well worth preliminary mention.
But let's get on to where our cases part,
If part they do. Let me propose a start.
(We're rivals in the badness of our case,
Remember, and must keep a solemn face.)
Space ails us moderns: we are sick with space.
Its contemplation makes us out as small
As a brief epidemic of microbes
That in a good glass may be seen to crawl
The patina of this the least of globes.
But have we there the advantage after all?
You were belittled into vilest worms
God hardly tolerated with his feet;
Which comes to the same thing in different terms.
We both are the belittled human race.
One as compared with God and one with space.
I had thought ours the more profound disgrace;
But doubtless this was only my conceit.
The cloister and the observatory saint
Take comfort in about the same complaint.
So science and religion really meet.

I can just hear you call your Palace class:
Come learn the Latin Eheu for alas.
You may not want to use it and you may.
O paladins, the lesson for today

Is how to be unhappy yet polite.
And at the summons Roland, Olivier,
And every sheepish paladin and peer,
Being already more than proved in fight,
Sits down in school to try if he can write
Like Horace in the true Horatian vein,
Yet like a Christian disciplined to bend
His mind to thinking always of the end.
Memento Mori and obey the Lord.
Art and religion love the somber chord.
Earth's a hard place in which to save the soul,
And could it be brought under state control,
So automatically we all were saved,
Its separateness from Heaven could be waived;
It might as well at once be kingdom-come.
(Perhaps it will be next millennium.)

But these are universals, not confined
To any one time, place, or human kind.
We're either nothing or a God's regret.
As ever when philosophers are met,
No matter where they stoutly mean to get,
Nor what particulars they reason from,
They are philosophers, and from old habit
They end up in the universal Whole
As unoriginal as any rabbit.

One age is like another for the soul.
I'm telling you. You haven't said a thing,
Unless I put it in your mouth to say.
I'm having the whole argument my way—
But in your favor—please to tell your King—
In having granted you all ages shine
With equal darkness, yours as dark as mine.
I'm liberal. You, you aristocrat
Won't know exactly what I mean by that.
I mean so altruistically moral
I never take my own side in a quarrel.
I'd lay my hand on his hand on his staff,
Lean back and have my confidential laugh,
And tell him I had read his Epitaph.

It sent me to the graves the other day.
The only other there was far away
Across the landscape with a watering pot
At his devotions in a special plot.

And he was there resuscitating flowers
(Make no mistake about its being bones);
But I was only there to read the stones
To see what on the whole they had to say
About how long a man may think to live,
Which is becoming my concern of late.
And very wide the choice they seemed to give;
The ages ranging all the way from hours
To months and years and many many years.
One man had lived one hundred years and eight.
But though we all may be inclined to wait
And follow some development of state,
Or see what comes of science and invention,
There is a limit to our time extension.
We all are doomed to broken-off careers,
And so's the nation, so's the total race.
The earth itself is liable to the fate
Of meaninglessly being broken off.
(And hence so many literary tears
At which my inclination is to scoff.)
I may have wept that any should have died
Or missed the chance, or not have been their best,
Or been their riches, fame, or love denied;
On me as much as any is the jest.
I take my incompleteness with the rest.
God bless himself can no one else be blessed.

I hold your doctrine of Memento Mori.
And were an epitaph to be my story
I'd have a short one ready for my own.
I would have written of me on my stone:
I had a lover's quarrel with the world.

Robert Frost

The Latest Decalogue

Thou shalt have one God only; who
Would be at the expense of two?
No graven images may be
Worshiped, except the currency:
Swear not at all; for, for thy curse
Thine enemy is none the worse:
At church on Sunday to attend
Will serve to keep the world thy friend:
Honor thy parents; that is, all
From whom advancement may befall:
Thou shalt not kill; but need'st not strive
Officiously to keep alive:
Do not adultery commit;
Advantage rarely comes of it:
Thou shalt not steal; an empty feat,
When it's so lucrative to cheat:
Bear not false witness; let the lie
Have time on its own wings to fly:
Thou shalt not covet, but tradition
Approves all forms of competition.

Arthur Hugh Clough

The Holy Office

Myself unto myself will give
This name, Katharsis-Purgative.
I, who disheveled ways forsook
To hold the poets' grammar-book,
Bringing to tavern and to brothel
The mind of witty Aristotle,
Lest bards in the attempt should err
Must here be my interpreter:
Wherefore receive now from my lip
Peripatetic scholarship.
To enter heaven, travel hell,
Be piteous or terrible
One positively needs the ease
Of plenary indulgences.
For every true-born mysticist
A Dante is, unprejudiced,
Who safe at ingle-nook, by proxy,
Hazards extremes of heterodoxy,
Like him who finds joy at a table
Pondering the uncomfortable.

Ruling one's life by common sense
How can one fail to be intense?
But I must not accounted be
One of that mumming company—
With him who hies him to appease
His giddy dames' frivolities
While they console him when he whinges
With gold-embroidered Celtic fringes—
Or him who sober all the day
Mixes a naggin in his play—
Or him whose conduct "seems to own"
His preference for a man of "tone"—
Or him who plays the ragged patch
To millionaires in Hazelpatch
But weeping after holy fast
Confesses all his pagan past—
Or him who will his hat unfix
Neither to malt nor crucifix
But show to all that poor-dressed be
His high Castilian courtesy—
Oh him who loves his Master dear—
Or him who drinks his pint in fear—
Or him who once when snug abed
Saw Jesus Christ without his head
And tried so hard to win for us
The long-lost works of Aeschylus.
But all these men of whom I speak
Make me the sewer of their clique.
That they may dream their dreamy dreams
I carry off their filthy streams
For I can do those things for them
Through which I lost my diadem,
Those things for which Grandmother Church
Left me severely in the lurch.
Thus I relieve their timid arses,
Perform my office of Katharsis.
My scarlet leaves them white as wool:
Through me they purge a bellyful.
To sister mummers one and all
I act as vicar-general
And for each maiden, shy and nervous,
I do a similar kind service.
For I detect without surprise
That shadowy beauty in her eyes,
The "dare not" of sweet maidenhood
That answers my corruptive "would,"

Whenever publicly we meet
She never seems to think of it;
At night when close in bed she lies
And feels my hand between her thighs
My little love in light attire
Knows the soft flame that is desire.
But Mammon places under ban
The uses of Leviathan
And that high spirit ever wars
On Mammon's countless servitors
Nor can they ever be exempt
From his taxation of contempt.
So distantly I turn to view
The shamblings of that motley crew,
Those souls that hate the strength that mine has
Steeled in the school of old Aquinas.
Where they have crouched and crawled and prayed
I stand, the self-doomed, unafraid,
Unfellowed, friendless and alone,
Indifferent as the herring-bone,
Firm as the mountain ridges where
I flash my antlers on the air.
Let them continue as is meet
To adequate the balance sheet.
Though they may labor to the grave
My spirit shall they never have
Nor make my soul with theirs as one
Till the Mahamanvantara be done:
And though they spurn me from their door
My soul shall spurn them evermore.

James Joyce

The English

The Germans live in Germany,
The Romans live in Rome,
The Turkeys live in Turkey,
But the English live at Home.

J. H. Goring

The Moon

You say it's made of silver,
I say it's made of cheese—
For I am an American
And say what I damn please.

Robert Beverly Hale

A Little Man

And I am only a little man
Living in pre-occupied Japan,
And I say please and pretty please
Give me a piece of your damn cheese.

Anonymous

Clerihew

Sir Christopher Wren
Said, "I am going to dine with some men.
If anybody calls
Say I am designing St. Paul's."

E. C. Bentley

An Old Man of Boulogne

There was an old man of Boulogne
Who sang a most topical song.
    It wasn't the words
    Which frightened the birds,
But the horrible double entendre.

Anonymous

A Dublin Limerick

*(Inspired by a Gray Day, in the Royal Hibernian Hotel,
Oct. 1953)*

There was a young man from Chapultepec,
Who invented a practical catapult
    Which tossed bindles and bones
    And brickbats and scones
And flattened Kemal Pasha Ataturk.

Ray Bradbury

House Plant

A foam of leaves applauds the crimson signal
Run up by the sun. In the window across the street
A man is shaving, a percolator talks to itself
And a bob-tail cat boxes with the sash cord.

Winthrop Palmer

Dionysus

A yellow chrysanthemum with furious hair
Dismisses, each to its own blank cubby hole,
The drum of politics, the Bristol board
Of life-at-court, and the dead cigar
Under the table at regimental headquarters.

Winthrop Palmer

The Martian Maid

When the Martian Maid knocked on my door
I opened it. Guess what I saw?
A scrawny body—straggly and small,
A head bigger than a basketball.
She looked at me and then she laughed.
I looked at her and thought her daft.
All of a sudden I looked and spied
Two other Martians at her side.
They thought that I was Exhibit A
In a freak show opened that day.
Then I awoke and to my delight
I found I was mentally all right.
I stood up straight and yelled, "Hurray!"
For it was only a book I had read today.

Brian Lazarus, Age 12

The Unknown Citizen

*(To JS/07/M/378 This Marble Monument Is Erected
by the State)*

He was found by the Bureau of Statistics to be
One against whom there was no official complaint,
And all the reports on his conduct agree
That, in the modern sense of an old-fashioned word, he was a
saint,
For in everything he did he served the Greater Community.
Except for the War till the day he retired
He worked in a factory and never got fired,
But satisfied his employers, Fudge Motors Inc.
Yet he wasn't a scab or odd in his views,
For his Union reports that he paid his dues,
(Our report on his Union shows it was sound)
And our Social Psychology workers found
That he was popular with his mates and liked a drink.
The Press are convinced that he bought a paper every day

And that his reactions to advertisements were normal in every
way.
Policies taken out in his name prove that he was fully insured,
And his Health-card shows he was once in hospital but left it
cured.
Both Producers Research and High-Grade Living declare
He was fully sensible to the advantages of the Installment Plan
And had everything necessary to the Modern Man,
A phonograph, a radio, a car and a frigidaire.
Our researchers into Public Opinion are content
That he held the proper opinions for the time of year;
When there was peace, he was for peace; when there was war,
he went.
He was married and added five children to the population,
Which our Eugenist says was the right number for a parent of
his generation,
And our teachers report that he never interfered with their
education.
Was he free? Was he happy? The question is absurd:
Had anything been wrong, we should certainly have heard.

W. H. Auden

The Family Fool

Oh! a private buffoon is a lighthearted loon,
  If you listen to popular rumor;
From morning to night he's so joyous and bright,
  And he bubbles with wit and good humor!
He's so quaint and so terse, both in prose and in verse;
  Yet though people forgive his transgression,
There are one or two rules that all Family Fools
  Must observe if they love their profession.
        There are one or two rules,
          Half-a-dozen, maybe,
        That all family fools,
          Of whatever degree,
    Must observe if they love their profession.

If you wish to succeed as a jester, you'll need
  To consider each person's auricular;
What is allright for B. would quite scandalize C.
  (For C. is so very particular);
And D. may be dull, and E.'s very thick skull
  Is as empty of brains as a ladle;
While F. is F sharp, and will cry with a carp,
  That he's known your best joke from his cradle!
      When your humor they flout,

You can't let yourself go;
And it *does* put you out
When a person says, "Oh!
I have known that old joke from my cradle!"

If your master is surly, from getting up early
  (And tempers are short in the morning),
An inopportune joke is enough to provoke
  Him to give you, at once, a month's warning.
Then if you refrain, he is at you again,
  For he likes to get value for money,
He'll ask then and there, with an insolent stare,
  "If you know that you're paid to be funny?"
          It adds to the tasks
              Of a merryman's place,
          When your principal asks,
              With a scowl on his face,
  If you know that you're paid to be funny?

Comes a Bishop, maybe, or a solemn D.D.—
  Oh! beware of his anger provoking
Better not pull his hair—don't stick pins in his chair;
  He won't understand practical joking.
If the jests that you crack have an orthodox smack,
  You may get a bland smile from these sages;
But should it, by chance, be imported from France,
  Half-a-crown is stopped out of your wages!
          It's a general rule,
              Though your zeal it may quench
          If the Family Fool
              Makes a joke that's *too* French,
  Half-a-crown is stopped out of his wages!

Though your head it may rack with a bilious attack,
  And your senses with toothache you're losing,
Don't be mopy and flat—they don't fine you for that
  If you're properly quaint and amusing!
Though your wife ran away with a soldier that day
  And took with her your trifle of money;
Bless your heart, they don't mind—they're exceedingly kind—
  They don't blame you—as long as you're funny!
          It's a comfort to feel
              If your partner should flit,
          Though *you* suffer a deal,
              They don't mind it a bit—
  They don't blame you—so long as you're funny!

                                        Sir W. S. Gilbert

Hudibras, the Presbyterian Knight

He was in logic a great critic,
Profoundly skill'd in analytic.
He could distinguish, and divide
A hair 'twixt South and South-West side:
On either which he would dispute,
Confute, change hands, and still confute.
He'd undertake to prove by force
Of argument, a man's no horse.
He'd prove a buzzard is no fowl,
And that a lord may be an owl,
A calf an Alderman, a goose a Justice,
And rooks Committee-men, and Trustees;
He'd run in debt by disputation,
And pay with ratiocination.
All this by syllogism, true
In mood and figure, he would do.
For rhetoric he could not ope
His mouth, but out there flew a trope:
And when he happened to break off
I' th' middle of his speech, or cough,
H' had hard words, ready to shew why,
And tell what rules he did it by.
Else when with greatest art he spoke,
You'd think he talk'd like other folk,
For all a rhetorician's rules,
Teach nothing but to name his tools,
His ordinary rate of speech
In loftiness of sound was rich,
A Babylonish dialect,
Which learned pedants much affect.
It was a parti-colour'd dress
Of patch'd and pybal'd languages:
'Twas English cut on Greek and Latin,
Like fustian heretofore on satin.
It had an odd promiscuous tone,
As if h' had talk'd three parts in one.
Which made some think when he did gabble,
Th' had heard three laborers of Babel;
Or Cerberus himself pronounce
A leash of languages at once.
This he as volubly would vent
As if his stock would ne'er be spent.
And truly to support that charge
He had supplies as vast and large.

For he could coin or counterfeit
New words with little or no wit:
Words so debas'd and hard, no stone
Was hard enough to touch them on.
And when with hasty noise he spoke 'em,
The ignorant for current took 'em.
That had the orator who once,
Did fill his mouth with pebble stones
When he harangu'd, but known his phrase,
He would have us'd no other ways.

. . . .

Beside he was a shrewd philosopher,
And had read every text and gloss over:
What e'er the crabbed'st author hath
He understood b' implicit faith,
What ever skeptic could inquire for;
For every why he had a wherefore;
Knew more than forty of them do,
As far as words and terms could go.
All which he understood by rote,
And as occasion serv'd, would quote;
No matter whether right or wrong:
They might be either said or sung.
His notions fitted things so well,
That which was which he could not tell;
But oftentimes mistook th' one
For th' other, as great clerks have done.
He could reduce all things to acts,
And knew their natures by abstracts,
Where entity and quiddity
The ghosts of defunct bodies fly;
Where truth in person does appear,
Like words congeal'd in northern air.
He knew what's what, and that's as high
As metaphysic wit can fly,
In school divinity as able
As he that hight Irrefragable;
Profound in all the nominal
And real ways beyond them all;
And with as delicate a hand,
Could twist as tough a rope of sand,
And weave fine cobwebs, fit for skull
That's empty when the moon is full;
Such as take lodgings in a head
That's to be let unfurnished.

He could raise scruples dark and nice,
And after solve 'em in a trice:
As if divinity had catch'd
The itch, of purpose to be scratch'd;
Or, like a mountebank, did wound
And stab her self with doubts profound,
Only to show with how small pain
The sores of faith are cur'd again;
Although by woeful proof we find,
They always leave a scar behind.
He knew the seat of Paradise,
Could tell in what degree it lies:
And as he was dispos'd, could prove it,
Below the moon, or else above it.
What Adam dreamt of when his bride
Came from her closet in his side:
Whether the Devil tempted her
By a High Dutch interpreter:
If either of them had a navel;
Who first made music malleable:
Whether the serpent at the fall
Had cloven feet, or none at all.
All this without a gloss or comment,
He would unriddle in a moment:
In proper terms, such as men smatter
When they throw out and miss the matter.
For his religion it was fit
To match his learning and his wit:
'Twas Presbyterian true blue,
For he was of that stubborn crew
Of errant saints, whom all men grant
To be the true Church Militant:
Such as do build their faith upon
The holy text of pike and gun;
Decide all controversies by
Infallible artillery;
And prove their doctrine orthodox
By apostolic blows and knocks;
Call fire and sword and desolation,
A godly-thorough-Reformation,
Which always must be carried on,
And still be doing, never done:
As if religion were intended
For nothing else but to be mended.
A sect, whose chief devotion lies
In odd perverse antipathies;

In falling out with that or this,
And finding somewhat still amiss:
More peevish, cross, and splenetic,
Than dog distract, or monkey sick.
That with more care keep Holy-day
The wrong, than others the right way:
Compound for sins, they are inclin'd to;
By damning those they have no mind to;
Still so perverse and opposite,
As if they worship'd God for spite,
The self-same thing they will abhor
One way, and long another for.
Free-will they one way disavow,
Another, nothing else allow.
All piety consists therein
In them, in other men all sin.
Rather than fail, they will defy
That which they love most tenderly,
Quarrel with minc'd pies, and disparage
Their best and dearest friend, plum-porridge;
Fat pig and goose itself oppose,
And blaspheme custard through the nose.
Th' Apostles of this fierce Religion,
Like Mahomet's, were ass and widgeon,
To whom our Knight, by fast instinct
Of wit and temper was so linked,
As if hypocrisy and non-sense
Had got th' advowson of his conscience.

Samuel Butler

A Round Dozen of Famous Limericks

I. ENGLISH LIBERAL

"I think," thought Sam Butler,
        "Truth ever lies
        In mean compromise."
What could be subtler
Than the thought of Sam Butler?

Geoffrey Taylor

II. JUST FOR THE RIDE

There was a young man of the Clyde,
Who went to a funeral and cried.
        When asked who was dead,
        He stammered and said,
"I don't know—I just came for the ride."

Anonymous

III. NOT JUST FOR THE RIDE

There was a young lady of Niger
Who smiled as she rode on a tiger:
        They came back from the ride
        With the lady inside
And the smile on the face of the tiger.

Anonymous

IV. IT PAYS

There was a young man of Montrose
Who had pockets in none of his clothes.
        When asked by his lass
        Where he carried his brass,
He said: "Darling, I pay through the nose."

Arnold Bennett

V. MY FACE

As a beauty I'm not a great star,
There are others more handsome, by far,
        But my face—I don't mind it
        For I am behind it,
It's the people in front get the jar!

Anthony Euwer

VI. A OLD MAN FROM PERU

There wa. an old man from Peru
Who dreamed he was eating his shoe.
        He woke in a fright
        In the middle of the night
And found it was perfectly true.   *Anonymous*

VII. EDOUARD

A bugler named Dougal MacDougal
Found ingenious ways to be frugal.
    He learned how to sneeze
    In various keys,
Thus saving the price of a bugle.

Ogden Nash

VIII. A HAPPY TIME

There was a young fellow named Hall,
Who fell in the spring in the fall;
    'Twould have been a sad thing
    If he'd died in the spring,
But he didn't—he died in the fall.

Anonymous

IX

A Turk by the name of Haroun
Ate whisky by means of a spoon.
    To one who asked why,
    This Turk made reply:
"To drink is forbidden, you loon."

Anonymous

X. OLD MAN OF ST. BEES

There was an old man of St. Bees,
Who was stung in the arm by a wasp;
    When they asked, "Does it hurt?"
    He replied, "No, it doesn't,
But I thought all the while 'twas a hornet!"

Sir W. S. Gilbert

XI

A decrepit old gasman, named Peter,
While hunting around his gas heater,
    Touched a leak with his light;
    He rose out of sight—
And, as everyone who knows anything about
    poetry can tell you, he also ruined the meter.

Anonymous

XII. REQUIEM

There was a young belle of old Natchez
Whose garments were always in patchez.
    When comment arose
    On the state of her clothes,
She drawled, "When Ah itchez, Ah scratchez."

Ogden Nash

Potpourri in Rhyme

I

A swarm of bees in May
Is worth a load of hay;
A swarm of bees in June
Is worth a silver spoon;
A swarm of bees in July
Is not worth a fly.

II

Man may work from sun to sun,
But woman's work is never done.

III

Fe, Fi, Fo, Fum!
I smell the blood of an Englishman;
Be he alive or be he dead,
I'll grind his bones to make my bread.

IV

Lives of great men all remind us
As their pages o'er we turn,
That we're apt to leave behind us
Letters that we ought to burn.

V

See the happy moron,
He doesn't give a damn.
I wish I were a moron—
My God, perhaps I am!

VI

You will eat, bye & bye,
In that glorious land above the sky;
Work and pray, live on hay,
You'll get pie in the sky when you die.

VII

Use it up and wear it out,
Make it do, or do without.

Anonymous

PART SIX

Invectives, Imprecations, and Other Blasts

Ancient Music

Winter is icumen in,
Lhude sing Goddamm,
Raineth drop and staineth slop,
And how the wind doth ramm!
     Sing: Goddamm.
Skiddeth bus and sloppeth us,
An ague hath my ham.
Freezeth river, turneth liver,
     Damn you, sing: Goddamm.
Goddamm, Goddamm, 'tis why I am, Goddamm,
     So 'gainst the winter's balm.
Sing goddamm, damm, sing Goddamm,
Sing goddamm, sing goddamm, DAMM.

Ezra Pound

The Traveler's Curse After Misdirection
(*From the Welsh*)

May they wander stage by stage
Of the same vain pilgrimage,
Stumbling on, age after age,
Night and day, mile after mile,
At each and every step, a stile;
At each and every stile, withal,
May they catch their feet and fall;
At each and every fall they take,
May a bone within them break;
And may the bones that break within
Not be, for variation's sake,
Now rib, now thigh, now arm, now shin,
But always, without fail, THE NECK.

Robert Graves

next to of course god america i

"next to of course god america i
love you land of the pilgrims' and so forth oh
say can you see by the dawn's early my
country 'tis of centuries come and go
and are no more what of it we should worry
in every language even deafanddumb
thy sons acclaim your glorious name by gorry
by jingo by gee by gosh by gum
why talk of beauty what could be more beautiful than these heroic happy dead
who rushed like lions to the roaring slaughter
they did not stop to think they died instead
then shall the voice of liberty be mute?"

He spoke. And drank rapidly a glass of water

e. e. cummings

To a Fat Lady Seen from the Train

O why do you walk through the fields in gloves,
    Missing so much and so much?
O fat white woman whom nobody loves,
Why do you walk through the fields in gloves,
When the grass is soft as the breast of doves
    And shivering-sweet to the touch?
O why do you walk through the fields in gloves,
    Missing so much and so much?

Frances Cornford

The Complete Misanthropist

I love to think of things I hate
      In moments of mopishness;
I hate people who sit up straight,
And youths who smirk about their "date,"
      And the dates who smirk no less.

I hate children who clutch and whine,
      And the arrogant, virtuous poor;
And critical connoisseurs of wine,
And everything that is called a shrine,
      And Art and Literature.

I hate eggs and I hate the hen;
      I hate the rooster, too.
I hate people who wield the pen,
I hate women and I hate men;
      And what's more, I hate you.

                              Morris Bishop

The Complaint of Chaucer to His Purse

To you, my purse, and to non other wight
Complayne I, for ye be my lady dere!
I am so sory, now that ye been light;
For certes, but ye make me hevy chere,
Me were as leef be layd upon my bere;
For whiche unto your mercy thus I crye:
Beth hevy ageyn, or elles moote I dye!

Now voucheth sauf this day, or hit be night,
That I of you the blisful soun may here,
Or see your colour lyk the sonne bright,
That of yelownesse hadde never pere.
Ye be my lyf, ye be myn hertes stere,
Quene of comfort and of good companye:
Beth hevy ageyn, or elles moote I dye!

Now purse, that be to me my lyves light,
And saveour, as doun in this world here,
Out of this toune help me through your might,
Sin that ye wole nat been my tresorere;
For I am shave as nye as any frere.
But yet I pray unto your curtesye:
Beth hevy ageyn, or elles moote I dye!

L'ENVOY DE CHAUCER

O conquerour of Brutes Albyon,
Which that by lyne and free eleccion
Ben verray king, this song to you I send;
And ye, that mowen al our harmes amend,
Have mind upon my supplicacioun!

Geoffrey Chaucer

A Satire Against Mankind

Were I, who, to my cost, already am
One of those strange, prodigious creatures, man,
A spirit free to choose for my own share
What sort of flesh and blood I pleased to wear,
I'd be a dog, a monkey, or a bear,
Or anything, but that vain animal,
Who is so proud of being rational.
The senses are too gross, and he'll contrive
A sixth to contradict the other five;
And before certain instinct will prefer
Reason, which fifty times for one does err—
Reason, an *ignis fatuus* of the mind,
Which leaves the light of nature, sense, behind.
Pathless and dangerous wand'ring ways it takes
Through error's fenny bogs and thorny brakes,
Whilst the misguided follower climbs with pain
Mountains of whimsies, heap'd in his own brain,
Stumbling from thought to thought, falls headlong down
Into doubt's boundless sea, where, like to drown,
Books bear him up a while and make him try
To swim with bladders of philosophy,
In hopes still to o'ertake the skipping light.
The vapor dances in his dazzled sight
Till, spent, it leaves him to eternal night.
Then old age and experience, hand in hand,
Lead him to death and make him understand
After a search so painful and so long,
That all his life he has been in the wrong.
Huddled in dirt [the] reas'ning engine lies
Who was so proud, so witty, and so wise.
Pride drew him in, as cheats their bubbles catch,
And made him venture to be made a wretch.
His wisdom did his happiness destroy,
Aiming to know the world he should enjoy;
And wit was his vain frivolous pretense

Of pleasing others at his own expense.
For wits are treated just like common whores;
First they're enjoyed, and then kicked out of doors.
The pleasure past, a threatening doubt remains,
That frights the enjoyer with succeeding pains.
Women and men of wit are dangerous tools,
And ever fatal to admiring fools.
Pleasure allures, and when the fops escape,
'Tis not that they're beloved, but fortunate,
And therefore what they fear, at least they hate. . . .
Be judge yourself, I'll bring it to the test,
Which is the basest creature, man or beast:
Birds feed on birds, beasts on each other prey;
But savage man alone does man betray.
Pressed by necessity, they kill for food;
Man undoes man to do himself no good.
With teeth and claws by Nature armed they hunt
Nature's allowance, to supply their want;
But man with smiles, embraces, friendships, praise,
Inhumanly his fellow's life betrays,
With voluntary pains works his distress,
Not through necessity, but wantonness.
For hunger or for love they bite or tear,
Whilst wretched man is still in arms for fear:
For fear he arms, and is of arms afraid;
From fear to fear successively betrayed.
Base fear, the source whence his best passions came,
His boasted honor, and his dear-bought fame,
The lust of power, to which he's such a slave,
And for the which alone he dares be brave;
To which his various projects are designed,
Which makes him generous, affable, and kind;
For which he takes such pains to be thought wise,
And screws his actions in a forced disguise;
Leads a most tedious life in misery,
Under laborious, mean hypocrisy.
Look to the bottom of his vast design,
Wherein man's wisdom, power, and glory join—
The good he acts, the ill he does endure,
'Tis all from fear, to make himself secure.
Merely for safety, after fame they thirst,
For all men would be cowards if they durst;
And honesty's against all common sense—
Men must be knaves; 'tis in their own defense.
Mankind's dishonest; if they think it fair,
Amongst known cheats, to play upon the square.

You'll be undone—
Nor can weak truth your reputation save;
The knaves will all agree to call you knave.
Wronged shall he live, insulted o'er, oppressed,
Who dares be less a villain than the rest.
Thus here you see what human nature craves,
Most men are cowards, all men should be knaves.
The difference lies, as far as I can see,
Not in the thing itself, but the degree;
And all the subject-matter of debate,
Is only, who's a knave of the first rate.

                          John Wilmot, Earl of Rochester

Poems in Praise of Practically Nothing

I

You buy some flowers for your table;
You tend them tenderly as you're able;
You fetch them water from hither and thither—
What thanks do you get for it all? They wither.

II

Only the wholesomest foods you eat;
You lave and you lave from your head to your feet;
The earth is not steadier on its axis
Than you in the matter of prophylaxis;
You go to bed early, and early you rise;
You scrub your teeth and you scour your eyes—
What thanks do you get for it all? Nephritis,
Pneumonia, appendicitis,
Renal calculus and gastritis.

III

You get a girl; and you say you love her;
You pan the comparative stars above her;
You roast the comparative roses below her;
You throw the bull that you'll never throw her—
What thanks do you get? The very first whozis
Who tips his mitt, with him she vamooses.

IV

You buy yourself a new suit of clothes;
The care you give it, God only knows;
The material, of course, is the very best yet;

You get it pressed and pressed and pressed yet;
You keep it free from specks so tiny—
What thanks do you get? The pants get shiny.

V

You leap out of bed; you start to get ready;
You dress and you dress till you feel unsteady;
Hours go by, and you're still busy
Putting on clothes, till your brain is dizzy.
Do you flinch, do you quit, do you go out naked?—
The least little button, you don't forsake it.
What thanks do you get? Well, for all this mess, yet
When night comes around you've got to undress yet.

Samuel Hoffenstein

Greetings of the Season

I wish my enemies would go to hell,
Noel! Noel! Noel! Noel! Noel!

Hilaire Belloc

Epigrams

AN ANSWER TO THE PARSON

"Why of the sheep do you not learn peace?"
"Because I don't want you to shear my fleece."

SIR JOSHUA REYNOLDS

When Sir Joshua Reynolds died
    All Nature was degraded;
The King dropped a tear into the Queen's ear,
    And all his pictures faded.

TO ENGLISH CONNOISSEURS

You must agree that Rubens was a fool,
And yet you make him master of your school,
And give more money for his slobberings
Than you will give for Raphael's finest things.
I understood Christ was a carpenter
And not a brewer's servant, my good Sir.

TO FLAXMAN

I mock thee not, though I by thee am mockèd;
Thou call'st me madman, but I call thee blockhead.

TO HUNT

You think Fuseli is not a Great Painter. I'm glad:
This is one of the best compliments he ever had.

A CHARACTER

Her whole life is an epigram, smart, smooth, and neatly
    penned,
Platted quite neat to catch applause, with a hang-noose at the
    end.   *William Blake*

Overheard at a Sculpture Show at a Museum

"Any floozie
Can look at a Brancusi!"

Anonymous

A Semi-revolution

I advocate a semi-revolution.
The trouble with a total revolution
(Ask any reputable Rosicrucian)
Is that it brings the same class up on top.
Executives of skillful execution
Will therefore plan to go halfway and stop.
Yes, revolutions are the only salves,
But they're one thing that should be done by halves.

Robert Frost

A Total Revolution
(An Answer for Robert Frost)

I advocate a total revolution.
The trouble with a semi-revolution,
It's likely to be slow as evolution.
Who wants to spend the ages in collusion
With Compromise, Complacence and Confusion?
As for the same class coming up on top
That's wholecloth from the propaganda shop;
The old saw says there's loads of room on top,
That's where the poor should really plan to stop.
And speaking of those people called the "haves,"
Who own the whole cow and must have the calves
(And plant the wounds so they can sell the salves)
They won't be stopped by doing things by halves.
I say that for a permanent solution
There's nothing like a total revolution!

P.S. And may I add by way of a conclusion
    I wouldn't dream to ask a Rosicrucian.

Oscar Williams

How Beastly the Bourgeois Is

How beastly the bourgeois is
especially the male of the species—

Presentable, eminently presentable—
shall I make you a present of him?
Isn't he handsome? isn't he healthy? Isn't he a fine specimen?
doesn't he look the fresh clean englishman, outside?
Isn't it god's own image? tramping his thirty miles a day
after partridges, or a little rubber ball?
wouldn't you like to be like that, well off, and quite the thing?

Oh, but wait!
Let him meet a new emotion, let him be faced with another
    man's need,
let him come home to a bit of moral difficulty, let life face him
    with a new demand on his understanding
and then watch him go soggy, like a wet meringue.
Watch him turn into a mess, either a fool or a bully.
Just watch the display of him, confronted with a new demand
    on his intelligence,
a new life-demand.

How beastly the bourgeois is
especially the male of the species—

Nicely groomed, like a mushroom
standing there so sleek and erect and eyeable—
and like a fungus, living on the remains of bygone life
sucking his life out of the dead leaves of greater life than his
    own.
And even so, he's stale, he's been there too long.
Touch him, and you'll find he's all gone inside
Just like an old mushroom, all wormy inside, and hollow
under a smooth skin and an upright appearance.

Full of seething, wormy, hollow feelings
rather nasty—
How beastly the bourgeois is!

Standing in their thousands, these appearances, in damp Eng-
    land
what a pity they can't all be kicked over
like sickening toadstools, and left to melt back, swiftly into the
    soil of England.

D. H. Lawrence

Song of the Open Road

I think that I shall never see
A billboard lovely as a tree.
Perhaps, unless the billboards fall,
I'll never see a tree at all.

Ogden Nash

Who's the Fool Now?

Martin said to his man,
    Fie! man, fie!
Oh, Martin said to his man,
    Who's the fool now?
Martin said to his man,
Fill thou the cup, and I the can;
Thou hast well drunken, man:
    Who's the fool now?

I see a sheep shearing corn,
    Fie! man, fie!
I see a sheep shearing corn,
    Who's the fool now?
I see a sheep shearing corn,
And a cuckoo blow his horn;
Thou hast well drunken, man:
    Who's the fool now?

I see a man in the moon,
    Fie! man, fie!
I see a man in the moon,
    Who's the fool now?
I see a man in the moon,
Clouting of St. Peter's shoon;
Thou hast well drunken, man:
    Who's the fool now?

I see a hare chase a hound,
    Fie! man, fie!
I see a hare chase a hound,
    Who's the fool now?
I see a hare chase a hound,
Twenty mile above the ground;
Thou hast well drunken, man:
    Who's the fool now?

I see a goose ring a hog,
  Fie! man, fie!
I see a goose ring a hog,
   Who's the fool now?
I see a goose ring a hog,
And a snail that bit a dog;
Thou hast well drunken, man:
   Who's the fool now?

I see a mouse catch the cat,
  Fie! man, fie!
I see a mouse catch the cat,
   Who's the fool now?
I see a mouse catch the cat,
And the cheese to eat the rat;
Thou hast well drunken, man:
   Who's the fool now? *Anonymous*

Witches' Charm, *From "Macbeth"*

FIRST WITCH: Round about the caldron go;
 In the poison'd entrails throw.
 Toad, that under cold stone
 Days and nights hast thirty-one
 Swelter'd venom sleeping got,
 Boil thou first i' the charmed pot.
ALL: Double, double toil and trouble;
 Fire burn and caldron bubble.

SECOND WITCH: Fillet of a fenny snake,
    In the caldron boil and bake;
    Eye of newt, and toe of frog,
    Wool of bat, and tongue of dog,
    Adder's fork, and blind-worm's sting,
    Lizard's leg, and howlet's wing,
    For a charm of powerful trouble,
    Like a hell-broth boil and bubble.
ALL: Double, double toil and trouble;
    Fire burn and caldron bubble.
THIRD WITCH: Scale of dragon, tooth of wolf,
    Witch's mummy, maw and gulf
    Of the ravin'd salt-sea shark,
    Root of hemlock digg'd i' the dark,
    Liver of blaspheming Jew,
    Gall of goat, and slips of yew
    Sliver'd in the moon's eclipse,
    Nose of Turk, and Tartar's lips,
    Finger of birth-strangled babe
    Ditch-deliver'd by a drab,
    Make the gruel thick and slab:
    Add thereto a tiger's chaudron,
    For the ingredients of our caldron.
ALL: Double, double toil and trouble;
    Fire burn and caldron bubble.
SECOND WITCH: Cool it with a baboon's blood,
    Then the charm is firm and good.

William Shakespeare

The Logical Vegetarian

You will find me drinking rum,
    Like a sailor in a slum,
You will find me drinking beer like a Bavarian,
    You will find me drinking gin
    In the lowest kind of inn,
Because I am a rigid Vegetarian.

So I cleared the inn of wine,
    And I tried to climb the sign,
And I tried to hail the constable as "Marion."
    But he said I couldn't speak
    And he bowled me to the Beak
Because I was a happy Vegetarian.

Oh, I knew a Doctor Gluck,
    And his nose it had a hook,

And his attitudes were anything but Aryan;
   So I gave him all the pork
   That I had, upon a fork;
Because I am myself a Vegetarian.

I am silent in the club,
I am silent in the pub,
I am silent on a bally peak in Darien;
   For I stuff away for life
   Shoving peas in with a knife,
Because I am at heart a Vegetarian.

No more the milk of cows
Shall pollute my private house
Than the milk of the wild mares of the Barbarian;
   I will stick to port and sherry,
   For they are so very, very,
So very, very, very Vegetarian.

G. K. Chesterton

Naming of Parts

Today we have naming of parts. Yesterday,
We had daily cleaning. And tomorrow morning,
We shall have what to do after firing. But today,
Today we have naming of parts. Japonica
Glistens like coral in all of the neighboring gardens,
   And today we have naming of parts.

This is the lower sling swivel. And this
Is the upper sling swivel, whose use you will see,
When you are given your slings. And this is the piling swivel,
Which in your case you have not got. The branches
Hold in the gardens their silent, eloquent gestures,
   Which in our case we have not got.

This is the safety catch, which is always released
With an easy flick of the thumb. And please do not let me
See anyone using his finger. You can do it quite easy
If you have any strength in your thumb. The blossoms
Are fragile and motionless, never letting anyone see
   Any of them using their fingers.

And this you can see is the bolt. The purpose of this
Is to open the breech, as you see. We can slide it
Rapidly backwards and forwards: we call this

Easing the spring. And rapidly backwards and forwards
The early bees are assaulting and fumbling the flowers:
   They call it easing the Spring.

They call it easing the Spring: it is perfectly easy
If you have any strength in your thumb: like the bolt,
And the breech, and the cocking-piece, and the point of
   balance,
Which in our case we have not got; and the almond blossom
Silent in all of the gardens and the bees going backwards and
   forwards,
   For today we have naming of parts.

Henry Reed

Wishes of an Elderly Man

(Wished at a Garden Party, June, 1914)

I wish I loved the Human Race;
I wish I loved its silly face;
I wish I liked the way it walks;
I wish I liked the way it talks;
And when I'm introduced to one
I wish I thought *What Jolly Fun!*

Walter Raleigh

Two Epigrams

I

The Elders at their services begin
With paper offerings. They release from sin
The catechumens on the couches lying
In visions, testimonies, prophesying:
Not, "Are you saved?" they ask, but in informal
Insistent query, "Brother, are you normal?"

II

You ask me how Contempt who claims to sleep
With every woman that has ever been
Can still maintain that women are skin deep?
They never let him any deeper in.

J. V. Cunningham

Rich and Poor; or, Saint and Sinner

The poor man's sins are glaring;
In the face of ghostly warning
   He is caught in the fact
   Of an overt act—
Buying greens on Sunday morning.

The rich man's sins are hidden
In the pomp of wealth and station;
   And escape the sight
   Of the children of light
Who are wise in their generation.

The rich man has a kitchen
And cooks to dress his dinner;
   The poor who would roast
   To the baker's must post,
And thus becomes a sinner.

The rich man has a cellar,
And a ready butler by him;
   The poor must steer
   For his pint of beer
Where the saint can't choose but spy him.

The rich man's painted windows
Hide the concerts of the quality;
   The poor can but share
   A cracked fiddle in the air,
Which offends all sound morality.

The rich man is invisible
In the crowd of his gay society;
   But the poor man's delight
   Is a sore in the sight,
And a stench in the nose of piety.

                                T. L. Peacock

The Pains of Education

Accursed the man, whom fate ordains, in spite,
And cruel parents teach, to read and write!
What need of letters? wherefore should we spell?
Why write our names? a mark will do as well.
Much are the precious hours of youth misspent

In climbing learning's rugged, steep ascent;
When to the top the bold adventurer's got,
He reigns, vain monarch o'er a barren spot,
Whilst in the vale of ignorance below
Folly and vice to rank luxuriance grow;
Honors and wealth pour in on every side,
And proud preferment rolls her golden tide.
O'er crabbèd authors life's gay prime to waste,
To cramp wild genius in the chains of taste,
To bear the slavish drudgery of schools,
And tamely stoop to every pedant's rules;
For seven long years debarr'd of liberal ease,
To plod in college trammels to degrees;
Beneath the weight of solemn toys to groan,
Sleep over books, and leave mankind unknown;
To praise each senior blockhead's threadbare tale,
And laugh till reason blush, and spirits fail;
Manhood with vile submission to disgrace,
And cap the fool, whose merit is his place,
Vice-Chancellors, whose knowledge is but small,
And Chancellors who nothing know at all.

Charles Churchill

The Golf Links

The golf links lie so near the mill
    That almost every day
The laboring children can look out
    And see the men at play.

Sarah N. Cleghorn

Fate and the Younger Generation

It is strange to think of the Annas, the Vronskys, the Pierres,
    all the Tolstoyan lot
wiped out.

And the Alyoshas and Dmitris and Myshkins and Stavrogins,
    the Dostoevsky lot
all wiped out.
And the Tchekov wimbly-wambly wet-legs all wiped out.

Gone! Dead, or wandering in exile with their feathers plucked,
anyhow, gone from what they were, entirely.

Will the Proustian lot go next?
And then our English imitation intelligentsia?
Is it the *Quos vult perdere Deus* business?

Anyhow the Tolstoyan lot simply asked for extinction:
Eat me up, dear peasant!—So the peasant ate him.
And the Dostoevsky lot wallowed in the thought:
Let me sin my way to Jesus!—So they sinned themselves off the
    face of the earth.
And the Tchekov lot: I'm too weak and lovable to live!—So
    they went.
Now the Proustian lot: Dear darling death, let me wriggle my
    way towards you
like the worm I am!—So he wriggled and got there.
Finally our little lot: I don't want to die, but by Jingo if I do!—
—Well, it won't matter so very much, either.

D. H. Lawrence

it was a goodly co

it was a goodly co
which paid to make man free
(for man is enslaved by a dread dizziz
and the sooner it's over the sooner to biz
don't ask me what it's pliz)

then up rose bishop budge from kew
a anglican was who
(With a rag and a bone and a hank of hair)'d
he picked up a thousand pounds or two
and he smote the monster merde

then up rose pride and up rose pelf
and ghibelline and guelph
and ladios and laddios
(on radios and raddios)
did save man from himself

ye duskiest despot's goldenest gal
did wring that dragon's tail
(for men must loaf and women must lay)
and she gave him a desdemonial
that took his breath away

all history oped her teeming womb
said demon for to doom
yea (fresh complexions being oke
with him) one william shakespeare broke
the silence of the tomb

then up rose mr lipshits pres
(who always nothing says)
and he kisséd the general menedjerr
and they smokéd a robert burns cigerr
to the god of things like they err

e. e. cummings

A Friend

Who borrows all your ready cash,
And with it cuts a mighty dash,
Proving the lender weak and rash?—
     Your friend!

Who finds out every secret fault,
Misjudges every word and thought,
And makes you pass for worse than nought?—
     Your friend!

Who wins your money at deep play,
Then tells you that the world doth say,
" 'Twere wise from clubs you kept away?"—
     Your friend!

Who sells you, for the longest price,
Horses, a dealer, in a trice,
Would find unsound and full of vice?—
     Your friend!

Who eats your dinners, then looks shrewd;
Wishes you had a cook like Ude,
For then much oftener would intrude?—
                                    Your friend!

Who tells you that you've shocking wine,
And owns that, though he sports not fine,
Crockford's the only place to dine?—
                                    Your friend!

Who wheedles you with words most fond
To sign for him a heavy bond,
"Or else, by jove, must quick abscond?"—
                                    Your friend!

Who makes you all the interest pay,
With principal, some future day,
And laughs at what you then may say?—
                                    Your friend!

Who makes deep love unto your wife,
Knowing you prize her more than life,
And breeds between you hate and strife?—
                                    Your friend!

Who, when you've got into a brawl,
Insists that out your man you call,
Then gets you shot, which ends it all?—
                                    Your friend!!!
                    Marguerite Power, Countess of Blessington

They Accuse Me

They accuse me—*Me*—the present writer of
The present poem—of—I know not what—
A tendency to underrate and scoff
At human power and virtue, and all that;
And this they say in language rather rough.
Good God! I wonder what they would be at!
I say no more than hath been said in Dante's
Verse, and by Solomon and by Cervantes;

By Swift, by Machiavel, by Rochefoucault,
By Fénelon, by Luther, and by Plato;
By Tillotson, and Wesley, and Rousseau,
Who knew this life was not worth a potato.

'Tis not their fault, nor mine, if this be so,—
For my part, I pretend not to be Cato,
Nor even Diogenes.—We live and die,
But which is best, you know no more than I.

Socrates said our only knowledge was
To know that nothing could be known; a pleasant
Science enough, which levels to an ass
Each man of wisdom, future, past, or present.
Newton (that proverb of the mind), alas!
Declared, with all his grand discoveries recent,
That he himself felt only "like a youth
Picking up shells by the great ocean—Truth."

Ecclesiastes said that All is vanity—
Most modern preachers say the same, or show it
By their examples of true Christianity:
In short, all know, or very soon may know it;
And in this scene of all-confess'd inanity,
By saint, by sage, by preacher, and by poet,
Must I restrain me, through the fear of strife,
From holding up the nothingness of life?

George Gordon, Lord Byron

I Wish My Tongue Were a Quiver

I wish my tongue were a quiver the size of a huge cask
Packed and crammed with long black venomous rankling darts.
I'd fling you more full of them, and joy in the task,
Than ever Sebastian was, or Caesar, with thirty-three swords
    in his heart.

I'd make a porcupine out of you, or a pincushion, say;
The shafts should stand so thick you'd look like a headless hen
Hung up by the heels, with the long bare red neck stretching,
    curving, and dripping away
From the soiled floppy ball of ruffled feathers standing on end.

You should bristle like those cylindrical brushes they use to
    scrub out bottles,
Not even to reach the kindly earth with the soles of your
    prickled feet,
And I would stand by and watch you wriggle and writhe,
    gurgling through the barbs in your throttle
Like a woolly caterpillar pinned on its back—man, that would
    be sweet.

L. A. Mackay

World War I

The officers get all the steak
And all we get is the bellyache.
The general got the croix-de-guerre,
And the son of a gun was never there.

World War II

The Wacs and Waves will win the war;
So what the hell are we fighting for?

World War III

I won't print and you won't see
The verses written on World War III.

Anonymous

The Chosen People

I   How odd   To choose
    Of God   The Jews.

W. N. Ewer

Two Replies

II   Oh no, it's not!
            God knows what's what!

quoted by John Davidson

III   But not so odd,   A Jewish God,
      As those who choose   Yet spurn the Jews.

Cecil Browne

Fifth Philosopher's Song

A million million spermatozoa,
    All of them alive:
Out of their cataclysm but one poor Noah
    Dare hope to survive.

And among that billion minus one
    Might have chanced to be
Shakespeare, another Newton, a new Donne—
    But that One was Me.

Shame to have ousted your betters thus,
    Taking ark while the others remained outside!
Better for all of us, forward Homunculus,
    If you'd quietly died!

Aldous Huxley

i sing of Olaf glad and big

i sing of Olaf glad and big
whose warmest heart recoiled at war:
a conscientious object-or

his wellbelovéd colonel (trig
westpointer most succinctly bred)
took erring Olaf soon in hand;
but—though an host of overjoyed
noncoms (first knocking on the head
him) do through icy waters roll
that helplessness which others stroke
with brushes recently employed
anent this muddy toiletbowl,
while kindred intellects evoke
allegiance per blunt instruments—
Olaf (being to all intents
a corpse and wanting any rag
upon what God unto him gave)
responds, without getting annoyed
"I will not kiss your f.ing flag"

straightway the silver bird looked grave
(departing hurriedly to shave)

but—though all kinds of officers
(a yearning nation's blueeyed pride)
their passive prey did kick and curse
until for wear their clarion
voices and boots were much the worse,
and egged the firstclassprivates on
his rectum wickedly to tease
by means of skillfully applied
bayonets roasted hot with heat—
Olaf (upon what were once knees)
does almost ceaselessly repeat
"there is some s. I will not eat"

our president, being of which
assertions duly notified
threw the yellowsonofabitch
into a dungeon, where he died

Christ (of His mercy infinite)
i pray to see; and Olaf, too

preponderatingly because
unless statistics lie he was
more brave than me: more blond than you.

e. e. cummings

The Curse

(To a Sister of an Enemy of the Author's Who Disapproved of "The Playboy")

Lord, confound this surly sister,
Blight her brow and blotch and blister,
Cramp her larynx, lung and liver,
In her guts a galling give her.

Let her live to earn her dinners
In Mountjoy with seedy sinners:
Lord, this judgment quickly bring,
And I'm your servant, J. M. Synge.

J. M. Synge

A Glass of Beer

The lanky hank of a she in the inn over there
Nearly killed me for asking the loan of a glass of beer;
May the devil grip the whey-faced slut by the hair,
And beat bad manners out of her skin for a year.

That parboiled ape, with the toughest jaw you will see
On virtue's path, and a voice that would rasp the dead,
Came roaring and raging the minute she looked at me,
And threw me out of the house on the back of my head!

If I asked her master he'd give me a cask a day;
But she, with the beer at hand, not a gill would arrange!
May she marry a ghost and bear him a kitten, and may
The High King of Glory permit her to get the mange.

James Stephens

A Score of Cruel Quatrains

I. TENDERHEARTEDNESS

Billy, in one of his nice new sashes,
Fell in the fire and was burnt to ashes;
Now, although the room grows chilly,
I haven't the heart to poke poor Billy.

Harry Graham

II. MISFORTUNES NEVER COME SINGLY

Making toast at the fireside,
Nurse fell in the grate and died;
And what makes it ten times worse,
All the toast was burnt with nurse.

Harry Graham

III. A PRACTICAL ANSWER

Says Hyam to Moses,
"Let's cut off our noses."
Says Moses to Hyam,
"Ma tear, who vould buy 'em?"

Shirley Brooks

IV. BURLESQUE

If the man who turnips cries,
Cry not when his father dies,
'Tis a proof that he had rather
Have a turnip than his father.

Samuel Johnson

V. DOCTOR FELL

I do not love thee, Doctor Fell,
The reason why I cannot tell,
But this one thing I know full well:
I do not love thee, Doctor Fell.

Thomas Brown

VI. WASTE

I had written to Aunt Maud,
Who was on a trip abroad,
When I heard she'd died of cramp
Just too late to save the stamp.

Harry Graham

VII. MR. JONES

"There's been an accident," they said,
"Your servant's cut in half; he's dead!"
"Indeed!" said Mr. Jones, "and please,
Send me the half that's got my keys."

Harry Graham

VIII. AUNT ELIZA

In the drinking well
   Which the plumber built her,
Aunt Eliza fell—
   We must buy a filter.

Harry Graham

IX. IT ISN'T THE COUGH

It isn't the cough
That carries you off;
It's the coffin
They carry you off in.

Anonymous

X

And the Lord said to Moses,
All the Jews shall have long noses,
Exceptin' Aaron
Who will have a squaaron.

Anonymous

XI. THE CRIMES OF LIZZIE BORDEN

Lizzie Borden with an axe,
Hit her father forty whacks,
When she saw what she had done,
She hit her mother forty-one.

Anonymous

XII. LIZZIE'S SISTER

Lizzie's sister with her pen
Hit her husband's tender wen,
When she saw what she had done,
She hit again and cried, "What fun!"

Anonymous

XIII. THE COXCOMB BIRD

The coxcomb bird, so talkative and grave,
That from his cage cries Cuckold, Whore, and Knave,
Though many a passenger he rightly call,
You hold him no Philosopher at all.

Alexander Pope

XIV. REVEILLE

The porter shouted, "Syracuse!"
And shook me hard and cried, "Excuse,
Ef you wa'n't goin' to La Crosse
This is where I'd wake you, Boss!"

Hughes Mearns

XV. A SHOT AT RANDOM

(In Imitation of Longfellow)

I shot an arrow into the air:
I don't know how it fell, or where;
But, strangely enough, at my journey's end,
I found it again in the neck of a friend.

D. B. W. Lewis

XVI. INFANT INNOCENCE

The Grizzly Bear is huge and wild;
He has devoured the infant child.
The infant child is not aware
It has been eaten by the bear.

A. E. Housman

XVII. THE RAIN

The rain it raineth every day,
    Upon the just and unjust fella,
But more upon the just, because
    The unjust hath the just's umbrella.

Anonymous

XVIII. TO AN ACQUAINTANCE

Thou speakest always ill of me,
I always speak well of thee:
But, spite of all our noise and pother,
The world believes nor one, nor t'other.

Anonymous

XIX. CRUEL CLEVER CAT

Sally, having swallowed cheese,
Directs down holes the scented breeze,
Enticing thus with baited breath
Nice mice to an untimely death. *Geoffrey Taylor*

XX

Auntie, did you feel no pain
    Falling from that apple tree?
Would you do it, please, again?
    'Cos my friend here didn't see.

Harry Graham

Boston

I come from the city of Boston,
The home of the bean and the cod,
Where the Cabots speak only to Lowells,
And the Lowells speak only to God.   *Anonymous*

Some Europeans

I

All those Germans
    Who save their tears
    For their own beers
Are in need of sermons.

II

(Written during the Vichy regime)

It isn't the stench   It's the gall
About the French;   That annoys us all.

III

The Russians
Aren't push-ins.
(By the White Cliffs of all Dovers!
Should I have said they aren't push-overs?)

Anonymous

From "Verses on the Death of Dr. Swift"

The time is not remote, when I
Must by the course of nature die,
When, I foresee, my special friends
Will try to find their private ends;
Tho' it is hardly understood
Which way my death can do them good,
Yet thus, methinks, I hear 'em speak:
"See, how the Dean begins to break!
Poor gentleman, he droops apace!
You plainly find it in his face.
That old vertigo in his head
Will never leave him till he's dead.
Besides, his memory decays:
He recollects not what he says;
He can not call his friends to mind;
Forgets the place where last he din'd;
Plies you with stories o'er and o'er;
He told them fifty times before.
How does he fancy we can sit
To hear his out-of-fashion'd wit?
But he takes up with younger folks,
Who for his wine will bear his jokes.
Faith! he must make his stories shorter,
Or change his comrades once a quarter;
In half the time he talks them round,
There must another set be found.

"For poetry he's past his prime:
He takes an hour to find a rhyme;
His fire is out, his wit decay'd,
His fancy sunk, his Muse a jade.
I'd have him throw away his pen;—
But there's no talking to some men!"
And then their tenderness appears,
By adding largely to my years;
"He's older than he would be reckon'd,
And well remembers Charles the Second.
He hardly drinks a pint of wine;
And that, I doubt, is no good sign.
His stomach too begins to fail;
Last year we thought him strong and hale;
But now he's quite another thing:
I wish he may hold out till Spring!"
Then hug themselves, and reason thus:
"It is not yet so bad with us!"

Behold the fatal day arrive!
"How is the Dean?"—"He's just alive."
Now the departing prayer is read.
"He hardly breathes"—"The Dean is dead."
Before the passing-bell begun,
The news through half the town has run.
"Oh! may we all for death prepare!
What has he left? and who's his heir?"
"I know no more than what the news is;
'Tis all bequeathed to public uses."
"To public use! a perfect whim!
What had the public done for him?
Mere envy, avarice, and pride:
He gave it all—but first he died.
And had the Dean in all the nation
No worthy friend, no poor relation?
So ready to do strangers good,
Forgetting his own flesh and blood?"

Now Grub Street wits are all employed;
With elegies the town is cloyed;
Some paragraph in every paper
To curse the Dean, or bless the Drapier.

The doctors, tender of their fame,
Wisely on me lay all the blame.
"We must confess his case was nice;
But he would never take advice.
Had he been ruled, for aught appears,
He might have lived these twenty years:
For, when we opened him, we found,
That all his vital parts were sound."

From Dublin soon to London spread,
'Tis told at court, "The Dean is dead."
Kind Lady Suffolk, in the spleen,
Runs laughing up to tell the Queen.
The Queen, so gracious, mild, and good,
Cries, "Is he gone? 'tis time he should.
He's dead, you say; why, let him rot:
I'm glad the medals were forgot.
I promised him, I own; but when?
I only was a princess then;
But now, as consort of a king,
You know, 'tis quite a different thing."

Now Chartres, at Sir Robert's levee,
Tells with a sneer the tidings heavy:
"Why, is he dead without his shoes?"

Cries Bob, "I'm sorry for the news:
Oh, were the wretch but living still,
And in his place my good friend Will!
Or had a miter on his head,
Provided Bolingbroke were dead!"

Now Curll his shop from rubbish drains:
Three genuine tomes of Swift's remains!
And then, to make them pass the glibber,
Revised by Tibbalds, Moore, and Cibber.
He'll treat me as he does my betters,
Publish my will, my life, my letters;
Revive the libels born to die,
Which Pope must bear, as well as I.

Here shift the scene, to represent
How those I love my death lament.
Poor Pope will grieve a month, and Gay
A week, and Arbuthnot a day.

St. John himself will scarce forbear
To bite his pen, and drop a tear.
The rest will give a shrug, and cry,
"I'm sorry—but we all must die!"

Indifference clad in wisdom's guise
All fortitude of mind supplies:
For how can stony bowels melt
In those who never pity felt?
When *we* are lashed, *they* kiss the rod,
Resigning to the will of God.

The fools, my juniors by a year,
Are tortured with suspense and fear;
Who wisely thought my age a screen,
When death approached, to stand between:
The screen removed, their hearts are trembling;
They mourn for me without dissembling.

My female friends, whose tender hearts
Have better learned to act their parts,
Receive the news in doleful dumps:
"The Dean is dead (and what is trumps?)
Then, Lord have mercy on his soul!
(Ladies, I'll venture for the vole.)
Six deans, they say, must bear the pall.
(I wish I knew what king to call.)
Madam, your husband will attend
The funeral of so good a friend?"
"No, madam, 'tis a shocking sight,
And he's engaged tomorrow night;
My Lady Club will take it ill,

If he should fail her at quadrille.
He loved the Dean—(I lead a heart,)
But dearest friends, they say, must part.
His time was come: he ran his race;
We hope he's in a better place."
    Why do we grieve that friends should die?
No loss more easy to supply.
One year is past; a different scene!
No further mention of the Dean;
Who now, alas! no more is miss'd
Than if he never did exist.
Where's now this fav'rite of Apollo!
Departed:—and his works must follow;
Must undergo the common fate;
His kind of wit is out of date.

    Some country squire to Lintot goes,
Inquires for "Swift in Verse and Prose."
Says Lintot, "I have heard the name;
He died a year ago."—"The same."
He searches all the shop in vain.
"Sir, you may find them in Duck Lane.
I sent them with a load of books,
Last Monday to the pastry-cook's.
To fancy they could live a year!
I find you're but a stranger here.
The Dean was famous in his time,
And had a kind of knack at rhyme.
His way of writing now is past;
The town has got a better taste;
I keep no antiquated stuff,
But spick and span I have enough.
Pray do but give me leave to show 'em;
Here's Colley Cibber's birthday poem.
This ode you never yet have seen,
By Stephen Duck, upon the queen.

.   .   .   .

    Suppose me dead; and then suppose
A club assembled at the Rose;
Where, from discourse of this and that,
I grow the subject of their chat.
And while they toss my name about,
With favor some, and some without,
One, quite indiff'rent in the cause,
My character impartial draws:
    "The Dean, if we believe report,
Was never ill receiv'd at court.

As for his works in verse and prose
I own myself no judge of those;
Nor can I tell what critics thought 'em:
But this I know, all people bought 'em,
As with a moral view design'd
To cure the vices of mankind;
And, if he often miss'd his aim,
The world must own it, to their shame,
The praise is his, and theirs the blame."
"Sir, I have heard another story:
He was a most confounded Tory,
And grew, or he is much belied,
Extremely dull before he died."
    "Can we the Drapier then forget?
Is not our nation in his debt?
'Twas he that writ the Drapier's letters!"
    "He should have left them for his betters;
We had a hundred abler men,
Nor need depend upon his pen.
Say what you will about his reading,
You never can defend his breeding;
Who in his satires running riot,
Could never leave the world in quiet,
Attacking, when he took the whim,
Court, city, camp—all one to him.
    "But why should he, except he slobbered,
Offend our patriot, great Sir Robert,
Whose counsels aid the sovereign power
To save the nation every hour?
What scenes of evil he unravels
In satires, libels, lying travels!
Not sparing his own clergy-cloth,
But eats into it, like a moth!"
    "His vein, ironically grave,
Exposed the fool and lashed the knave,
To steal a hint was never known,
But what he writ was all his own.
    "He never thought an honor done him,
Because a duke was proud to own him,
Would rather slip aside and choose
To talk with wits in dirty shoes;
Despised the fools with stars and garters,
So often seen caressing Chartres.
He never courted men in station,
Nor persons held in admiration;
Of no man's greatness was afraid,

Because he sought for no man's aid.
Though trusted long in great affairs,
He gave himself no haughty airs;
Without regarding private ends,
Spent all his credit for his friends;
And only chose the wise and good;
No flatterers, no allies in blood;
But succored virtue in distress,
And seldom failed of good success;
As numbers in their hearts must own,
Who, but for him, had been unknown.

.   .   .   .

"By innocence and resolution,
He bore continual persecution;
While numbers to preferment rose,
Whose merits were, to be his foes;
When even his own familiar friends,
Intent upon their private ends,
Like renegadoes now he feels,
Against him lifting up their heels.
"The Dean did, by his pen, defeat
An infamous destructive cheat;
Taught fools their interest how to know,
And gave them arms to ward the blow.
Envy has owned it was his doing,
To save that hapless land from ruin;
While they who at the steerage stood,
And reaped the profit, sought his blood.
"To save them from their evil fate,
In him was held a crime of state.
A wicked monster on the bench,
Whose fury blood could never quench;
As vile and profligate a villain,
As modern Scroggs, or old Tresilian;
Who long all justice had discarded,
Nor feared he God, nor man regarded;
Vowed on the Dean his rage to vent,
And make him of his zeal repent:
But Heaven his innocence defends,
The grateful people stand his friends;
Not strains of law, nor judge's frown,
Nor topics brought to please the crown,
Nor witness hired, nor jury pick'd,
Prevail to bring him in convict.
"In exile, with a steady heart,
He spent his life's declining part;

Where folly, pride, and faction sway,
Remote from St. John, Pope, and Gay."
"Alas, poor Dean! his only scope
Was to be held a misanthrope.
This into gen'ral odium drew him,
Which if he liked, much good may't do him.
His zeal was not to lash our crimes,
But discontent against the times;
For had we made him timely offers
To raise his post, or fill his coffers,
Perhaps he might have truckled down,
Like other brethren of his gown.
For party he would scarce have bled;
I say no more—because he's dead.
What writings has he left behind?
I hear, they're of a different kind;
A few in verse; but most in prose—
Some high-flown pamphlets, I suppose;—
All scribbled in the worst of times,
To palliate his friend Oxford's crimes,
To praise Queen Anne, nay more, defend her,
As never fav'ring the Pretender;
Or libels yet conceal'd from sight,
Against the court to show his spite;
Perhaps his travels, part the third;
I lie at every second word—
Offensive to a loyal ear:
But not one sermon, you may swear."
"His friendships there, to few confined
Were always of the middling kind;
No fools of rank, a mongrel breed,
Who fain would pass for lords indeed:
Where titles give no right or power,
And peerage is a wither'd flower;
He would have held it a disgrace,
If such a wretch had known his face.
On rural squires, that kingdom's bane,
He vented oft his wrath in vain;
[Biennial] squires to market brought;
Who sell their souls and [votes] for nought;
The [nation stripped,] go joyful back,
To ———— the church, their tenants rack,
Go snacks with [rogues and rapparees,]
And keep the peace to pick up fees;
In every job to have a share,
A jail or barrack to repair;

And turn the tax for public roads,
Commodious to their own abodes.
    "Perhaps I may allow the Dean,
Had too much satire in his vein;
And seem'd determined not to starve it,
Because no age could more deserve it.
Yet malice never was his aim;
He lash'd the vice, but spared the name.
No individual could resent,
Where thousands equally were meant;
His satire points at no defect,
But what all mortals may correct;
For he abhorr'd that senseless tribe
Who call it humor when they gibe:
He spared a hump, or crooked nose,
Whose owners set not up for beaux.
True genuine dullness moved his pity,
Unless it offer'd to be witty.
Those who their ignorance confess'd,
He ne'er offended with a jest;
But laughed to hear an idiot quote
A verse from Horace learn'd by rote.
    "Vice, if it e'er can be abash'd,
Must be or ridiculed or lash'd.
If you resent it, who's to blame?
He neither knew you nor your name.
Should vice expect to 'scape rebuke,
Because its owner is a duke?
    "He knew an hundred pleasant stories,
With all the turns of Whigs and Tories;
Was cheerful to his dying day;
And friends would let him have his way.
    "He gave the little wealth he had
To build a house for fools and mad;
And show'd by one satiric touch
No nation wanted it so much.
That kingdom he hath left his debtor.
I wish it soon may have a better.
And, since you dread no farther lashes
Methinks you may forgive his ashes." *Jonathan Swift*

Farewell, Rewards and Fairies

Farewell, rewards and fairies,
    Good housewives now may say,
For now foul sluts in dairies
    Do fare as well as they.

And though they sweep their hearths no less
    Than maids were wont to do,
Yet who of late for cleanliness
    Finds sixpence in her shoe?

Lament, lament, old Abbeys,
    The Fairies' lost command!
They did but change Priests' babies,
    But some have changed your land.
And all your children, sprung from thence,
    Are now grown Puritans,
Who live as Changelings ever since
    For love of your domains.

At morning and at evening both
    You merry were and glad,
So little care of sleep or sloth
    These pretty ladies had;
When Tom came home from labor,
    Or Cis to milking rose,
Then merrily went their tabor,
    And nimbly went their toes.

Witness those rings and roundelays
    Of theirs, which yet remain,
Were footed in Queen Mary's days
    On many a grassy plain;
But since of late, Elizabeth,
    And, later, James came in,
They never danced on any heath
    As when the time hath been.

By which we note the Fairies
    Were of the old Profession.
Their songs were "Ave Mary's,"
    Their dances were Procession.
But now, alas, they all are dead;
    Or gone beyond the seas;
Or farther for Religion fled;
    Or else they take their ease.

A tell-tale in their company
    They never could endure!
And whoso kept not secretly
    Their mirth, was punished, sure;
It was a just and Christian deed
    To pinch such black and blue.
Oh how the commonwealth doth want
    Such Justices as you!   *Richard Corbet*

The Lie

Go, Soul, the body's guest,
Upon a thankless arrant:
Fear not to touch the best;
The truth shall be thy warrant:
Go, since I needs must die,
And give the world the lie.

Say to the court, it glows
And shines like rotten wood;
Say to the church, it shows
What's good, and doth no good:
If church and court reply
Then give them both the lie.

Tell potentates, they live
Acting by others' action;
Not loved unless they give,
Not strong but by a faction:
If potentates reply,
Give potentates the lie.

Tell men of high condition,
That manage the estate,
Their purpose is ambition,
Their practice only hate:
And if they once reply,
Then give them all the lie.

Tell them that brave it most,
They beg for more by spending,
Who, in their greatest cost,
Seek nothing but commending:
And if they make reply,
Then give them all the lie.

Tell zeal it wants devotion;
Tell love it is but lust:
Tell time it is but motion;
Tell flesh it is but dust:
And wish them not reply,
For thou must give the lie.

Tell age it daily wasteth;
Tell honor how it alters;
Tell beauty how she blasteth;
Tell favor how it falters:
And as they shall reply,
Give every one the lie.

Tell wit how much it wrangles
In tickle points of niceness;
Tell wisdom she entangles
Herself in over-wiseness:
And when they do reply,
Straight give them both the lie.

Tell physic of her boldness;
Tell skill it is pretension;
Tell charity of coldness;
Tell law it is contention:
And as they do reply,
So give them still the lie.

Tell fortune of her blindness;
Tell nature of decay;
Tell friendship of unkindness;
Tell justice of delay:
And if they will reply,
Then give them all the lie.

Tell arts they have no soundness,
But vary by esteeming;
Tell schools they want profoundness,
And stand too much on seeming:
If arts and schools reply,
Give arts and schools the lie.

Tell faith it's fled the city;
Tell how the country erreth;
Tell manhood shakes off pity
And virtue least preferreth:
And if they do reply,
Spare not to give the lie.

So when thou hast, as I
Commanded thee, done blab-
bing
—Although to give the lie

Deserves no less than stab-
bing—
Stab at thee he that will,
No stab the soul can kill.

Sir Walter Raleigh

Mac Flecknoe

All human things are subject to decay,
And, when Fate summons, monarchs must obey:
This Flecknoe found, who, like Augustus, young
Was called to empire and had governed long:
In prose and verse was owned, without dispute
Through all the realms of Nonsense, absolute.
This aged prince now flourishing in peace,
And blest with issue of a large increase,
Worn out with business, did at length debate
To settle the succession of the state;
And pond'ring which of all his sons was fit
To reign, and wage immortal war with wit,
Cried, " 'Tis resolved; for Nature pleads that he
Should only rule, who most resembles me:
Shadwell alone my perfect image bears,
Mature in dullness from his tender years;
Shadwell alone of all my sons is he
Who stands confirmed in full stupidity.
The rest to some faint meaning make pretense,
But Shadwell never deviates into sense.
Some beams of wit on other souls may fall,
Strike through and make a lucid interval;
But Shadwell's genuine night admits no ray,
His rising fogs prevail upon the day:
Besides, his goodly fabric fills the eye
And seems designed for thoughtless Majesty:
Thoughtless as Monarch Oaks that shade the plain,
And, spread in solemn state, supinely reign.
Heywood and Shirley were but types of thee,
Thou last great prophet of tautology:
Even I, a dunce of more renown than they,

Was sent before but to prepare thy way:
And coarsely clad in Norwich drugget came
To teach the nations in thy greater name.
My warbling lute, the lute I whilom strung,
When to King John of Portugal I sung,
Was but the prelude to that glorious day,
When thou on silver Thames did'st cut thy way,
With well-timed oars before the Royal Barge,
Swelled with the pride of thy celestial charge;
And, big with Hymn, commander of an host,
The like was ne'er in Epsom blankets tossed.
Methinks I see the new Arion sail,
The lute still trembling underneath thy nail.
At thy well-sharpened thumb from shore to shore
The treble squeaks for fear, the basses roar:
Echoes from Pissing-Alley, Shadwell call,
And Shadwell they resound from Aston hall.
About thy boat the little fishes throng,
As at the morning toast that floats along.
Sometimes as prince of thy harmonious band,
Thou wield'st thy papers in thy threshing hand.
St. André's feet ne'er kept more equal time,
Not ev'n the feet of thy own Psyche's rhyme:
Though they in number as in sense excel,
So just, so like tautology they fell
That, pale with envy, Singleton forswore
The lute and sword which he in triumph bore,
And vowed he ne'er would act Villerius more."
Here stopped the good old sire; and wept for joy,
In silent raptures of the hopeful boy.
All arguments, but most his plays, persuade
That for anointed dullness he was made.

Close to the walls which fair Augusta bind,
(The fair Augusta much to fears inclin'd)
An ancient fabric raised t'inform the sight,
There stood of yore, and Barbican it hight:
A watch tower once, but now, so fate ordains,
Of all the pile an empty name remains.
From its old ruins brothel-houses rise,
Scenes of lewd loves, and of polluted joys,
Where their vast courts the mother-strumpets keep,
And, undisturb'd by watch, in silence sleep.
Near these a Nursery erects its head,
Where queens are formed, and future heroes bred:
Where unfledged actors learn to laugh and cry,
Where infant punks their tender voices try,

And little Maximins the gods defy.
Great Fletcher never treads in buskins here,
Nor greater Jonson dares in socks appear.
But gentle Simkin just reception finds
Amid this monument of vanished minds;
Pure clinches, the suburbian Muse affords;
And Panton waging harmless war with words.
Here Flecknoe, as a place to fame well known,
Ambitiously designed his Shadwell's throne.
For ancient Decker prophesied long since,
That in this pile should reign a mighty prince,
Born for a scourge of wit, and flail of sense,
To whom true dullness should some Psyches owe,
But worlds of misers from his pen should flow;
Humorists and hypocrites it should produce,
Whole Raymond families and tribes of Bruce.

  Now Empress Fame had published the renown
Of Shadwell's coronation through the town.
Rous'd by report of fame, the nations meet,
From near Bun Hill and distant Wa'ling Street,
No Persian carpets spread th' imperial way,
But scattered limbs of mangled poets lay;
From dusty shops neglected authors come,
Martyrs of pies and relics of the bum.
Much Heywood, Shirley, Ogleby there lay,
But loads of Shadwell almost choked the way.
Bilked stationers for yeomen stood prepar'd
And Herringman was captain of the guard.
The hoary prince in majesty appear'd,
High on a throne of his own labors rear'd.
At his right hand our young Ascanius sat,
Rome's other hope and pillar of the state.
His brows thick fogs, instead of glories, grace,
And lambent dullness played around his face.
As Hannibal did to the altars come,
Sworn by his sire a mortal foe to Rome;
So Shadwell swore, nor should his vow be vain,
That he till death true dullness would maintain;
And, in his father's right, and realm's defense,
Ne'er to have peace with wit, nor truce with sense.
The king himself the sacred unction made,
As king by office, and as priest by trade:
In his sinister hand, instead of ball,
He placed a mighty mug of potent ale;
Love's kingdom to his right he did convey,
At once his scepter and his rule of sway;
Whose righteous lore the prince had practic'd young

And from whose loins recorded Psyche sprung.
His temples, last, with poppies were o'erspread,
That nodding seemed to consecrate his head:
Just at that point of time, if fame not lie,
On his left hand twelve reverend owls did fly.
So Romulus, 'tis sung, by Tiber's Brook,
Presage of sway from twice six vultures took.
Th' admiring throng loud acclamations make
And omens of his future empire take.
The sire then shook the honors of his head,
And from his brows damps of oblivion shed
Full on the filial dullness: long he stood,
Repelling from his breast the raging god;
At length burst out in his prophetic mood:
    "Heavens bless my son, from Ireland let him reign
To far Barbadoes on the western main;
Of his dominion may no end be known,
And greater than his father's be his throne.
Beyond love's kingdom let him stretch his pen";
He paused, and all the people cried "Amen."
Then thus continued he, "My son, advance
Still in new impudence, new ignorance.
Success let others teach, learn thou from me
Pangs without birth, and fruitless industry.
Let Virtuosos in five years be writ;
Yet not one thought accuse thy toil of wit.
Let gentle George in triumph tread the stage,
Make Dorimant betray, and Loveit rage;
Let Cully, Cockwood, Fopling, charm the pit,
And in their folly show the writer's wit.
Yet still thy fools shall stand in thy defense
And justify their author's want of sense.
Let 'em be all by thy own model made
Of dullness and desire no foreign aid,
That they to future ages may be known,
Not copies drawn, but issue of thy own.
Nay, let thy men of wit too be the same,
All full of thee, and differing but in name;
But let no alien Sedley interpose
To lard with wit thy hungry Epsom prose.
And when false flowers of rhetoric thou would'st cull,
Trust Nature, do not labor to be dull;
But write thy best, and top; and in each line
Sir Formal's oratory will be thine.
Sir Formal, though unsought, attends thy quill,
And does thy northern dedications fill.
Nor let false friends seduce thy mind to fame,

By arrogating Jonson's hostile name.
Let Father Flecknoe fire thy mind with praise
And Uncle Ogleby thy envy raise.
Thou art my blood, where Jonson has no part:
What share have we in Nature or in Art?
Where did his wit on learning fix a brand
And rail at arts he did not understand?
Where made he love in Prince Nicander's vein,
Or swept the dust in Psyche's humble strain?
Where sold he bargains, 'Whip-stich, kiss my arse,'
Promis'd a play and dwindled to a farce?
When did his muse from Fletcher scenes purloin,
As thou whole Etheredge dost transfuse to thine?
But so transfused as oils on waters flow,
His always floats above, thine sinks below.
This is thy province, this thy wondrous way,
New humors to invent for each new play:
This is that boasted bias of thy mind,
By which one way, to dullness, 'tis inclined.
Which makes thy writings lean on one side still,
And, in all changes, that way bends thy will.
Nor let thy mountain belly make pretense
Of likeness: thine's a tympany of sense.
A tun of man in thy large bulk is writ,
But sure thou'rt but a kilderkin of wit.
Like mine thy gentle numbers feebly creep;
Thy tragic muse gives smiles, thy comic sleep.
With whate'er gall thou sett'st thy self to write,
Thy inoffensive satires never bite.
In thy felonious heart though venom lies,
It does but touch thy Irish pen, and dies.
Thy genius calls thee not to purchase fame
In keen iambics, but mild anagram:
Leave writing plays, and choose for thy command
Some peaceful province in acrostic land.
There thou mayest wings display, and altars raise,
And torture one poor word ten thousand ways;
Or, if thou would'st thy different talents suit,
Set thy own songs, and sing them to thy lute."
He said, but his last words were scarcely heard,
For Bruce and Longvil had a trap prepar'd,
And down they sent the yet declaiming bard.
Sinking he left his drugget robe behind,
Borne upwards by a subterranean wind.
The mantle fell to the young prophet's part
With double portion of his father's art.   *John Dryden*

PART SEVEN

The Bawdy House

The Tunnynge of Elynour Rummynge

(See Glossary at the end of the poem.)

Tell you I chyll,
If that ye wyll
A whyle be styll,
Of a comely gyll
That dwelt on a hyll:
But she is not gryll,
For she is somewhat sage
And well worne in age;
For her vysage
It would aswage
A mannes corage.

Her lothly lere
Is nothynge clere,
But ugly of chere,
Droupy and drowsy,
Scurvy and lowsy;
Her face all bowsy,
Comely crinkled
Woundersly wrynkled,
Lyke a rost pygges eare,
Brystled wyth here.
Her lewde lyppes twayne,

191

They slaver, men sayne,
Lyke a ropy rayne,
A gummy glayre:
She is ugly fayre:
Her nose somdele hoked,
And camously croked,
Never stoppynge,
But ever droppynge;
Her skynne lose and slacke,
Grained lyke a sacke;
With a croked backe.
Her eyen gowndy
Are full unsoundy,
For they are blered;
And she gray hered;
Jawed lyke a jetty;
A man would have pytty
To se how she is gumbed,
Fyngered and thumbed,
Gently jointed,
Gresed and anoynted
Up to the knockels;
The bones of her huckels
Lyke as they were with
    buckels
Togyther made fast:
Her youth is farre past:
Foted lyke a plane,
Legged lyke a crane;
And yet she wyll jet
Lyke a jollivet,
In her furred flocket,
And gray russet rocket,
With symper the cocket.
Her huke of Lincoln grene,
It had been hers, I wene,

More than fourty yere;
And so doth it apere,
For the grene bare thredes
Loke lyke sere wedes,
Wyddered lyke hay,
The woll worn away;
And yet, I dare saye
She thynketh herselfe gaye
Upon the holy daye,
Whan she doth her aray,
And gyrdeth in her gytes,
Stytched and pranked with
    pletes;
Her kyrtel Bristow red,
With clothes upon her hed
That wey a sowe of led,
Wrythen in wonder wyse,
After the Saracens gyse,
With a whym wham,
Knyt with a trym tram,
Upon her brayne pan,
Lyke an Egyptian,
Capped about:
Whan she goeth out
Herselfe for to shewe,
She dryveth downe the dewe
With a payre of heles
As brode as two wheles;
She hobles as a gose
With her blanket hose
Over the falowe;
Her shoone smered with
    talowe,
Gresed upon dyrt
That baudeth her skyrt.

PRIMUS PASSUS

And this comely Dame,
I understande, her name
Is Elynour Rummynge,
At home in her wonnynge;
And as men say
She dwelt in Sothray,

In a certayne stede
Besyde Lederhede.
She is a tonnysh gyb;
The devyll and she be syb.
But to make up my tale,
She breweth noppy ale,

And maketh therof port sale
To travellars, to tynkers,
To sweters, to swynkers,
And all good ale drynkers,
That wyll nothynge spare,
But drynke till they stare
And brynge themselfe bare,
With, Now aware the mare
And let us sley care
As wyse as an hare!
Come who so wyll
To Elynour on the hyll,
Wyth, Fyll the cup, fyll,
And syt there by styll,
Erly or late:
Thither cometh Kate,
Cysly and Sare,
With theyr legges bare,
And also theyr fete
Hardely full unswete;
With theyr heles dagged,
Theyr kyrtelles all to-jagged
Theyr smockes all to-ragged,
Wyth tytters and tatters;
Brynge dysshes and platters,
Wyth all theyr myght runnynge
To Elynour Rummynge
To have of her tunnynge:
She leneth them on the same,

And thus begynneth the game.
Some wenches come unlased,
Some huswyves come unbrased,
With theyr naked pappes
That flyppes and flappes;
It wygges and it wagges,
Like tawny saffron bagges;
A sorte of foule drabbes
All scurvy with scabbes:
Some be flybytten;
Some skewed as a kytten;
Some wyth a sho clout
Bynde theyr heddes about;
Some have no herelace,
Theyr lockes about theyr face,
Theyr tresses untrust,
All full of unlust;
Some loke strawry,
Some cawry mawry;
Full untydy tegges,
Lyke rotten egges.
Such a lewde sorte
To Elynour resorte
From tyde to tyde:
Abyde, abyde,
And to you shall be tolde
Howe hyr ale is solde
To mawte and to molde.

SECUNDUS PASSUS

Some have no mony
That thyder commy,
For theyr ale to pay,
That is a shreud aray;
Elynour swered, Nay,
Ye shall not beare away
My ale for nought,
By hym that be bought!
With, Hey, dogge, hay,
Have these hogges away!
With, Get me a staffe,

The swyne eate my draffe!
Stryke the hogges with a clubbe,
They have dronke up my swyllynge tubbe!
For, be there never so much prese,
These swyne go to the hye dese,
The sowe wyth her pygges;
The bore his tayle wrygges,

His rumpe also he frygges
Agaynst the hye benche!
With, Fo, ther is a stenche!
Gather up, thou wenche;
Seest thou not what is fall?
Take up dyrt and all,
And bere out of the hall:
God gyve it yll prevyinge,
Clenly as yvell chevyinge!
But let us turne playne,
There we lefte agayne.
For, as yll a patch as that,
The hennes ron in the
    mashfat;
For they go to roust
Streyght over the ale joust,
And donge, whan it commes,
In the ale tunnes.
Then Elynour taketh
The mashe bolle, and shaketh
The hennes donge away,
And skommeth it into a tray
Whereas the yeest is,
Wyth her maungy fystis:
And somtyme she blennes
The donge of her hennes
And the ale togither;
And sayeth, Gossyp, com
    hyther,
This ale shal be thycker,
And flowre the more quicker;
For I may tell you
I lerned it of a Jewe,
Whan I began to brewe,

And I have founde it trew;
Drinke now whyle it is new;
An ye may it broke,
It shall make you loke
Yonger than ye be
Yeres two or thre,
For ye may prove it by me;
Beholde, she sayde, and se
How bryght I am of ble!
Ich am not cast away,
That can my husbond say,
Whan we kys and play
In lust and in lyking;
He calleth me his whytyng,
His mullyng and his mytyng,
His nobbes and his conny,
His swetyng and his honny,
With, Bas, my pretty bonny,
Thou art worth good and
    monny.
Thus make I my falyre fonny,
Til that he dreme and dronny;
For, after all our sport,
Than wyll he rout and snort;
Than swetely together we ly,
As two pygges in a sty.

To cease me semeth best,
And of this tale to rest,
And for to leve this letter,
Because it is no better,
And because it is no swetter;
We wyll no farther ryme
Of it at this tyme . . .

                    John Skelton

Bas: kiss	Draffe: hogwash	Gyll: girl	Snort: snore
Baudeth: befouls	Dronny: drone	Gose: goose	Trym Tram:
Ble: complexion	Falyre: fellow	Here: hair	pretty trifle
Camously croked:	Fonny: love-silly	Huke: mantle	Wonnynge: dwelling
pug-noses	Flocket: loose gown	Huckels: hips	Woll: wool
Cocket: coquette	Glayre: snot	Jet: strut	Yvell chevyinge:
Chyll: will	Gryll: grim	Lere: skin	evil ending

Portrait of the Artist as a Prematurely Old Man

It is common knowledge to every schoolboy and even every
  Bachelor of Arts,
That all sin is divided into two parts.
One kind of sin is called a sin of commission, and that is very
  important,
And it is what you are doing when you are doing something
  you ortant,
And the other kind of sin is just the opposite and is called a
  sin of omission and is equally bad in the eyes of all right-
  thinking people, from Billy Sunday to Buddha,
And it consists of not having done something you shudda.
I might as well give you my opinion of these two kinds of sin
  as long as, in a way, against each other we are pitting them,
And that is, don't bother your head about sins of commission
  because however sinful, they must at least be fun or else you
  wouldn't be committing them.
It is the sin of omission, the second kind of sin,
That lays eggs under your skin.
The way you get really painfully bitten
Is by the insurance you haven't taken out and the checks you
  haven't added up the stubs of and the appointments you
  haven't kept and the bills you haven't paid and the letters
  you haven't written.
Also, about sins of omission there is one particularly painful
  lack of beauty,
Namely, it isn't as though it had been a riotous red letter day
  or night every time you neglected to do your duty;
You didn't get a wicked forbidden thrill
Every time you let a policy lapse or forgot to pay a bill;
You didn't slap the lads in the tavern on the back and loudly
  cry Whee,
Let's all fail to write just one more letter before we go home,
  and this round of unwritten letters is on me.
No, you never get any fun
Out of the things you haven't done,
But they are the things that I do not like to be amid,
Because the suitable things you didn't do give you a lot more
  trouble than the unsuitable things you did.
The moral is that it is probably better not to sin at all, but if
  some kind of sin you must be pursuing,
Well, remember to do it by doing rather than by not doing.

Ogden Nash

The Naked and the Nude

For me, the naked and the nude
(By lexicographers construed
As synonyms that should express
The same deficiency of dress
Or shelter) stand as wide apart
As love from lies, or truth from art.

Lovers without reproach will gaze
On bodies naked and ablaze;
The Hippocratic eye will see
In nakedness, anatomy;
And naked shines the Goddess when
She mounts her lion among men.

The nude are bold, the nude are sly
To hold each treasonable eye.
While draping, by a showman's trick,
Their dishabille in rhetoric,
They grin a mock-religious grin
Of scorn at those of naked skin.

The naked, therefore, who compete
Against the nude may know defeat,
Yet when they both together tread
The briary pastures of the dead,
By Gorgons with long whips pursued,
How naked go the sometimes nude!

Robert Graves

A Round of Infamous Limericks

I

There was an old party of Lyme,
Who lived with three wives at one time.
    When asked, "Why the third?"
    He replied, "One's absurd,
And bigamy, sir, is a crime!"

Anonymous

II

There once was a maid with such graces,
That her curves cried aloud for embraces.
    "You look," said McGee,
    "Like a million to me—
Invested in *all* the right places!"

Anonymous

III. MENDELIAN THEORY

There was a young woman called Starkie,
Who had an affair with a darky.
    The result of her sins
    Was quadruplets, not twins—
One black, and one white, and two khaki.

Anonymous

IV. REAL ESTATE

There was a young lady of Wantage
Of whom the Town Clerk took advantage.
    Said the County Surveyor,
    "Of course you must pay her;
You've altered the line of her frontage."

Anonymous

V

There was a young lady named Rood,
Who was such an absolute prude
    That she pulled down the blind
    When changing her mind,
Lest curious eye should intrude.

Anonymous

VI

There was a lady of Erskine,
Who had a remarkably fair skin.
    When I said to her, "Mabel,
    You look well in your sable,"
She replied, "I look best in my bearskin."

Anonymous

VII

There was a young lady of Kent,
Who said that she knew what it meant
    When men asked her to dine,
    And served cocktails and wine;
She knew, oh she knew!—but she went!

Anonymous

VIII

There was a young maid from Madras,
Who had a magnificent ass;
    Not rounded and pink,
    As you probably think—
It was gray, had long ears, and ate grass.

Anonymous

IX

There was a young chap not so nice
Who indulged in bigamy twice;
    He said, "One is a bore,
    I'd rather have more—
The plural of spouse is called spice."

Anonymous

X. BENJAMIN

There was a brave girl of Connecticut
Who flagged the express with her petticut,
    Which critics defined
    As presence of mind,
But deplorable absence of ecticut.

Ogden Nash

XI

The last time I slept with the queen
She said, as I whistled, *"Ich dien.*
    Please put the light out,
    It's royalty's night out,
The queen may be had but not seen."

Dylan Thomas

XII

There was an old man from Antigua,
Whose wife said, "My dear, what a pig you are!"
 He replied, "O my queen,
 Is it manners you mean,
Or do you refer to my fig-u-a?"

Anonymous

XIII

A beautiful lady named Psyche
Is loved by a fellow named Yche.
 One thing about Ych
 The lady can't lych
Is his beard, which is dreadfully spyche.

Anonymous

XIV

Said a great Congregational preacher
To a hen, "You're a beautiful creature."
 And the hen, just for that,
 Laid an egg in his hat,
And thus did the Hen reward Beecher.

Anonymous

XV. A LIMERICK ON LIMERICKS

A limerick gets laughs anatomical
Into space that is quite economical.
 But the good ones I've seen
 So seldom are clean,
And the clean ones so seldom are comical.

Anonymous

XVI. THE FOLKWAYS OF SODOM

There once was a Warden of Wadham
Who approved of the folkways of Sodom,
 For a man might—he said—
 Have a very poor head,
But be a fine fellow, at bottom.

E. W.

XVII. LIMBERICK

It's time to make love. Douse the glim.
The fireflies twinkle and dim.
 The stars lean together
 Like birds of a feather,
And the loin lies down with the limb.

Conrad Aiken

Song for the Clatter-Bones

God rest that Jewy woman,
Queen Jezebel, the bitch
Who peeled the clothes from her shoulder-bones
Down to her spent teats
As she stretched out of the window
Among the geraniums, where
She chaffed and laughed like one half daft
Titivating her painted hair—

King Jehu he drove to her,
She tipped him a fancy beck;
But he from his knacky sidecar spoke,
"Who'll break that dewlapped neck?"
And so she was thrown from the window;
Like Lucifer she fell
Beneath the feet of the horses and they beat
The light out of Jezebel.

That corpse wasn't planted in clover;
Ah, nothing of her was found
Save those grey bones that Hare-foot Mike
Gave me for their lovely sound;
And as once her dancing body
Made star-lit princes sweat,
So I'll just clack: though her ghost lacks a back
There's music in the old bones yet.

F. R. Higgins

She Was Poor, but She Was Honest

She was poor, but she was honest,
    Victim of the squire's whim:
First he loved her, then he left her,
    And she lost her honest name.

Then she ran away to London,
    For to hide her grief and shame;
There she met another squire,
    And lost her name again.

See her riding in her carriage,
    In the Park and all so gay:
All the nibs and nobby persons
    Come to pass the time of day.

See the little old-world village
   Where her aged parents live,
Drinking the champagne she sends them;
   But they never can forgive.

In the rich man's arms she flutters,
   Like a bird with broken wing:
First he loved her, then he left her,
   And she hasn't got a ring.

See him in the splendid mansion,
   Entertaining with the best,
While the girl that he has ruined,
   Entertains a sordid guest.

See him in the House of Commons,
   Making laws to put down crime,
While the victim of his passions
   Trails her way through mud and slime.

Standing on the bridge at midnight,
   She says: "Farewell, blighted Love."
There's a scream, a splash—Good Heavens!
   What is she a-doing of?

Then they drag her from the river,
   Water from her clothes they wrang,
For they thought that she was drownded;
   But the corpse got up and sang:

"It's the same the whole world over,
   It's the poor that gets the blame,
It's the rich that gets the pleasure.
   Isn't it a blooming shame?"

Anonymous

True Romance

O the girl with the eyes
Of pearls in a vise
And the neck of a chalk
   palisade
And the boy in the pose
Of a scarecrow in clothes
And the voice of a weak
   lemonade
Fell in love
Fell in love
As naturally
As any old you or me.

But the girl was so proud
She never allowed
How she'd no family tree
To the boy who was rich
And engaged to a bitch
With a smirk and a high bony
   knee.
He felt tied
He felt tied
As naturally
As any old you or me.

So that all he could do
Was stew and eat crow
And deny his shriveling
   glands
While the girl from below
With her mouth in an O
Lay down by the sea in the
   sands
Feeling pooped
Feeling pooped
As naturally
As any old you or me.

Then the girl from above
Cried love was not love
Without petting or jiving or
   gin.
So he followed her west
Till he caught her undressed

In the arms of a guy with a
   grin
Whom he shot
Whom he shot
As naturally
As any old you or me.

Then he buttoned his vest
And turned his nose east
Like the bird who crows
   when it flies
And there on a beach
Like a ravishing fish
Lay the girl with the valuable
   eyes
Looking gone
Looking gone
As naturally
As any old you or me.

Without giving a thought
To should he or ought
He lay down by her soft un-
   derside
And so stirred her up
That she opened a lip
And she cried and she cried
   o she cried
Feeling thrilled
Feeling thrilled
As naturally
As any old you or me.

Then the sea opened up
And out of it jumped
A preacher who crooned I'm
   your chum.
So without getting wet
They were sterlingly wed
With a hint of a junior to
   come.
How we wept
How we wept (you and me)
As unnaturally
As any old loon up a tree.

Edwin Honig

He That Marries a Merry Lass

He that marries a merry lass,
  He has most cause to be sad:
For let her go free in her merry tricks,
  She'll work his patience mad.
But he that marries a scold, a scold,
  He has most cause to be merry:
    For when she's in her fits,
    He may cherish his wits,
  With singing, hey down derry!
He that weds a roaring girl,
  That will both scratch and fight,
    Though he study all day
    To make her away,
  Will be glad to please her at night.
And he that copes with a sullen wench,
  That scarce will speak at all,
    Her doggedness more
    Than a scold or a whore
  Will penetrate his gall.
He that's matched with a turtle dove,
  That has no spleen about her,
    Shall waste so much life,
    In love of his wife,
  He had better be without her.

Anonymous

I Once Was a Maid

I once was a maid, tho' I cannot tell when,
And still my delight is in proper young men:
Some one of a troop of dragoons was my daddie,
No wonder I'm fond of a sodger laddie.
        Sing, lal de lal, &c.

The first of my loves was a swaggering blade,
To rattle the thundering drum was his trade;
His leg was so tight, and his cheek was so ruddy,
Transported I was with my sodger laddie.

But the godly old chaplain left him in the lurch;
The sword I forsook for the sake of the church:
He ventur'd the soul, and I risked the body,
'Twas then I proved false to my sodger laddie.

Full soon I grew sick of my sanctified sot,
The regiment at large for a husband I got;

From the gilded spontoon to the fife I was ready,
I askèd no more but a sodger laddie.

But the peace it reduc'd me to beg in despair,
Till I met my old boy in a Cunningham fair;
His rags regimental, they flutter'd so gaudy,
My heart is rejoic'd at a sodger laddie.

And now I have liv'd—I know not how long,
And still I can join in a cup and a song;
But whilst with both hands I can hold the glass steady,
Here's to thee, my hero, my sodger laddie!

Robert Burns

The Milton Abbas Rhyme

(The chapel at Milton Abbas in Dorsetshire was dedicated to
St. Catherine, the Patron saint of spinsters.)

St. Catherine, St. Catherine,
O lend me your aid,
And grant that I never
May die an old maid!

But any one better
Than no one, St. Catherine!

A husband, St. Catherine!
Handsome, St. Catherine!
Rich, St. Catherine!

A husband, St. Catherine!
A good one, St. Catherine!

Young, St. Catherine!
SOON, St. Catherine!

Anonymous

The Ruined Maid

"O, 'Melia, my dear, this does everything crown!
Who would have supposed I should meet you in Town?
And whence such fair garments, such prosperi-ty?"—
"O didn't you know I'd been ruined?" said she.

—"You left us in tatters, without shoes or socks,
Tired of digging potatoes, and spudding up docks;
And now you've gay bracelets and bright feathers three!"—
"Yes: that's how we dress when we're ruined," said she.

—"At home in the barton you said 'thee' and 'thou.'
And 'thik oon,' and 'theas oon,' and 'to'other'; but now
Your talking quite fits 'ee for high compa-ny!"
"Some polish is gained with one's ruin," said she.

—"Your hands were like paws then, your face blue and bleak,
But now I'm bewitched by your delicate cheek,
And your little gloves fit as on any la-dy!"—
"We never do work when we're ruined," said she.

—"You used to call home life a hag-ridden dream,
And you'd sigh, and you'd sock; but at present you seem
To know not of megrims or melancho-ly!"—
"True. One's pretty lively when ruined," said she.

—"I wish *I* had feathers, a fine sweeping gown,
And a delicate face, and could strut about Town!"—
"My dear—a raw country girl, such as you be,
Cannot quite expect that. You ain't ruined," said she.

Thomas Hardy

Oh, Please Don't Get Up!

There is one form of life to which I unconditionally surrender,
Which is the feminine gender.
Like lightning and thunder, women are awe-inspiring
phenomena,
And they have a custom which many men might well adopt,
which is to gird themselves in devices that reduce or at
least repress their abdomena,
And they have a traditional rite which is handed down from
mother to daughter,
Which is that they always have to wash their face with cold
cream instead of water.
Also, I think there must be some great difference in the way
men and women are built,
Because women walk around all day wearing shoes that a man
would break his neck the first step he took in them because where a man's shoe has a heel a woman's shoe has
a stilt,
So I often wonder who started this rumor about woman being
the clinging vine and man the mighty oak or elm,
And I have an idea that the phrase "weaker sex" was coined
by some woman to disarm some man she was preparing
to overwhelm,
Because certainly a man shod like a woman would just have
to sit down all day, and yet my land!
Women not only don't have to sit, but prefer to stand,
Because their pleasure in standing up is exquisite,
As everybody knows who has ever watched a woman pay a
call or a visit,
Because at first they will sit in a chair,
And their heart may be in the highlands, but it certainly isn't
there,
And their conversation is unspontaneous,
And their topics are trifling and miscellaneous,
But finally, after an uncomfortable while,

Their faces brighten with the well-I-must-be-running-along-
          now smile,
And they get to their feet and the front door,
And the Old Mother of Waters surges over the levee with a
          roar,
Because the proportions of feminine social chitchat are con-
          stant, always;
One part of sitting down in the sitting room to four parts
          standing up saying good-by in foyers and hallways,
Which is why I think that when it comes to physical prowess,
Why woman is a wow, or should I say a wowess.

                                                   Ogden Nash

A Ballad of the Good Lord Nelson

The Good Lord Nelson had a swollen gland,
Little of the scripture did he understand
Till a woman led him to the promised land
          Aboard the Victory, Victory O.

Adam and Evil and a bushel of figs
Meant nothing to Nelson who was keeping pigs,
Till a woman showed him the various rigs
          Aboard the Victory, Victory O.

His heart was softer than a new-laid egg,
Too poor for loving and ashamed to beg,
Till Nelson was taken by the Dancing Leg
          Aboard the Victory, Victory O.

Now he up and did up his little tin trunk
And he took to the ocean on his English junk,
Turning like the hour-glass in his lonely bunk
          Aboard the Victory, Victory O.

The Frenchman saw him a-coming there
With the one-piece eye and the valentine hair,

With the safety-pin sleeve and occupied air
    Aboard the Victory, Victory O.

Now you all remember the message he sent
As an answer to Hamilton's discontent—
There were questions asked about it in the Parliament
    Aboard the Victory, Victory O.

Now the blacker the berry, the thicker comes the juice.
Think of Good Lord Nelson and avoid self-abuse,
For the empty sleeve was no mere excuse
    Aboard the Victory, Victory O.

"England Expects" was the motto he gave
When he thought of little Emma out on Biscay's wave,
And remembered working on her like a galley-slave
    Aboard the Victory, Victory O.

The first Great Lord in our English land
To honor the Freudian command,
For a cast in the bush is worth two in the hand
    Aboard the Victory, Victory O.

Now the Frenchman shot him there as he stood
In the rage of battle in a silk-lined hood
And he heard the whistle of his own hot blood
    Aboard the Victory, Victory O.

Now stiff on a pillar with a phallic air
Nelson stylites in Trafalgar Square
Reminds the British what once they were
    Aboard the Victory, Victory O.

If they'd treat their women in the Nelson way
There'd be fewer frigid husbands every day
And many more heroes on the Bay of Biscay
    Aboard the Victory, Victory O.

Lawrence Durrell

Head and Heart

    I put my hand upon my heart
    And swore that we should never part—
    I wonder what I should have said
    If I had put it on my head.

C. D. B. Ellis

Bagpipe Music

It's no go the merrygoround, it's no go the rickshaw,
All we want is a limousine and a ticket for the peepshow.
Their knickers are made of crepe-de-chine, their shoes are
    made of python,
Their halls are lined with tiger rugs and their walls with heads
    of bison.

John MacDonald found a corpse, put it under the sofa,
Waited till it came to life and hit it with a poker,
Sold its eyes for souvenirs, sold its blood for whiskey,
Kept its bones for dumbbells to use when he was fifty.

It's no go the Yogi-Man, it's no go Blavatsky,
All we want is a bank balance and a bit of skirt in a taxi.

Annie MacDougall went to milk, caught her foot in the
    heather,
Woke to hear a dance record playing of Old Vienna.
It's no go your maidenheads, it's no go your culture,
All we want is a Dunlop tire and the devil mend the puncture.

The Laird o'Phelps spent Hogmanay declaring he was sober,
Counted his feet to prove the fact and found he had one foot
    over.
Mrs. Carmichael had her fifth, looked at the job with repulsion,
Said to the midwife "Take it away; I'm through with over-
    production."

All we want is a mother's help and a sugar-stick for the baby.
It's no go the gossip column, it's no go the Ceilidh,

Willie Murray cut his thumb, couldn't count the damage,
Took the hide of an Ayrshire cow and used it for a bandage.
His brother caught three hundred cran when the seas were
    lavish,
Threw the bleeders back in the sea and went upon the parish.

It's no go the Herring Board, it's no go the Bible,
All we want is a packet of fags when our hands are idle.

It's no go the picture palace, it's no go the stadium,
It's no go the country cot with a pot of pink geraniums.
It's no go the Government grants, it's no go the elections,
Sit on your arse for fifty years and hang your hat on a pension.

It's no go my honey love, it's no go my poppet;
Work your hands from day to day, the winds will blow the
      profit.
The glass is falling hour by hour, the glass will fall for ever,
But if you break the bloody glass you won't hold up the
      weather.   *Louis MacNeice*

News Item

> Men seldom make passes
> At girls who wear glasses   *Dorothy Parker*

Second News Item

> Now, aren't men asses
> Who seldom make passes
> At girls who wear glasses?   *Anonymous*

Sylvia the Fair

Sylvia the fair, in the bloom of fifteen,
Felt an innocent warmth as she lay on the green;
She had heard of a pleasure, and something she guessed
By the towsing and tumbling and touching her breast;
She saw the men eager, but was at a loss
What they meant by their sighing and kissing so close;

Chorus: By their praying and whining,
      And clasping and twining,
      And panting and wishing,
      And sighing and kissing,
      And sighing and kissing so close.

Ah, she cried, ah, for a languishing maid
In a country of Christians to die without aid!
Not a Whig or a Tory or Trimmer at least,
Or a Protestant parson or Catholic priest,
To instruct a young virgin that is at a loss
What they meant by their sighing and kissing so close;

Cupid in shape of a swain did appear;
He saw the sad wound, and in pity drew near,
Then showed her his arrow and bid her not fear,
For the pain was no more than a maiden may bear;
When the balm was infused, she was not at a loss
What they meant by their sighing and kissing so close.
                                                John Dryden

Penal Servitude for Mrs. Maybrick

She Will Not Have to Climb Golden Stairs

The Maybrick trial is over now, there's been a lot of jaw,
    Of doctors' contradiction, and expounding of the law;
She had Sir Charles Russell to defend her as we know,
    But tho' he tried his very best it all turned out no go.

Chorus: But Mrs. Maybrick will not have to climb the golden
            stairs;
       Tho' the Jury's found her guilty and she nearly said her
            prayers;
       She's at another kind of mashing and at it she must
            stop,
       Old Berry he's took down a peg with his big long drop.

Now at the trial the doctors had a very gay old time,
    They all told different stories about this cruel crime;
Some said that Mr. Maybrick to death had dosed himself,
    While others said it was his wife that put him on the shelf.

Then came the servants' story how the flypapers were found,
    In fact it seems the missis had arsenic all around,
In food and drink of every kind, in cupboard and in box,
    In handkerchiefs, and even in the pockets of her frocks.

Next came the waiter's story about her trip to town,
    Which proved that from the virtue of a wife she had fell
        down,
And when a woman like her from her husband goes astray,
    It plainly shows she wishes that he was out of the way.

Then came the fatal letter that fairly cooked her goose,
    It seemed to say to Brierly that she soon meant to be loose;
And tho' she made a statement to explain it all away,
    The Jury wouldn't have it, you are guilty they did say.

Then to each gay and flighty wife may this a warning be,
    Don't write to any other man or sit upon his knee;
When once you start like Mrs. Maybrick perhaps you couldn't
        stop,
    So stick close to your husband and keep clear of Berry's
        drop.

Anonymous

Ballade un Peu Banale

The bellow of good Master Bull
    Astoundeth gentil Cow
That standeth in the meadow cool
    Where cuckoo singeth now.

She stoppeth in a moony trance
    Beneath the timeless trees,
While ebon-bellied shad-flies dance
    About her milk-white knees.

He snuffeth her from distant field—
    Sly Farmer Pimp approves:
To him the gates and latches yield;
    He smiles upon their loves.

Bull boometh from the briary bush,
    Advances, tail aloft—
The meadow grass is long and lush,
    The oozy turf is soft.

He stampeth with his foremost foot,
    His nostrils breathing bale;
Uncouth, unhallowed is his suit;
    The vestal turneth tail.

He feinteth with his ivory horn,
    Bites rump, bites flank, bites nape—
Sweet Saviour, of a Virgin born,
    How shall this maid escape!

He chaseth her to pasture wall;
    She maketh stand, poor bird!
He wields his tail like an iron flail.
    Alas! he presseth hard!

.   .   .   .   .   .

I like to think sweet Jesus Christ,
    For His dear Mother's sake,
By some miraculous device,
    Her to Himself did take;

That her preserv'd Virginity
    Flutes holy flats and sharps
In that divine vicinity
    Where Eliot's hippo harps.

                        A. J. M. Smith

Poetic Thought

Oh Moon! when I look on thy beautiful face,
Careering along through the boundaries of space,
The question has frequently come to my mind,
If ever I'll gaze on thy glorious behind.

Anonymous
(Ascribed to Edmund Gosse's serving maid)

On a Painted Woman

To youths, who hurry thus away,
  How silly your desire is
At such an early hour to pay
  Your compliments to Iris.

Stop, prithee, stop, ye hasty beaux,
  No longer urge this race on;
Though Iris has put on her clothes,
  She has not put her face on.

P. B. Shelley

ponder, darling, these busted statues

(ponder, darling, these busted statues
of yon motheaten forum be aware
notice what hath remained
—the stone cringes
clinging to the stone, how obsolete

lips utter their extant smile. . . .
remark

a few deleted of texture
or meaning monuments and dolls

resist Them Greediest Paws of careful
time all of which is extremely
unimportant) whereas Life

matters if or

when the your- and my-
idle vertical worthless
self unite in a peculiarly
momentary

partnership (to instigate
constructive
                    Horizontal
business. . . . even so, let us make haste
—consider well this ruined aqueduct

lady,
which used to lead something into somewhere)
                                        e. e. cummings

All's Well That Ends Well

A Friend of mine was married to a scold,
To me he came, and all his troubles told.
Said he, "She's like a woman raving mad."
"Alas! my friend," said I, "that's very bad!"
"No, not so bad," said he; "for, with her, true
I had both house and land, and money too."
    "That was well," said I;
    "No, not so well," said he;
    "For I and her own brother
    Went to law with one another;
    I was cast, the suit was lost,
And every penny went to pay the cost."
    "That was bad," said I;
    "No, not so bad," said he:
"For we agreed that he the house should keep,
And give to me four score of Yorkshire sheep
All fat, and fair, and fine, they were to be."
"Well, then," said I, "sure that was well for thee?"
    "No, not so well," said he;
    "For, when the sheep I got,
    They every one died of the rot."
    "That was bad," said I;
    "No, not so bad," said he;

"For I had thought to scrape the fat
    And keep it in an oaken vat;
Then into tallow melt for winter store."
"Well, then," said I, "that's better than before?"
    " 'Twas not so well," said he;
    "For having got a clumsy fellow
    To scrape the fat and melt the tallow;
Into the melting fat the fire catches,
    And, like brimstone matches,
    Burnt my house to ashes."
    "That was bad," said I;
"No! not so bad," said he; "for, what is best,
My scolding wife has gone among the rest."

Anonymous

A Joke Versified

"Come, come," said Tom's father, "at your time of life,
There's no longer excuse for thus playing the rake—
It is time you should think, boy, of taking a wife."—
"Why so it is, father,—whose wife shall I take?"

Thomas Moore

Miss Twye

Miss Twye was soaping her breasts in her bath
When she heard behind her a meaning laugh
And to her amazement she discovered
A wicked man in the bathroom cupboard.

Gavin Ewart

No Platonic Love

Tell me no more of minds embracing minds,
    And hearts exchang'd for hearts;
That spirits spirits meet, as winds do winds,
    And mix their subt'lest parts;
That two unbodied essences may kiss,
And then like Angels, twist and feel one Bliss.

It was that silly thing that once was wrought
    To practice this thin love;
I'd climb'd from sex to soul, from soul to thought;
    But thinking there to move,
Headlong I rolled from thought to soul, and then
From soul I lighted at the sex again.

As some strict down-looked men pretend to fast,
    Who yet in closets eat;

So lovers who profess they spirits taste,
  Feed yet on grosser meat;
I know they boast they souls to souls convey,
Howe'r they meet, the body is the way.

Come, I will undeceive thee, they that tread
  Those vain aerial ways,
Are like young heirs and alchemists misled
  To waste their wealth and days,
For searching thus to be for ever rich,
They only find a med'cine for the itch.

William Cartwright

Tell Me a Word

Tell me a word
That you've often heard
Yet it makes you squint
If you see it in print!

D. H. Lawrence

The Bee Is Such a Busy Soul

The bee is such a busy soul
It has no time for birth control,
And that is why in times like these
There are so many sons of bees.

Anonymous

Down, Wanton, Down!

Down, wanton, down! Have you no shame
That at the whisper of Love's name,
Or Beauty's, presto! up you raise
Your angry head and stand at gaze?

Poor bombard-captain, sworn to reach
The ravelin and effect a breach—
Indifferent what you storm or why,
So be that in the breach you die!

Love may be blind, but Love at least
Knows what is man and what mere beast;
Or Beauty wayward, but requires
More delicacy from her squires.

Tell me, my witless, whose one boast
Could be your staunchness at the post,

When were you made a man of parts
To think fine and profess the arts?

Will many-gifted Beauty come
Bowing to your bald rule of thumb,
Or Love swear loyalty to your crown?
Be gone, have done! Down, wanton, down!

Robert Graves

The Maid's Longing

A maiden of late
Whose name was Sweet Kate,
She dwelt in London near Aldersgate;
Now list to my ditty, declare it I can,
She would have a child without help of a man.

To a doctor she came,
A man of great fame,
Whose deep skill in physick report did proclaim,
Quoth she, Mr. Doctor show me if you can,
How I may conceive without help of a man.

Then listen, quoth he,
Since it must be,
This wondrous strange med'cine I'll show presently;
Take nine pound of thunder, six legs of a swan,
And you shall conceive without help of a man.

The wool of a frog,
The juice of a log,
Well parboil'd together in the skin of a hog,
With the egg of a moon calf, if get it you can,
And you shall conceive without help of a man.

Nine drops of rain
Brought hither from Spain,
With the blast of a bellows quite over the main,
With eight quarts of brimstone brew'd in a can,
And you shall conceive without help of a man.

Six pottles of lard,
Squeez'd from rock hard,
With nine turkey eggs, each as long as a yard,
With pudding of hailstones well bak'd in a pan,
And you shall conceive without help of a man.

These medicines are good,
And approved have stood,
Well temper'd together with a pottle of blood
Squeez'd from a grasshopper and the nail of a swan,
To make maids conceive without help of a man.

Anonymous

The Chaste Arabian Bird

'Tis the Arabian bird alone
Lives chaste, because there is but one.
But had kind nature made them two,
They would like doves and sparrows do.

John Wilmot, Earl of Rochester

On the Upright Judge, Who Condemned the "Drapier's" Printer

In church your grandsire cut his throat;
To do the job too long he tarried:
He should have had my hearty vote
To cut his throat before he married.

Jonathan Swift

Reflections on Ice-Breaking

Candy
Is dandy

But Liquor
Is quicker.

Ogden Nash

Footnote to the Renaissance

The Castrati
Had trouble getting naughty.

Enid Williams

Who Walks by the Dockside

Who walks by the dockside
In furs and peroxide
Was once a daughter
And purveyed laughter.

R. G. G. Price

She Crosses Her Knees

She crosses her knees:
That's the kind of girl she's.

Anonymous

Volume II (Kinsey)

Kinsey! Thy pages studiously rehearse
How female still may go from pet to worse;
Deliverance from frustration is thy tale—
How few delivered, though, by first-class male.

David Daiches

French Lisette

(*A Ballad of Maida Vale*)

Who strolls so late, for mugs a bait,
In the mists of Maida Vale,
Sauntering past a stucco gate
Fallen, but hardly frail?

You can safely bet that it's French Lisette,
The Pearl of Pottsdown Square,
On the game she has made her name
And rather more than her share.

In a coat of coney with her passport phoney
She left her native haunts,
For an English surname exchanging *her* name
And then took up with a ponce.

Now a meaning look conceals the hook
Some innocent fish will swallow,
Chirping "Hello, darling!" like a cheeky starling
She'll turn, and he will follow.

For her eyes are blue and her eyelids too
And her smile's by no means cryptic,
Her perm's as firm as if waved with glue,
She plies an orange lipstick.

And orange-red is her perky head
Under a hat like a tiny pie—
A pie on a tart, it might be said,
Is redundant, but oh, how spry!

From the distant tundra to snuggle under her
Chin a white fox was conveyed,
And with winks and leerings and Woolworth earrings
She's all set up for trade.

Now who comes here replete with beer?
A quinquagenarian clerk

Who in search of Life has left "the wife"
and "the kiddies" in Tufnell Park.

Dear sir, beware! for sex is a snare
And all is not true that allures.
Good sir, come off it! She means to profit
By this little weakness of yours:

Too late for alarm! Exotic charm
Has caught in his gills like a gaff,
He goes to his fate with a hypnotized gait,
The slave of her silvery laugh,

And follows her in to her suite of sin,
Her self-contained bower of bliss,
They enter her flat, she takes his hat,
And he hastens to take a kiss.

Ah, if only he knew that concealed from view
Behind a "folk-weave" curtain
Is her fancy man, called Dublin Dan,
His manner would be less certain,

His bedroom eyes would express surprise,
His attitude less languor,
He would watch his money, not call her "Honey,"
And be seized with fear or anger.

Of the old technique one need scarcely speak,
But oh, in the quest for Romance
'Tis folly abounding in a strange surrounding
To be divorced from one's pants.

Willam Plomer

To His Mistress Going to Bed

Come, Madam, come, all rest my powers defy,
Until I labor, I in labor lie.
The foe oft-times having the foe in sight,
Is tired with standing though he never fight.
Off with that girdle, like heaven's zone glittering,
But a far fairer world encompassing.
Unpin that spangled breastplate which you wear,
That th'eyes of busy fools may be stopped there.
Unlace your self, for that harmonious chime
Tells me from you that now it is bed time.
Off with that happy busk, which I envy,
That still can be, and still can stand so nigh.
Your gown going off, much beauteous state reveals,
As when from flowery meads th'hill's shadow steals.
Off with that wiry coronet and show
That hairy diadem which on you doth grow:
Now off with those shoes, and then safely tread
In this love's hallowed temple, this soft bed.
In such white robes, heaven's angels used to be
Received by men; thou angel bringst with thee
A heaven like Mahomet's paradise; and though
Ill spirits walk in white, we easily know,
By this these angels from an evil sprite,
Those set our hairs, but these our flesh upright.
    License my roving hands, and let them go
Before, behind, between, above, below.
O my America! my new-found-land,
My kingdom, safeliest when with one man manned,
My mine of precious stones, my Emperie,
How blest am I in this discovering thee!
To enter in these bonds, is to be free;
Then where my hand is set, my seal shall be.
    Full nakedness! All joys are due to thee,
As souls unbodied, bodies unclothed must be,
To taste whole joys. Gems which you women use
Are like Atlanta's balls, cast in men's views,
That when a fool's eye lighteth on a Gem,
His earthly soul may covet theirs, not them.
Like pictures, or like books' gay coverings made
For laymen, are all women thus arrayed;
Themselves are mystic books, which only we
(Whom their imputed grace will dignify)
Must see revealed. Then since that I may know,
As liberally, as to a midwife, show

Thy self: cast all, yea, this white linen hence,
There is no penance, much less innocence;
To teach thee, I am naked first; why then
What needst thou have more covering than a man.

John Donne

The Angel

I asked a thief to steal me a peach:
He turn'd up his eyes.
I ask'd a lithe lady to lie her down:
Holy and meek she cries.
As soon as I went an angel came:
He wink'd at the thief
And smil'd at the dame,
And without one word spoke
Had a peach from the tree,
And 'twixt earnest and joke
Enjoy'd the Lady.

William Blake

The Ballad of Persse O'Reilly

Have you heard of one Humpty Dumpty
How he fell with a roll and a rumble
And curled up like Lord Olofa Crumple
By the bull of the Magazine Wall,
   Chorus: Of the Magazine Wall,
        Hump, helmet and all?

He was one time our King of the Castle
Now he's kicked about like a rotten old parsnip,
And from Green street he'll be sent by order of his Worship
To the penal jail of Mountjoy!
   Chorus: To the jail of Mountjoy!
        Jail him and joy.

He was fafafather of all schemes for to bother us
Slow coaches and immaculate contraceptives for the populace,
Mare's milk for the sick, seven dry Sundays a week,
Openair love and religion's reform,
   Chorus: And religious reform,
        Hideous in form.

Arrah, why, says you, couldn't he manage it?
I'll go bail, my fine dairyman darling,

Like the bumping bull of the Cassidys
All your butter is in your horns.
   Chorus: His butter is in his horns.
        Butter his horns!

(Repeat)   Hurrah there, Hosty, frosty Hosty, change that
        shirt on ye,
        Rhyme the rann, the king of all ranns!

           Balbaccio, balbuccio!
We had chaw chaw chops, chairs, chewing gum, the chicken-
    pox and china chambers
Universally provided by this soffsoaping salesman.
Small wonder He'll Cheat E'erawan our local lads nick-
    named him
When Chimpden first took the floor
   Chorus: With his bucketshop store
        Down Bargainweg, Lower.

So snug he was in his hotel premises sumptuous
But soon we'll bonfire all his trash, tricks and trumpery
And 'tis short till sheriff Clancy'll be winding up his unlimited
    company
With the bailiff's bom at the door,
   Chorus: Bimbam at the door.
        Then he'll bum no more.

Sweet bad luck on the waves washed to our island
The hooker of that hammerfast viking
And Gall's curse on the way when Eblana bay
Saw his black and tan man-o'-war.
   Chorus: Saw his man-o'-war.
        On the harbor bar.

Where from? roars Poolbeg. Cookingha'pence, he bawls Don-
    nezmoi scampitle, wick an wipin'fampiny
Fingal Mac Oscar Onesine Bargearse Boniface
Thok's min gammelhole Norveegickers moniker
Og as ay are at gammelhore Norveegickers cod.
   Chorus: A Norwegian camel old cod.
        He is, begod.

Lift it, Hosty, lift it, ye devil ye! up with the rann, the rhym-
    ing rann!

It was during some fresh water garden pumping
Or, according to the *Nursing Mirror*, while admiring the
    monkeys

That our heavyweight heathen Humpharey
Made bold a maid to woo
   Chorus: Woohoo, what'll she doo!
          The general lost her maidenloo!

He ought to blush for himself, the old hayheaded philosopher,
For to go and shove himself that way on top of her.
Begob, he's the crux of the catalogue
Of our antediluvial zoo,
   Chorus: Messrs. Billing and Coo.
          Noah's larks, good as noo.

He was joulting by Wellinton's monument
Our rotorious hippopopotamuns
When some bugger let down the backtrap of the omnibus
And he caught his death of fusiliers,
   Chorus: With his rent in his rears.
          Give him six years.

'Tis sore pity for his innocent poor children
But look out for his missus legitimate!
When that frew gets a grip of old Earwicker
Won't there be earwigs on the green?
   Chorus: Big earwigs on the green,
          The largest ever you seen.

   Suffoclose! Shikespower! Seudodanto! Anonymoses!

Then we'll have a free trade Gaels' band and mass meeting
For to sod the brave son of Scandiknavery,
And we'll bury him down on Oxmanstown
Along with the devil and Danes,
   Chorus: With the deaf and dumb Danes,
          And all their remains.

And not all the king's men nor his horses
Will resurrect his corpus
For there's no true spell in Connacht or hell
   (bis) That's able to raise a Cain.

                            James Joyce

Man, Man, Man

Man, man, man is for the woman made,
And the woman made for man;
As the spur is for the jade,
As the scabbard for the blade,
As for digging is the spade,
   As for liquor is the can,
So man, man, man, is for the woman made,
   And the woman made for man.

As the scepter's to be swayed,
As for Night's the serenade,
   As for pudding is the pan,
   As to cool us is the fan,
So man, man, man, is for the woman made,
   And the woman made for man.

Be she widow, wife or maid,
Be she wanton, be she staid,
Be she well- or ill-arrayed,
   Shrew, slut, or harridan,
Yet man, man, man, is for the woman made,
   And the woman made for man.

Anonymous

From "The Old Wife's Tale"

When as the rye reach to the chin,
And chopcherry, chopcherry ripe within,
Strawberries swimming in the cream,
And schoolboys playing in the stream;
   Then O, then O, then O my true love said,
    Till that time come again,
  She could not live a maid.
                George Peele

Here's to the Maiden

Here's to the maiden of bashful fifteen;
Now to the widow of fifty;
Here's to the flaunting extravagant quean;
And here's to the housewife that's thrifty:

  Chorus: Let the toast pass,
      Drink to the lass:
      I'll warrant she'll prove
      An excuse for the glass.

Here's to the charmer whose dimples we prize;
Now to the damsel with none, Sir;
Here's to the girl with a pair of blue eyes;
And now to the nymph with but one, Sir:

Here's to the maid with a bosom of snow;
Now to her that's as brown as a berry;
Here's to the wife with a face full of woe;
And now to the damsel that's merry:

For let her be clumsy or let her be slim;
Young or ancient, I care not a feather;
So fill up a bumper, nay, fill to the brim;
And let us e'en toast 'em together:
                Richard Brinsley Sheridan

Frankie and Johnny

Frankie and Johnny were lovers.
O my Gawd how they did love!
They swore to be true to each other,
As true as the stars above.
He was her man but he done her wrong.

Frankie and Johnny went walking,
Johnny in a brand new suit.

Frankie went walking with Johnny,
Said: "O Gawd don't my Johnny look cute."
He was her man but he done her wrong.

Frankie went down to Memphis,
Went on the morning train,
Paid a hundred dollars,
Bought Johnny a watch and chain.
He was her man but he done her wrong.

Frankie lived in a crib-house,
Crib-house with only two doors,
Gave her money to Johnny,
He spent it on those parlor whores.
He was her man but he done her wrong.

Frankie went down to the hock-shop,
Went for a bucket of beer,
Said: "O, Mr. Bartender,
Has my loving Johnny been here?
He is my man but he's doing me wrong."

"I don't want to make you no trouble.
I don't want to tell you no lie,
But I saw Johnny an hour ago
With a girl name Nelly Bly.
He is your man but he's doing you wrong."

Frankie went down to the hotel.
She didn't go there for fun,
'Cause underneath her kimono
She toted a 44 gun.
He was her man but he done her wrong.

Frankie went down to the hotel.
She rang the front-door bell,
Said: "Stand back all you chippies
Or I'll blow you all to hell.
I want my man for he's doing me wrong."

Frankie looked in through the keyhole
And there before her eye
She saw her Johnny on the sofa
A-loving up Nelly Bly.
He was her man; he was doing her wrong.

Frankie threw back her kimono,
Took out a big 44,

Root-a-toot-toot, three times she shoot
Right through that hardware door.
He was her man but was doing her wrong.

Johnny grabbed up his Stetson,
Said, "O my Gawd Frankie don't shoot."
But Frankie pulled hard on the trigger
And the gun went root-a-toot-toot.
She shot her man who was doing her wrong.

"Roll me over easy,
Roll me over slow,
Roll me over on my right side
'Cause my left side hurts me so.
I was her man but I done her wrong."

Johnny he was a gambler,
He gambled for the gain;
The very last words he ever said
Were—"High-low Jack and the game."
He was her man but he done her wrong.

"Bring out your rubber-tired buggy,
Bring out your rubber-tired hack;
I'll take my Johnny to the graveyard
But I won't bring him back.
He was my man but he done me wrong.

"Lock me in that dungeon,
Lock me in that cell,
Lock me where the north-east wind
Blows from the corner of Hell.
I shot my man 'cause he done me wrong."

Frankie went down to the Madame,
She went down on her knees.
"Forgive me, Mrs. Halcombe,
Forgive me if you please
For shooting my man 'cause he done me wrong."

"Forgive you Frankie darling,
Forgive you I never can,
Forgive you, Frankie darling,
For shooting your only man,
For he was your man though he done you wrong."

It was not murder in the first degree,
It was not murder in the third.

A woman simply shot her man
As a hunter drops a bird.
She shot her man 'cause he done her wrong.

Frankie said to the Sheriff,
"What do you think they'll do?"
The Sheriff said to Frankie,
"It's the electric chair for you.
You shot your man 'cause he done you wrong."

Frankie sat in the jailhouse,
Had no electric fan,
Told her little sister:
"Don't you marry no sporting man.
I had a man but he done me wrong."

Frankie heard a rumbling,
Away down in the ground;
Maybe it was little Johnny
Where she had shot him down.
He was her man, but he done her wrong.

Once more I saw Frankie,
She was sitting in the chair
Waiting for to go and meet her God
With the sweat dripping out of her hair.
He was her man, but he done her wrong.

This story has no moral,
This story has no end,
This story only goes to show
That there ain't no good in men.
He was her man but he done her wrong.

Anonymous

PART EIGHT

Eat, Drink, and Be Merry

Grace

Good bread,
   Good meat;
Good God!
   Let's eat!

Anonymous

The Five Reasons for Drinking

If all be true that I do think,
There are five reasons we should drink;
Good wine—a friend—or being dry—
Or lest we should be by and by—
Or any other reason why.

Henry Aldrich

Hymn to the Belly

Room! room! make room for the bouncing Belly,
First father of sauce and deviser of jelly;
Prime master of arts and the giver of wit,
That found out the excellent engine, the spit,
The plow and the flail, the mill and the hopper,
The hutch and the boulter, the furnace and copper,
The oven, the bavin, the mawkin, the peel,
The hearth and the range, the dog and the wheel.
He, he first invented the hogshead and tun,
The gimlet and vise too, and taught 'em to run;
And since, with the funnel and hippocras bag,
He's made of himself that now he cries swag;
Which shows, though the pleasure be but of four inches,
Yet he is a weasel, the gullet that pinches
Of any delight, and not spares from his back
Whatever to make of the belly a sack.
Hail, hail, plump paunch! O the founder of taste,
For fresh meats or powdered, or pickle or paste!
Devourer of broiled, baked, roasted or sod!
And emptier of cups, be they even or odd!
All which have now made thee so wide i' the waist,
As scarce with no pudding thou art to be laced;
But eating and drinking until thou dost nod,
Thou break'st all thy girdles and break'st forth a god.

Ben Jonson

The Epicure

Underneath this myrtle shade,
On flowery beds supinely laid,
With odorous oils my head o'erflowing,
And around it roses growing,
What should I do but drink away
The heat and troubles of the day?
In this more than kingly state
Love himself on me shall wait.
Fill to me, Love! nay, fill it up!
And mingled cast into the cup
Wit and mirth and noble fires,
Vigorous health and gay desires.
The wheel of life no less will stay
In a smooth than rugged way:
Since it equally doth flee,
Let the motion pleasant be.
Why do we precious ointments shower?—

Nobler wines why do we pour?—
Beauteous flowers why do we spread
Upon the monuments of the dead?
Nothing they but dust can show.
Or bones that hasten to be so.
Crown me with roses while I live,
Now your wines and ointments give:
After death I nothing crave,
Let me alive my pleasures have:
All are Stoics in the grave.

Abraham Cowley

Jolly Good Ale and Old

I cannot eat but little meat,
  My stomach is not good;
But sure I think that I can drink
  With him that wears a hood.
Though I go bare, take ye no care,
  I nothing am a-cold;
I stuff my skin so full within
  Of jolly good ale and old.
Chorus: Back and side go bare, go bare;
      Both feet and hand go cold;
      But, belly, God send thee good ale enough,
      Whether it be new or old.

I love no roast but a nut-brown toast,
  And a crab laid in the fire;
A little bread shall do me stead;
  Much bread I not desire.
No frost nor snow, nor wind, I trow,
  Can hurt me if I wold;
I am so wrapped and thoroughly lapped
  Of jolly good ale and old.

And Tib, my wife, that as her life
  Loveth well good ale to seek,
Full oft drinks she till ye may see
  The tears run down her cheek:
Then doth she trowl to me the bowl
  Even as a maltworm should,
And saith, "Sweetheart, I took my part
  Of this jolly good ale and old."

Now let them drink till they nod and wink,
  Even as good fellows should do;
They shall not miss to have the bliss
  Good ale doth bring men to;
And all poor souls that have scoured bowls
  Or have them lustily trolled,
God save the lives of them and their wives,
  Whether they be young or old.

Anonymous

Cakes and Ale

I gave her Cakes and I gave her Ale,
  I gave her Sack and Sherry;
I kissed her once and I kissed her twice,
  And we were wondrous merry.

I gave her Beads and Bracelets fine,
  I gave her Gold down derry.
I thought she was afeard till she stroked my Beard,
  And we were wondrous merry.

Merry my Hearts, merry my Cocks, merry my Sprights.
  Merry merry merry my hey down derry.
I kissed her once and I kissed her twice,
  And we were wondrous merry.

Anonymous

The Careless Gallant

Let us drink and be merry, dance, joke, and rejoice,
With claret and sherry, theorbo and voice,
The changeable world to our joy is unjust,
All treasure's uncertain, then down with your dust;
  In frolics dispose your pounds, shillings, and pence,
  For we shall be nothing a hundred years hence.

We'll sport and be free with Frank, Betty, and Dolly,
Have lobsters and oysters to cure melancholy,
Fish dinners will make a man spring like a flea,
Dame Venus, love's lady, was born of the sea,
    With her and with Bacchus we'll tickle the sense,
    For we shall be past it a hundred years hence.

Your beautiful bit, that hath all eyes upon her,
That her honesty sells for a hogo of honor,
Whose lightness and brightness doth cast such a splendor,
That none are thought fit but the stars to attend her;
    Though now she seems pleasant and sweet to the sense,
    Will be damnably moldy a hundred years hence.

Your usurer that in the hundred takes twenty,
Who wants in his wealth, and pines in his plenty,
Lays up for a season which he shall ne'er see,
The year of one thousand, eight hundred and three,
    Shall have changed all his bags, his houses and rents,
    For a worm-eaten coffin a hundred years hence.

Your Chancery-lawyer who by subtlety thrives,
In spinning a suit to the length of three lives,
A suit which the client doth wear out in slavery,
Whilst pleader makes conscience a cloak for his knavery,
    Can boast of his cunning but i' th' present tense,
    For *non est inventus* a hundred years hence.

Then why should we turmoil in cares and in fears,
And turn our tranquillity to sighs and tears?
Let's eat, drink and play, ere the worms do corrupt us,
For I say that, *Post mortem nulla voluptas;*
    Let's deal with our Damsels, that we may from thence
    Have broods to succeed us a hundred years hence.

I never could gain satisfaction upon
Your dreams of a bliss when we're cold as a stone,
The Sages call us Drunkards, Gluttons, and Wenchers,
But we find such morsels, upon their own trenchers:
    For Abigail, Hannah, and sister Prudence,
    Will simper to nothing a hundred years hence.

The butterfly courtier, that pageant of state,
The mousetrap of honor and May-game of fate,
With all his ambitions, intrigues, and his tricks,
Must die like a clown, and then drop into Styx,

His plots against death are too slender a fence,
For he'll be out of place a hundred years hence.

Yea, the poet himself that so loftily sings,
As he scorns any subjects, but heroes or kings,
Must to the capricios of fortune submit,
And often be counted a fool for his wit,
    Thus beauty, wit, wealth, law, learning and sense,
    All comes to nothing a hundred years hence.

Thomas Jordan

Nursery Rhyme for the Tender-Hearted

Scuttle, scuttle, little roach—
How you run when I approach:
Up above the pantry shelf,
Hastening to secrete yourself.

Most adventurous of vermin,
How I wish I could determine
How you spend your hours of ease,
Perhaps reclining on the cheese.

Cook has gone, and all is dark—
Then the kitchen is your park:
In the garbage heap that she leaves
Do you browse among the tea leaves?

How delightful to suspect
All the places you have trekked:
Does your long antenna whisk its
Gentle tip across the biscuits?

Do you linger, little soul,
Drowsing in our sugar bowl?
Or, abandonment most utter,
Shake a shimmy on the butter?

Do you chant your simple tunes
Swimming in the baby's prunes?
Then, when dawn comes, do you slink
Homeward to the kitchen sink?

Timid roach, why be so shy?
We are brothers, thou and I.
In the midnight, like yourself,
I explore the pantry shelf!   *Christopher Morley*

Rye Whisky

I'll eat when I'm hungry,
 I'll drink when I'm dry;
If the hard times don't kill me,
 I'll lay down and die.

Chorus:
Rye whisky, rye whisky,
 Rye whisky, I cry,
If I don't get rye whisky,
 I surely will die.

I'll tune up my fiddle,
 And I'll rosin my bow,
I'll make myself welcome,
 Wherever I go.

Beefsteak when I'm hungry,
 Red liquor when I'm dry,
Greenbacks when I'm hard
 up,
 And religion when I die.

They say I drink whisky,
 My money's my own,
All them that don't like me,
 Can leave me alone.

Sometimes I drink whisky,
 Sometimes I drink rum,
Sometimes I drink brandy,
 At other times none.

But if I get boozy,
 My whisky 's my own,
And them that don't like me,
 Can leave me alone.

Jack o' diamonds, jack o'
 diamonds,
 I know you of old,
You've robbed my poor
 pockets
 Of silver and gold.

Oh, whisky, you villain,
 You've been my downfall,
You've kicked me, you've
 cuffed me—
 But I love you for all.

If the ocean was whisky,
 And I was a duck,
I'd dive to the bottom,
 To get one sweet suck.

But the ocean ain't whisky
 And I ain't a duck,
So we'll round up the cattle
 And then we'll get drunk.

My foot 's in my stirrup,
 My bridle 's in my hand,
I'm leaving sweet Lillie,
 The fairest in the land.

Her parents don't like me,
 They say I'm too poor;
They say I'm unworthy
 To enter her door.

Sweet milk when I'm hungry,
 Rye whisky when I'm dry,
If a tree don't fall on me,
 I'll live till I die.

I'll drink my own whisky,
 I'll make my own stew;
If I get drunk, madam,
 It's nothing to you.

I'll drink my own whisky,
 I'll drink my own wine;
Some ten thousand bottles
 I've killed in my time.

I've no wife to quarrel,
 No babies to bawl;
The best way of living
 Is no wife at all.

Way up on Cinch Mountain
 I wander alone;
I'm as drunk as the devil,
 Oh, let me alone.

You may boast of your
 knowledge
 En' brag of your sense,
'Twill all be forgotten
 A hundred years hence.
     Anonymous

Liquor and Longevity

The horse and mule live thirty years
And nothing know of wines and beers.
The goat and sheep at twenty die
And never taste of Scotch or Rye.
The cow drinks water by the ton
And at eighteen is mostly done.
The dog at fifteen cashes in
Without the aid of rum and gin.
The cat in milk and water soaks
And then in twelve short years it croaks.
The modest, sober, bone-dry hen
Lays eggs for nogs, then dies at ten.
All animals are strictly dry:
They sinless live and swiftly die;
But sinful, ginful rum-soaked men
Survive for three score years and ten,
And some of them, a very few,
Stay pickled till they're ninety-two.   *Anonymous*

When That St. George Had Slain His Dragon

When that St. George had slain his dragon
He sat down and had his flagon;
    And, wit ye well,
    Within a spell
He had a mostly pleasant jag on.   *Anonymous*

Take the Glass Away

Take the glass away:—
    I know I hadn't oughter:—
I'll take a pledge—I will—
    I never will drink water.   *Anonymous*

Toast

Here's to those who love us,
And here's to those who don't,
A smile for those who are willing to,
And a tear for those who won't.   *Anonymous*

Riddle

Here is a riddle most abstruse:
Canst read the answer right?
Why is it that my tongue grows loose
Only when I grow tight?   *Anonymous*

Beer

A man to whom illness was chronic,
When told that he needed a tonic,
    Said, "Oh, Doctor, dear,
      Won't you please make it beer?"
"No, no," said the Doc, "that's Teutonic."

Anonymous

Unforgivable and Unforgiven

With Peter I refuse to dine:
His jokes are older than his wine.

With Paul I have not lately dined:
My jokes were broader than his mind.

C. D. B. Ellis

La Carte

    It takes much art
    To choose à la carte
    For less than they quote
    For the table d'hôte.

Justin Richardson

An Epicure

An epicure, dining at Crewe,
Found quite a large mouse in his stew.
    Said the waiter, "Don't shout,
    And wave it about,
Or the rest will be wanting one, too!"

Anonymous

Peas

    I always eat peas with honey,
    I've done it all my life,
    They do taste kind of funny,
    But it keeps them on the knife.

Anonymous

A Young Fellow Named Sydney

There was a young fellow named Sydney,
Who drank till he ruined his kidney.
    It shriveled and shrank,
    As he sat there and drank,
But he'd had a good time at it, didn't he?

Anonymous

PART NINE

Unlikely Tales

Mrs. Mary Blaize

Good people all, with one accord,
    Lament for Madam Blaize,
Who never wanted a good word—
    From those who spoke her praise.

The needy seldom pass'd her door,
    And always found her kind;
She freely lent to all the poor—
    Who left a pledge behind.

238

She strove the neighborhood to please
  With manners wondrous winning;
And never followed wicked ways—
  Unless when she was sinning.

At church, in silks and satins new
  With hoop of monstrous size,
She never slumbered in her pew—
  But when she shut her eyes.

Her love was sought, I do aver,
  By twenty beaux and more;
The King himself has followed her—
  When she has walk'd before.

But now, her wealth and finery fled,
  Her hangers-on cut short-all:
The doctors found, when she was dead,—
  Her last disorder mortal.

Let us lament, in sorrow sore,
  For Kent Street well may say,
That had she lived a twelvemonth more,—
  She had not died today.   *Oliver Goldsmith*

Elegy on the Death of a Mad Dog

Good people all, of every sort,
  Give ear unto my song;
And if you find it wond'rous short,
  It cannot hold you long.

In Islington there was a man,
  Of whom the world might say,
That still a godly race he ran,
  Whene'er he went to pray.

A kind and gentle heart he had,
  To comfort friends and foes;
The naked every day he clad,
  When he put on his clothes.

And in that town a dog was found,
  As many dogs there be,
Both mongrel, puppy, whelp, and hound,
  And curs of low degree.

This dog and man at first were friends;
　　But when a pique began,
The dog, to gain some private ends,
　　Went mad and bit the man.

Around from all the neighboring streets
　　The wond'ring neighbors ran,
And swore the dog had lost its wits,
　　To bit so good a man.

The wound it seem'd both sore and sad
　　To every Christian eye;
And while they swore the dog was mad,
　　They swore the man would die.

But soon a wonder came to light,
　　That showed the rogues they lied:
The man recover'd of the bite,
　　The dog it was that died.　　　　*Oliver Goldsmith*

The Bunyip and the Whistling Kettle

I knew a most superior camper
　　Whose methods were absurdly wrong,
He did not live on tea and damper
　　But took a little stove along.

And every place he came to settle
　　He spread with gadgets saving toil,
He even had a whistling kettle
　　To warn him it was on the boil.

Beneath the waratahs and wattles,
　　Boronia and coolibah,
He scattered paper, cans and bottles,
　　And parked his nasty little car.

He camped, this sacrilegious stranger
　　(The moon was at the full that week),
Once in a spot that teemed with danger
　　Besides a bunyip-haunted creek.

He spread his junk but did not plunder,
　　Hoping to stay the weekend long;
He watched the bloodshot sun go under
　　Across the silent billabong.

He ate canned food without demurring,
   He put the kettle on for tea.
He did not see the water stirring
   Far out beside a sunken tree.

Then, for the day had made him swelter
   And night was hot and tense to spring,
He donned a bathing suit in shelter
   And left the firelight's friendly ring.

He felt the water kiss and tingle.
   He heard the silence—none too soon!
A ripple broke against the shingle,
   And dark with blood it met the moon.

Abandoned in the hush, the kettle
   Screamed as it guessed its master's plight,
And loud it screamed, the lifeless metal,
   Far into the malicious night.   *John Manifold*

The Deacon's Masterpiece or, The Wonderful "One-Hoss Shay"

A Logical Story

Have you heard of the wonderful one-hoss shay,
That was built in such a logical way
It ran a hundred years to a day,
And then, of a sudden, it—ah, but stay,
I'll tell you what happened without delay,
Scaring the parson into fits,
Frightening people out of their wits,—
Have you ever heard of that, I say?

Seventeen hundred and fifty-five.
Georgius Secundus was then alive,—
Snuffy old drone from the German hive.
That was the year when Lisbon-town
Saw the earth open and gulp her down,

And Braddock's army was done so brown,
Left without a scalp to its crown.
It was on the terrible Earthquake-day
That the Deacon finished the one-hoss shay.

Now in building of chaises, I tell you what,
There is always *somewhere* a weakest spot,—
In hub, tire, felloe, in spring or thill,
In panel, or crossbar, or floor, or sill,
In screw, bolt, thoroughbrace,—lurking still,
Find it somewhere you must and will,—
Above or below, or within or without,—
And that's the reason, beyond a doubt,
That a chaise *breaks down,* but doesn't *wear out.*

But the Deacon swore (as Deacons do,
With an "I dew vum," or an "I tell *yeou*")
He would build one shay to beat the taown
'n' the keounty 'n' all the kentry raoun';
It should be so built that it *couldn'* break daown:
"Fur," said the Deacon, " 't 's mighty plain
Thut the weakes' place mus' stan' the strain;
'n' the way t' fix it, uz I maintain, is only jest
T' make that place uz strong uz the rest."

So the Deacon inquired of the village folk
Where he could find the strongest oak,
That couldn't be split nor bent nor broke,—
That was for spokes and floor and sills;
He sent for lancewood to make the thills;
The crossbars were ash, from the straightest trees,
The panels of whitewood, that cuts like cheese,
But lasts like iron for things like these;
The hubs of logs from the "Settler's ellum,"—
Last of its timber,—they couldn't sell 'em,
Never an axe had seen their chips,
And the wedges flew from between their lips,
Their blunt ends frizzled like celery-tips;
Step and prop-iron, bolt and screw,
Spring, tire, axle, and linchpin too,
Steel of the finest, bright and blue;
Thoroughbrace bison-skin, thick and wide;
Boot, top, dasher, from tough old hide
Found in the pit when the tanner died.
That was the way he "put her through."
"There!" said the Deacon, "naow she'll dew!"

Do! I tell you, I rather guess
She was a wonder, and nothing less!
Colts grew horses, beards turned gray,
Deacon and deaconess dropped away,
Children and grandchildren—where were they?
But there stood the stout old one-hoss shay
As fresh as on Lisbon-earthquake-day!

EIGHTEEN HUNDRED;—it came and found
The Deacon's masterpiece strong and sound.
Eighteen hundred increased by ten;—
"Hahnsum kerridge" they called it then.
Eighteen hundred and twenty came;—
Running as usual; much the same.
Thirty and forty at last arrive,
And then come fifty, and FIFTY-FIVE.

Little of all we value here
Wakes on the morn of its hundredth year
Without both feeling and looking queer.
In fact, there's nothing that keeps its youth,
So far as I know, but a tree and truth.
(This is a moral that runs at large;
Take it.—You're welcome.—No extra charge.)

FIRST OF NOVEMBER,—the Earthquake-day,—
There are traces of age in the one-hoss shay,
A general flavor of mild decay,
But nothing local, as one may say.
There couldn't be,—for the Deacon's art
Had made it so like in every part
That there wasn't a chance for one to start.
For the wheels were just as strong as the thills
And the floor was just as strong as the sills,
And the panels just as strong as the floor,
And the whippletree neither less nor more,
And the back-crossbar as strong as the fore,
And spring and axle and hub *encore.*
And yet, *as a whole,* it is past a doubt
In another hour it will be *worn out!*

First of November, fifty-five!
This morning the parson takes a drive.
Now, small boys, get out of the way!
Here comes the wonderful one-hoss shay,
Drawn by a rat-tailed, ewe-necked bay.
"Huddup!" said the parson.—Off went they.

The parson was working his Sunday's text,—
Had got to *fifthly*, and stopped perplexed
At what the—Moses—was coming next.
All at once the horse stood still,
Close by the meet'n'-house on the hill.
First a shiver, and then a thrill,
Then something decidedly like a spill,—
And the parson was sitting upon a rock,
At half past nine by the meet'n'-house clock,—
Just the hour of the Earthquake shock!

What do you think the parson found,
When he got up and stared around?
The poor old chaise in a heap or mound,
As if it had been to the mill and ground!
You see, of course, if you're not a dunce,
How it went to pieces all at once,—
All at once, and nothing first,—
Just as bubbles do when they burst.

End of the wonderful one-hoss shay.
Logic is logic. That's all I say.

O. W. Holmes

The Dong with a Luminous Nose

When awful darkness and silence reign
Over the great Gromboolian plain,
   Through the long, long wintry nights;—
When the angry breakers roar
As they beat on the rocky shore;—
   When Storm clouds brood on the towering heights
Of the Hills of the Chankly Bore:

Then, through the vast and gloomy dark,
There moves what seems a fiery spark,
   A lonely spark with silvery rays
   Piercing the coal-black night,—
   A meteor strange and bright:
Hither and thither the vision strays,
   A single lurid light.

Slowly it wanders,—pauses,—creeps,—
Anon it sparkles,—flashes and leaps;
And ever as onward it gleaming goes
A light on the Bong-tree stems it throws.

And those who watch at that midnight hour
From Hall or Terrace, or lofty Tower,
Cry, as the wild light passes along,—
    "The Dong!—the Dong!
  The wandering Dong through the forest goes!
    The Dong! the Dong!
  The Dong with a luminous Nose!"

     Long years ago
  The Dong was happy and gay,
Till he fell in love with a Jumbly Girl
  Who came to those shores one day,
For the Jumblies came in a Sieve, they did,—
Landing at eve near the Zemmery Fidd
    Where the Oblong Oysters grow,
  And the rocks are smooth and gray.
And all the woods and the valleys rang
With the Chorus they daily and nightly sang,—
    "Far and few, far and few,
     Are the lands where the Jumblies live;
    Their heads are green, and their hands are blue,
    And they went to sea in a sieve."

Happily, happily passed those days!
    While the cheerful Jumblies stayed;
  They danced in circlets all night long,
  To the plaintive pipe of the lively Dong,
    In moonlight, shine, or shade.
For day and night he was always there
By the side of the Jumbly Girl so fair,
With her sky-blue hands, and her sea-green hair.
Till the morning came of that hateful day
When the Jumblies sailed in their sieve away,
And the Dong was left on the cruel shore
Gazing—gazing for evermore,—
Ever keeping his weary eyes on
That pea-green sail on the far horizon,—
Singing the Jumbly Chorus still
As he sat all day on the grassy hill,—
    "Far and few, far and few,
     Are the lands where the Jumblies live;
    Their heads are green, and their hands are blue,
    And they went to sea in a sieve."

But when the sun was low in the West,
  The Dong arose and said,—
  "What little sense I once possessed

Has quite gone out of my head!"
And since that day he wanders still
By lake and forest, marsh and hill,
Singing—"O somewhere, in valley or plain
Might I find my Jumbly Girl again!
For ever I'll seek by lake and shore
Till I find my Jumbly Girl once more!"

Playing a pipe with silvery squeaks,
Since then his Jumbly Girl he seeks,
And because by night he could not see,
He gathered the bark of the Twangum Tree
      On the flowery plain that grows.
      And he wove him a wondrous Nose,—
A Nose as strange as a Nose could be!
Of vast proportions and painted red,
And tied with cords to the back of his head.
      —In a hollow rounded space it ended
With a luminous lamp within suspended,
            All fenced about
            With a bandage stout
      To prevent the wind from blowing it out;—
And with holes all round to send the light,
In gleaming rays on the dismal night.

And now each night, and all night long,
Over those plains still roams the Dong;
And above the wail of the Chimp and Snipe
You may hear the squeak of his plaintive pipe
While ever he seeks, but seeks in vain
To meet with his Jumbly Girl again;
Lonely and wild—all night he goes,—
The Dong with a luminous Nose!
And all who watch at the midnight hour,
From Hall or Terrace, or lofty Tower,
Cry, as they trace the Meteor bright,
Moving along through the dreary night,—
      "This is the hour when forth he goes,
      The Dong with a luminous Nose!
      Yonder—over the plain he goes;
            He goes!
            He goes;
      The Dong with a luminous Nose!"

                                                    Edward Lear

Mr. and Mrs. Discobbolos

Mr. and Mrs. Discobbolos
   Climbed to the top of a wall,
  And they sate to watch the sunset sky
  And to hear the Nupiter Piffkin cry
   And the Biscuit Buffalo call.
They took up a roll and some Camomile tea,
And both were as happy as happy could be—
    Till Mrs. Discobbolos said,—
     "Oh! W! X! Y! Z!
    It has just come into my head—
Suppose we should happen to fall!!!!!
     Darling Mr. Discobbolos!

"Suppose we should fall down flumpetty
   Just like two pieces of stone!
  Onto the thorns,—or into the moat!
  What would become of your new green coat?
   And might you not break a bone?
It never occurred to me before—
That perhaps we shall never go down any more!"
    And Mrs. Discobbolos said—
     "Oh! W! X! Y! Z!
    What put it into your head
To climb up this wall?—my own
     Darling Mr. Discobbolos?"

Mr. Discobbolos answered,—
    "At first it gave me pain,—
  And I felt my ears turn perfectly pink
  When your exclamation made me think
   We might never get down again!
But now I believe it is wiser far
To remain for ever just where we are."—

And Mr. Discobbolos said,
"Oh! W! X! Y! Z!
It has just come into my head—
We shall never go down again—
                Dearest Mrs. Discobbolos!"

So Mr. and Mrs. Discobbolos
        Stood up, and began to sing,
    "Far away from hurry and strife
    Here we will pass the rest of life,
        Ding a dong, ding dong, ding!
We want no knives nor forks nor chairs,
No tables nor carpets nor household cares,
        From worry of life we've fled—
        Oh! W! X! Y! Z!
    There is no more trouble ahead
    Sorrow or any such thing—
                For Mr. and Mrs. Discobbolos!"

Mr. and Mrs. Discobbolos
    Lived on the top of the wall,
For twenty years, a month, and a day,
Till their hair had grown all pearly gray,
    And their teeth began to fall.
They never were ill, or at all dejected,
By all admired, and by some respected,
        Till Mrs. Discobbolos said,
        "Oh! W! X! Y! Z!
    It has just come into my head,
    We have no more room at all—
                Darling Mr. Discobbolos!

"Look at our six fine boys!
    And our six sweet girls so fair!
Upon this wall they have all been born,
And not one of the twelve has happened to fall
    Through my maternal care!
Surely they should not pass their lives
Without any chance of husbands or wives!"
        And Mrs. Discobbolos said,
        "Oh! W! X! Y! Z!
    Did it never come into your head
    That our lives must be lived elsewhere,
                Dearest Mr. Discobbolos?

"They have never been at a ball,
    Nor have even seen a bazaar!

Nor have heard folks say in a tone all hearty,
'What loves of girls (at a garden party)
Those Misses Discobbolos are!'
Morning and night it drives me wild
To think of the fate of each darling child!"
But Mr. Discobbolos said,
"Oh! W! X! Y! Z!
What has come to your fiddledum head!
What a runcible goose you are!
Octopod Mrs. Discobbolos!"

Suddenly Mr. Discobbolos
Slid from the top of the wall;
And beneath it he dug a dreadful trench,
And filled it with dynamite, gunpowder gench,
And aloud he began to call—
"Let the wild bee sing,
And the blue bird hum!
For the end of your lives has certainly come!"
And Mrs. Discobbolos said,
"Oh! W! X! Y! Z!
We shall presently all be dead,
On this ancient runcible wall,
Terrible Mr. Discobbolos!"

Pensively, Mr. Discobbolos
Sat with his back to the wall;
He lighted a match, and fired the train,
And the mortified mountain echoed again
To the sound of an awful fall!
And all the Discobbolos family flew
In thousands of bits to the sky so blue,
And no one was left to have said,
"Oh! W! X! Y! Z!
Has it come into anyone's head
That the end has happened to all
Of the whole of the Clan Discobbolos?"

Edward Lear

Incidents in the Life of My Uncle Arly

O my aged Uncle Arly!
Sitting on a heap of Barley
Thro' the silent hours of night,—
Close beside a leafy thicket:—
On his nose there was a Cricket,—
In his hat a Railway Ticket
(But his shoes were far too tight).

Long ago, in youth, he squander'd
All his goods away, and wander'd
To the Tiniskoop hills afar.
There on golden sunsets blazing,
Every evening found him gazing,—
Singing,—"Orb! you're quite amazing!
How I wonder what you are!"

Like the ancient Medes and Persians,
Always by his own exertions
He subsisted on those hills;—
Whiles,—by teaching children spelling,—
Or at times by merely yelling,—
Or at intervals by selling
"Propter's Nicodemus Pills."

Later, in his morning rambles
He perceived the moving brambles—
Something square and white disclose;—
'Twas a First-class Railway Ticket;
But, on stooping down to pick it
Off the ground,—a pea-green Cricket
Settled on my uncle's Nose.

Never—Never more,—oh! never,
Did that Cricket leave him ever,—
Dawn or evening, day or night;—
Clinging as a constant treasure,—
Chirping with a cheerious measure,—
Wholly to my uncle's pleasure
(Though his shoes were far too tight).

So for three and forty winters,
Till his shoes were worn to splinters,
All those hills he wandered o'er,—
Sometimes silent;—sometimes yelling;—

Till he came to Borley-Melling,
Near his old ancestral dwelling
(But his shoes were far too tight).

On a little heap of Barley
Died my aged Uncle Arly,
And they buried him one night;—
Close beside the leafy thicket;—
There,—his hat and Railway Ticket;—
There,—his ever-faithful Cricket
(But his shoes were far too tight).

Edward Lear

The Gipsy Laddie

It was late in the night when the Squire came home
Inquiring for his lady.
His servant made a sure reply:
She's gone with the gipsum Davy.

Chorus: Rattle tum a gipsum gipsum
Rattle tum a gipsum Davy.

O go catch up my milk-white steed,
The black one's not so speedy,
I'll ride all night till broad daylight,
Or overtake my lady.

He rode and he rode till he came to the town,
He rode till he came to Barley.
The tears came rolling down his cheeks,
And then he spied his lady.

It's come go back, my dearest dear,
Come go back, my honey;
It's come go back, my dearest dear,
And you never shall lack for money.

I won't go back, my dearest dear,
I won't go back, my honey:
For I wouldn't give a kiss from gipsum's lips
For you and all your money.

It's go pull off those snow-white gloves,
A-made of Spanish leather,
And give to me your lily-white hand,
And bid farewell for ever.

It's she pulled off those snow-white gloves,
A-made of Spanish leather,
And gave to him her lily-white hand,
And bade farewell for ever.

She soon ran through her gay clothing,
Her velvet shoes and stockings;
Her gold ring off her finger's gone,
And the gold plate off her bosom.

O once I had a house and land,
Featherbed and money;
But now I've come to an old straw pad
With the gipsies dancing round me.

Anonymous

Nottamun Town

In Nottamun Town not a soul would look up,
Not a soul would look up, not a soul would look down,
Not a soul would look up, not a soul would look down,
To tell me the way to Nottamun Town.

I rode a big horse that was called a gray mare,
Gray mane and tail, gray stripes down his back,
Gray mane and tail, gray stripes down his back,
There weren't a hair on him but what was called black.

She stood so still, she threw me to the dirt,
She tore my hide and bruised my shirt;
From stirrup to stirrup I mounted again
And on my ten toes I rode over the plain.

Met the King and the Queen and a company of men
A-walking behind and a-riding before.
A stark naked drummer came walking along
With his hands in his bosom a-beating his drum.

Sat down on a hot and cold frozen stone,
Ten thousand stood round me yet I was alone.
Took my heart in my hand to keep my head warm.
Ten thousand got drowned that never were born.

Anonymous

Nightmare

When you're lying awake with a dismal headache, and repose
    is taboo'd by anxiety,
I conceive you may use any language you choose to indulge in,
    without impropriety;
For your brain is on fire—the bedclothes conspire of usual
    slumber to plunder you:
First your counterpane goes, and uncovers your toes, and your
    sheet slips demurely from under you;
Then the blanketing tickles—you feel like mixed pickles—so
    terribly sharp is the pricking,
And you're hot, and you're cross, and you tumble and toss till
    there's nothing 'twixt you and the ticking.
Then the bedclothes all creep to the ground in a heap, and you
    pick 'em all up in a tangle;
Next your pillow resigns and politely declines to remain at its
    usual angle!
Well, you get some repose in the form of a doze, with hot
    eyeballs, and head ever aching,
But your slumbering teems with such horrible dreams that
    you'd very much better be waking;
For you dream you are crossing the Channel, and tossing about
    in a steamer from Harwich—
Which is something between a large bathing machine and a
    very small second-class carriage—
And you're giving a treat (penny ice and cold meat) to a party
    of friends and relations—
They're a ravenous horde—and they all came on board at
    Sloane Square and South Kensington Stations.
And bound on that journey you find your attorney (who
    started that morning from Devon);
He's a bit undersized, and you don't feel surprised when he tells
    you he's only eleven.

Well, you're driving like mad with this singular lad (by-the-bye
    the ship's now a four-wheeler),

And you're playing round games, and he calls you bad names
    when you tell him that "ties pay the dealer."

But this you can't stand, so you throw up your hand, and you
    find you're as cold as an icicle,

In your shirt and your socks (the black silk with gold clocks),
    crossing Salisbury Plain on a bicycle:

And he and the crew are on bicycles too—which they've some-
    how or other invested in—

And he's telling the tars all the particu*lars* of a company he's
    interested in—

It's a scheme of devices, to get at low prices all goods from
    cough mixtures to cables

(Which tickled the sailors) by treating retailers, as though they
    were all vege*tables*—

You get a good spadesman to plant a small tradesman (first
    take off his boots with a boot-tree),

And his legs will take root, and his fingers will shoot, and
    they'll blossom and bud like a fruit-tree—

From the greengrocer tree you get grapes and green pea, cauli-
    flower, pineapple, and cranberries,

While the pastrycook plant cherry brandy will grant, apple
    puffs, and three-corners, and Banburys—

The shares are a penny, and ever so many are taken by
    Rothschild and Baring,

And just as a few are allotted to you, you awake with a shudder
    despairing—

You're a regular wreck, with a crick in your neck, and no
    wonder you snore, for your head's on the floor, and
    you've needles and pins from your soles to your shins,
    and your flesh is a-creep, for your left leg's asleep, and
    you've cramp in your toes, and a fly on your nose, and
    some fluff in your lung, and a feverish tongue, and a
    thirst that's intense, and a general sense that you haven't
    been sleeping in clover;

But the darkness has passed, and it's daylight at last, and
    the night has been long—ditto ditto my song—and
    thank goodness they're both of them over!

Sir W. S. Gilbert

Ballad

I

The auld wife sat at her ivied door,
   (Butter and eggs and a pound of cheese)
A thing she had frequently done before;
   And her spectacles lay on her apron'd knees.

The piper he piped on the hill-top high,
   (Butter and eggs and a pound of cheese)
Till the cow said "I die," and the goose ask'd "Why?"
   And the dog said nothing, but search'd for fleas.

The farmer he strode through the square farmyard;
   (Butter and eggs and a pound of cheese)
His last brew of ale was a trifle hard—
   The connection of which with the plot one sees.

The farmer's daughter hath frank blue eyes;
   (Butter and eggs and a pound of cheese)
She hears the rooks caw in the windy skies,
   As she sits at her lattice and shells her peas.

The farmer's daughter hath ripe red lips;
   (Butter and eggs and a pound of cheese)
If you try to approach her, away she skips
   Over tables and chairs with apparent ease.

The farmer's daughter hath soft brown hair
   (Butter and eggs and a pound of cheese)
And I met with a ballad, I can't say where,
   Which wholly consisted of lines like these.

II

She sat with her hands 'neath her dimpled cheeks
   (Butter and eggs and a pound of cheese)
And spake not a word. While a lady speaks
   There is hope, but she didn't even sneeze.

She sat, with her hands 'neath her crimson cheeks;
   (Butter and eggs and a pound of cheese)
She gave up mending her father's breeks,
   And let the cat roll in her new chemise.

She sat, with her hands 'neath her burning cheeks,
   (Butter and eggs and a pound of cheese)

And gazed at the piper for thirteen weeks;
　　The she follow'd him out o'er the misty leas.

Her sheep follow'd her, as their tails did them.
　　(Butter and eggs and a pound of cheese)
And this song is consider'd a perfect gem,
　　And as to the meaning, it's what you please.

　　　　　　　　　　　　　　　　　C. S. Calverley

Faithless Nellie Gray

Ben Battle was a soldier bold,
　　And used to war's alarms;
But a cannonball took off his legs,
　　So he laid down his arms.

Now as they bore him off the field,
　　Said he, "Let others shoot,
For here I leave my second leg,
　　And the Forty-second Foot!"

The army surgeons made him limbs:
　　Said he:—"They're only pegs:
But there's as wooden members quite
　　As represent my legs!"

Now Ben he loved a pretty maid,
　　Her name was Nellie Gray:
So he went to pay her his devours
　　When he'd devoured his pay!

But when he called on Nellie Gray,
   She made him quite a scoff;
And when she saw his wooden legs
   Began to take them off!

"O, Nellie Gray! O, Nellie Gray!
   Is this your love so warm?
The love that loves a scarlet coat
   Should be more uniform!"

She said, "I loved a soldier once,
   For he was blythe and brave;
But I will never have a man
   With both legs in the grave!

"Before you had those timber toes,
   Your love I did allow,
But then, you know, you stand upon
   Another footing now!"

"O, Nellie Gray! O, Nellie Gray!
   For all your jeering speeches,
At duty's call, I left my legs
   In Badajos's *breaches*!"

"Why, then," she said, "you've lost the feet
   Of legs in war's alarms,
And now you cannot wear your shoes
   Upon your feats of arms!"

"Oh, false and fickle Nellie Gray;
   I know why you refuse:—
Though I've no feet—some other man
   Is standing in my shoes!

"I wish I ne'er had seen your face;
   But now, a long farewell!
For you will be my death, alas!
   You will not be my Nell!"

Now when he went from Nellie Gray,
   His heart so heavy got—
And life was such a burthen grown,
   It made him take a knot!

So round his melancholy neck,
　　A rope he did entwine,
And, for his second time in life,
　　Enlisted in the Line!

One end he tied around a beam,
　　And then removed his pegs,
And as his legs were off,—of course
　　He soon was off his legs!

And there he hung, till he was dead
　　As any nail in town,—
For though distress had cut him up,
　　It could not cut him down!

A dozen men sat on his corpse,
　　To find out why he died—
And they buried Ben in four crossroads,
　　With a *stake* in his inside!

Thomas Hood

The Hunting of the Snark

FIT THE FIRST: THE LANDING

"Just the place for a Snark!" the Bellman cried,
　　As he landed his crew with care;
Supporting each man on the top of the tide
　　By a finger entwined in his hair.

"Just the place for a Snark! I have said it twice:
　　That alone should encourage the crew.
Just the place for a Snark! I have said it thrice:
　　What I tell you three times is true."

The crew was complete: it included a Boots—
　　A marker of Bonnets and Hoods—
A Barrister, brought to arrange their disputes—
　　And a Broker, to value their goods.

A Billiard-marker, whose skill was immense,
　　Might perhaps have won more than his share—
But a Banker, engaged at enormous expense,
　　Had the whole of their cash in his care.

There was also a Beaver, that paced on the deck,
　　Or would sit making lace in the bow:

And had often (the Bellman said) saved them from wreck,
  Though none of the sailors knew how.

There was one who was famed for the number of things
  He forgot when he entered the ship:
His umbrella, his watch, all his jewels and rings,
  And the clothes he had bought for the trip.

He had forty-two boxes, all carefully packed,
  With his name painted clearly on each:
But, since he omitted to mention the fact,
  They were all left behind on the beach.

The loss of his clothes hardly mattered, because
  He had seven coats on when he came,
With three pair of boots—but the worst of it was,
  He had wholly forgotten his name.

He would answer to "Hi!" or to any loud cry,
  Such as "Fry me!" or "Fritter my wig!"
To "What-you-may-call-um!" or "What-was-his-name!"
  But especially "Thing-um-a-jig!"

While, for those who preferred a more forcible word,
  He had different names from these:
His intimate friends called him "Candle-ends,"
  And his enemies "Toasted-cheese."

"His form is ungainly—his intellect small—"
  (So the Bellman would often remark)
"But his courage is perfect! And that, after all,
  Is the thing that one needs with a Snark."

He would joke with hyenas, returning their stare
  With an impudent wag of the head:
And he once went a walk, paw-in-paw, with a bear,
  "Just to keep up its spirits," he said.

He came as a Baker: but owned, when too late—
  And it drove the poor Bellman half-mad—
He could only bake Bride-cake—for which, I may state,
  No materials were to be had.

The last of the crew needs especial remark,
  Though he looked an incredible dunce:
He had just one idea—but, that one being "Snark,"
  The good Bellman engaged him at once.

He came as a Butcher: but gravely declared,
   When the ship had been sailing a week,
He could only kill Beavers. The Bellman looked scared,
   And was almost too frightened to speak:

But at length he explained, in a tremulous tone,
   There was only one Beaver on board;
And that was a tame one he had of his own,
   Whose death would be deeply deplored.

The Beaver, who happened to hear the remark,
   Protested, with tears in its eyes,
That not even the rapture of hunting the Snark
   Could atone for that dismal surprise!

It strongly advised that the Butcher should be
   Conveyed in a separate ship:
But the Bellman declared that would never agree
   With the plans he had made for the trip:

Navigation was always a difficult art,
   Though with only one ship and one bell:
And he feared he must really decline, for his part,
   Undertaking another as well.

The Beaver's best course was, no doubt, to procure
   A secondhand dagger-proof coat—
So the Baker advised it—and next, to insure
   Its life in some Office of note:

This the Banker suggested, and offered for hire
   (On moderate terms), or for sale,
Two excellent Policies, one Against Fire,
   And one Against Damage From Hail.

Yet still, ever after that sorrowful day,
   Whenever the Butcher was by,
The Beaver kept looking the opposite way,
   And appeared unaccountably shy.

FIT THE SECOND: THE BELLMAN'S SPEECH

The Bellman himself they all praised to the skies—
   Such a carriage, such ease and such grace!
Such solemnity, too! One could see he was wise,
   The moment one looked in his face!

He had bought a large map representing the sea,
   Without the least vestige of land:

And the crew were much pleased when they found it to be
    A map they could all understand.

"What's the good of Mercator's North Poles and Equators,
    Tropics, Zones, and Meridian Lines?"
So the Bellman would cry: and the crew would reply
    "They are merely conventional signs!

"Other maps are such shapes, with their islands and capes!
    But we've got our brave Captain to thank"
(So the crew would protest) "that he's bought *us* the best—
    A perfect and absolute blank!"

This was charming, no doubt: but they shortly found out
    That the Captain they trusted so well
Had only one notion for crossing the ocean,
    And that was to tingle his bell.

He was thoughtful and grave—but the orders he gave
    Were enough to bewilder a crew.
When he cried "Steer to starboard, but keep her head larboard!"
    What on earth was the helmsman to do?

Then the bowsprit got mixed with the rudder sometimes:
    A thing, as the Bellman remarked,
That frequently happens in tropical climes,
    When a vessel is, so to speak, "snarked."

But the principal failing occurred in the sailing,
    And the Bellman, perplexed and distressed,
Said he *had* hoped, at least, when the wind blew due East,
    That the ship would *not* travel due West!

But the danger was past—they had landed at last,
    With their boxes, portmanteaus, and bags:
Yet at first sight the crew were not pleased with the view,
    Which consisted of chasms and crags.

The Bellman perceived that their spirits were low,
    And repeated in musical tone
Some jokes he had kept for a season of woe—
    But the crew would do nothing but groan.

He served out some grog with a liberal hand,
    And bade them sit down on the beach:
And they could not but own that their Captain looked grand,
    As he stood and delivered his speech.

"Friends, Romans, and countrymen, lend me your ears!"
    (They were all of them fond of quotations:
So they drank to his health, and they gave him three cheers,
    While he served out additional rations).

"We have sailed many months, we have sailed many weeks,
    (Four weeks to the month you may mark),
But never as yet ('tis your Captain who speaks)
    Have we caught the least glimpse of a Snark!

"We have sailed many weeks, we have sailed many days,
    (Seven days to the week I allow),
But a Snark, on the which we might lovingly gaze,
    We have never beheld till now!

"Come, listen, my men, while I tell you again
    The five unmistakable marks
By which you may know, wheresoever you go,
    The warranted genuine Snarks.

"Let us take them in order. The first is the taste,
    Which is meager and hollow, but crisp:
Like a coat that is rather too tight in the waist,
    With a flavor of Will-o'-the-Wisp.

"Its habit of getting up late you'll agree
    That it carries too far, when I say
That it frequently breakfasts at five-o'clock tea,
    And dines on the following day.

"The third is its slowness in taking a jest.
    Should you happen to venture on one,
It will sigh like a thing that is deeply distressed:
    And it always looks grave at a pun.

"The fourth is its fondness for bathing-machines,
    Which it constantly carries about,
And believes that they add to the beauty of scenes—
    A sentiment open to doubt.

"The fifth is ambition. It next will be right
    To describe each particular batch:
Distinguishing those that have feathers, and bite,
    From those that have whiskers, and scratch.

"For, although common Snarks do no manner of harm,
    Yet I feel it my duty to say
Some are Boojums—" The Bellman broke off in alarm,
    For the Baker had fainted away.

FIT THE THIRD: THE BAKER'S TALE

They roused him with muffins—they roused him with ice—
  They roused him with mustard and cress—
They roused him with jam and judicious advice—
  They set him conundrums to guess.

When at length he sat up and was able to speak,
  His sad story he offered to tell;
And the Bellman cried "Silence! Not even a shriek!"
  And excitedly tingled his bell.

There was silence supreme! Not a shriek, not a scream,
  Scarcely even a howl or a groan,
As the man they called "Ho!" told his story of woe
  In an antediluvian tone.

"My father and mother were honest, though poor—"
  "Skip all that!" cried the Bellman in haste.
"If it once becomes dark, there's no chance of a Snark—
  We have hardly a minute to waste!"

"I skip forty years," said the Baker, in tears,
  "And proceed without further remark
To the day when you took me aboard of your ship
  To help you in hunting the Snark.

"A dear uncle of mine (after whom I was named)
  Remarked, when I bade him farewell—"
"Oh, skip your dear uncle!" the Bellman exclaimed,
  As he angrily tingled his bell.

"He remarked to me then," said that mildest of men,
  " 'If your Snark be a Snark, that is right:
Fetch it home by all means—you may serve it with greens,
  And it's handy for striking a light.

" 'You may seek it with thimbles—and seek it with care,
  You may hunt it with forks and hope;
You may threaten its life with a railway share;
  You may charm it with smiles and soap—' "

("That's exactly the method," the Bellman bold
  In a hasty parenthesis cried,
"That's exactly the way I have always been told
  That the capture of Snarks should be tried!")

" 'But oh, beamish nephew, beware of the day,
  If your Snark be a Boojum! For then

You will softly and suddenly vanish away,
   And never be met with again!'

"It is this, it is this that oppresses my soul,
   When I think of my uncle's last words:
And my heart is like nothing so much as a bowl
   Brimming over with quivering curds!

"It is this, it is this—" "We have had that before!"
   The Bellman indignantly said.
And the Baker replied "Let me say it once more.
   It is this, it is this that I dread!

"I engage with the Snark—every night after dark—
   In a dreamy delirious fight:
I serve it with greens in those shadowy scenes,
   And I use it for striking a light:

"But if ever I meet with a Boojum, that day,
   In a moment (of this I am sure),
I shall softly and suddenly vanish away—
   And the notion I cannot endure!"

FIT THE FOURTH: THE HUNTING

The Bellman looked uffish, and wrinkled his brow.
   "If only you'd spoken before!
It's excessively awkward to mention it now,
   With the Snark, so to speak, at the door!

"We should all of us grieve, as you well may believe,
   If you never were met with again—
But surely, my man, when the voyage began,
   You might have suggested it then?

"It's excessively awkward to mention it now—
   As I think I've already remarked."
And the man they called "Hi!" replied, with a sigh,
   "I informed you the day we embarked.

"You may charge me with murder—or want of sense—
   (We are all of us weak at times):
But the slightest approach to a false pretense
   Was never among my crimes!

"I said it in Hebrew—I said it in Dutch—
   I said it in German and Greek:
But I wholly forgot (and it vexes me much)
   That English is what you speak!"

" 'Tis a pitiful tale," said the Bellman, whose face
    Had grown longer at every word:
"But, now that you've stated the whole of your case,
    More debate would be simply absurd.

"The rest of my speech" (he exclaimed to his men)
    "You shall hear when I've leisure to speak it.
But the Snark is at hand, let me tell you again!
    'Tis your glorious duty to seek it!

"To seek it with thimbles, to seek it with care;
    To pursue it with forks and hope;
To threaten its life with a railway share;
    To charm it with smiles and soap!

"For the Snark's a peculiar creature, that won't
    Be caught in a commonplace way.
Do all that you know, and try all that you don't:
    Not a chance must be wasted today!

"For England expects—I forbear to proceed:
    'Tis a maxim tremendous, but trite:
And you'd best be unpacking the things that you need
    To rig yourself out for the fight."

Then the Banker endorsed a blank check (which he
        crossed),
    And changed his loose silver for notes.
The Baker with care combed his whiskers and hair.
    And shook the dust out of his coats.

The Boots and the Broker were sharpening a spade—
    Each working the grindstone in turn:
But the Beaver went on making lace, and displayed
    No interest in the concern:

Though the Barrister tried to appeal to its pride,
    And vainly proceeded to cite
A number of cases, in which making laces
    Had been proved an infringement of right.

The maker of Bonnets ferociously planned
    A novel arrangement of bows:
While the Billiard-marker with quivering hand
    Was chalking the tip of his nose.

But the Butcher turned nervous, and dressed himself fine,
    With yellow kid gloves and a ruff—

Said he felt it exactly like going to dine,
    Which the Bellman declared was all "stuff."

"Introduce me, now there's a good fellow," he said,
    "If we happen to meet it together!"
And the Bellman, sagaciously nodding his head,
    Said "That must depend on the weather."

The Beaver went simply galumphing about,
    At seeing the Butcher so shy:
And even the Baker, though stupid and stout,
    Made an effort to wink with one eye.

"Be a man!" cried the Bellman in wrath, as he heard
    The Butcher beginning to sob.
"Should we meet with the Jubjub, that desperate bird,
    We shall need all our strength for the job!"

FIT THE FIFTH: THE BEAVER'S LESSON

They sought it with thimbles, they sought it with care;
    They pursued it with forks and hope;
They threatened its life with a railway share;
    They charmed it with smiles and soap.

Then the Butcher contrived an ingenious plan
    For making a separate sally;
And had fixed on a spot unfrequented by man,
    A dismal and desolate valley.

But the very same plan to the Beaver occurred:
    It had chosen the very same place:
Yet neither betrayed, by a sign or a word,
    The disgust that appeared in his face.

Each thought he was thinking of nothing but "Snark"
    And the glorious work of the day;
And each tried to pretend that he did not remark
    That the other was going that way.

But the valley grew narrow and narrower still,
    And the evening got darker and colder,
Till (merely from nervousness, not from good will)
    They marched along shoulder to shoulder.

Then a scream, shrill and high, rent the shuddering sky,
    And they knew that some danger was near:
The Beaver turned pale to the tip of its tail,
    And even the Butcher felt queer.

He thought of his childhood, left far far behind—
   That blissful and innocent state—
The sound so exactly recalled to his mind
   A pencil that squeaks on a slate!

" 'Tis the voice of the Jubjub!" he suddenly cried.
   (This man, that they used to call "Dunce.")
"As the Bellman would tell you," he added with pride,
   "I have uttered that sentiment once.

" 'Tis the note of the Jubjub! Keep count, I entreat.
   You will find I have told it you twice.
'Tis the song of the Jubjub! The proof is complete.
   If only I've stated it thrice."

The Beaver had counted with scrupulous care,
   Attending to every word:
But it fairly lost heart, and outgrabe in despair,
   When the third repetition occurred.

It felt that, in spite of all possible pains,
   It had somehow contrived to lose count,
And the only thing now was to rack its poor brains
   By reckoning up the amount.

"Two added to one—if that could but be done,"
   It said, "with one's fingers and thumbs!"
Recollecting with tears how, in earlier years,
   It had been no pains with its sums.

"The thing can be done," said the Butcher, "I think
   The thing must be done, I am sure.
The thing shall be done! Bring me paper and ink,
   The best there is time to procure."

The Beaver brought paper, portfolio, pens,
   And ink in unfailing supplies:
While strange creepy creatures came out of their dens,
   And watched them with wondering eyes.

So engrossed was the Butcher, he heeded them not,
   As he wrote with a pen in each hand,
And explained all the while in a popular style
   Which the Beaver could well understand.

"Taking Three as the subject to reason about—
   A convenient number to state—

We add Seven, and Ten, and then multiply out
   By One Thousand diminished by Eight.

"The result we proceed to divide, as you see,
   By Nine Hundred and Ninety and Two:
Then subtract Seventeen, and the answer must be
   Exactly and perfectly true.

"The method employed I would gladly explain,
   While I have it so clear in my head,
If I had but the time and you had but the brain—
   But much yet remains to be said.

"In one moment I've seen what has hitherto been
   Enveloped in absolute mystery,
And without extra charge I will give you at large
   A Lesson in Natural History."

In his genial way he proceeded to say
   (Forgetting all laws of propriety,
And that giving instruction, without introduction,
   Would have caused quite a thrill in Society),

"As to temper the Jubjub's a desperate bird,
   Since it lives in perpetual passion:
Its taste in costume is entirely absurd—
   It is ages ahead of the fashion:

"But it knows any friend it has met once before:
   It never will look at a bribe:
And in charity meetings it stands at the door,
   And collects—though it does not subscribe.

"Its flavor when cooked is more exquisite far
   Than mutton, or oysters, or eggs:
(Some think it keeps best in an ivory jar,
   And some, in mahogany kegs:)

"You boil it in sawdust: you salt it in glue:
   You condense it with locusts and tape:
Still keeping one principal object in view—
   To preserve its symmetrical shape."

The Butcher would gladly have talked till next day,
   But he felt that the Lesson must end,
And he wept with delight in attempting to say
   He considered the Beaver his friend.

While the Beaver confessed, with affectionate looks
   More eloquent even than tears,
It had learned in ten minutes far more than all books
   Would have taught it in seventy years.

They returned hand-in-hand, and the Bellman, unmanned
   (For a moment) with noble emotion,
Said "This amply repays all the wearisome days
   We have spent on the billowy ocean!"

Such friends, as the Beaver and Butcher became,
   Have seldom if ever been known;
In winter or summer, 'twas always the same—
   You could never meet either alone.

And when quarrels arose—as one frequently finds
   Quarrels will, spite of every endeavor—
The song of the Jubjub recurred to their minds,
   And cemented their friendship for ever!

FIT THE SIXTH: THE BARRISTER'S DREAM

They sought it with thimbles, they sought it with care;
   They pursued it with forks and hope;
They threatened its life with a railway share;
   They charmed it with smiles and soap.

But the Barrister, weary of proving in vain
   That the Beaver's lace-making was wrong,
Fell asleep, and in dreams saw the creature quite plain
   That his fancy had dwelt on so long.

He dreamed that he stood in a shadowy Court,
   Where the Snark, with a glass in its eye,
Dressed in gown, bands, and wig, was defending a pig
   On the charge of deserting its sty.

The Witnesses proved, without error or flaw,
   That the sty was deserted when found:
And the Judge kept explaining the state of the law
   In a soft undercurrent of sound.

The indictment had never been clearly expressed,
   And it seemed that the Snark had begun,
And had spoken three hours, before any one guessed
   What the pig was supposed to have done.

The Jury had each formed a different view
   (Long before the indictment was read),

And they all spoke at once, so that none of them knew
  One word that the others had said.

"You must know—" said the Judge: but the Snark exclaimed
    "Fudge!
  That statute is obsolete quite!
Let me tell you, my friends, the whole question depends
  On an ancient manorial right.

"In the matter of Treason the pig would appear
  To have aided, but scarcely abetted:
While the charge of Insolvency fails, it is clear,
  If you grant the plea 'never indebted.'

"The fact of Desertion I will not dispute:
  But its guilt, as I trust, is removed
(So far as relates to the costs of this suit)
  By the Alibi which has been proved.

"My poor client's fate now depends on your votes."
  Here the speaker sat down in his place,
And directed the Judge to refer to his notes
  And briefly to sum up the case.

But the Judge said he never had summed up before;
  So the Snark undertook it instead,
And summed it so well that it came to far more
  Than the Witnesses ever had said!

When the verdict was called for, the Jury declined,
  As the word was so puzzling to spell;
But they ventured to hope that the Snark wouldn't mind
  Undertaking that duty as well.

So the Snark found the verdict, although, as it owned,
  It was spent with the toils of the day:
When it said the word "GUILTY!" the Jury all groaned,
  And some of them fainted away.

Then the Snark pronounced sentence, the Judge being quite
  Too nervous to utter a word:
When it rose to its feet, there was silence like night,
  And the fall of a pin might be heard.

"Transportation for life" was the sentence it gave,
  "And *then* to be fined forty pound."

The Jury all cheered, though the Judge said he feared
    That the phrase was not legally sound.

But their wild exultation was suddenly checked
    When the jailer informed them, with tears,
Such a sentence would have not the slightest effect,
    As the pig had been dead for some years.

The Judge left the Court, looking deeply disgusted:
    But the Snark, though a little aghast,
As the lawyer to whom the defense was intrusted,
    Went bellowing on to the last.

Thus the Barrister dreamed, while the bellowing seemed
    To grow every moment more clear:
Till he woke to the knell of a furious bell,
    Which the Bellman rang close to his ear.

FIT THE SEVENTH: THE BANKER'S FATE

They sought it with thimbles, they sought it with care;
    They pursued it with forks and hope;
They threatened its life with a railway share;
    They charmed it with smiles and soap.

And the Banker, inspired with a courage so new
    It was matter for general remark,
Rushed madly ahead and was lost to their view
    In his zeal to discover the Snark.

But while he was seeking with thimbles and care,
    A Bandersnatch swiftly drew nigh
And grabbed at the Banker, who shrieked in despair,
    For he knew it was useless to fly.

He offered large discount—he offered a check
    (Drawn "to bearer") for seven-pounds-ten:
But the Bandersnatch merely extended its neck
    And grabbed at the Banker again.

Without rest or pause—while those frumious jaws
    Went savagely snapping around—
He skipped and he hopped, and he floundered and flopped,
    Till fainting he fell to the ground.

The Bandersnatch fled as the others appeared
    Led on by that fear-stricken yell:

And the Bellman remarked "It is just as I feared!"
  And solemnly tolled on his bell.

He was black in the face, and they scarcely could trace
  The least likeness to what he had been:
While so great was his fright that his waistcoat turned
      white—
  A wonderful thing to be seen!

To the horror of all who were present that day,
  He uprose in full evening dress,
And with senseless grimaces endeavored to say
  What his tongue could no longer express.

Down he sank in a chair—ran his hands through his hair—
  And chanted in mimsiest tones
Words whose utter inanity proved his insanity,
  While he rattled a couple of bones.

"Leave him here to his fate—it is getting so late!"
  The Bellman exclaimed in a fright.
"We have lost half the day. And further delay,
  And we sha'n't catch a Snark before night!"

FIT THE EIGHTH: THE VANISHING

They sought it with thimbles, they sought it with care;
  They pursued it with forks and hope;
They threatened its life with a railway share;
  They charmed it with smiles and soap.

They shuddered to think that the chase might fail,
  And the Beaver, excited at last,
Went bounding along on the tip of his tail,
  For the daylight was nearly past.

"There is Thingumbob shouting!" the Bellman said.
  "He is shouting like mad, only hark!
He is waving his hands, he is wagging his head,
  He has certainly found a Snark!"

They gazed in delight, while the Butcher exclaimed
  "He was always a desperate wag!"
They beheld him—their Baker—their hero unnamed—
  On the top of a neighboring crag,

Erect and sublime, for one moment of time,
  In the next, that wild figure they saw

(As if stung by a spasm) plunge into a chasm,
   While they waited and listened in awe.

"It's a Snark!" was the sound that first came to their ears,
   And seemed almost too good to be true.
Then followed a torrent of laughter and cheers:
   Then the ominous words "It's a Boo—"

Then, silence. Some fancied they heard in the air
   A weary and wandering sigh
That sounded like "— jum!" but the others declare
   It was only a breeze that went by.

They hunted till darkness came on, but they found
   Not a button, or feather, or mark,
By which they could tell that they stood on the ground
   Where the Baker had met with the Snark.

In the midst of the word he was trying to say,
   In the midst of his laughter and glee,
He had softly and suddenly vanished away—
   For the Snark *was* a Boojum, you see.

Lewis Carroll

Odd but True

Oh that my Lungs could bleat like butter'd Peas;
But bleating of my lungs hath Caught the itch,
And are as mangy as the Irish seas
That doth engender windmills on a Bitch.

I grant that Rainbows being lull'd asleep,
Snort like a woodknife in a Lady's eyes;
Which makes her grieve to see a pudding creep,
For Creeping puddings only please the wise.

Not that a hard row'd herring should presume
To swing a tyth pig in a Catskin purse;
For fear the hailstones which did fall at Rome,
By lessening of the fault should make it worse.

For 't is most certain Winter woolsacks grow
From geese to swans if men could keep them so,
Till that the sheep shorn Planets gave the hint
To pickle pancakes in Geneva print.

Some men there were that did suppose the sky
Was made of Carbonado'd Antidotes;
But my opinion is, a Whale's left eye,
Need not be coined all King *Harry* groates.

The reason's plain, for Charon's Western barge
Running a tilt at the subjunctive mood,
Beckoned to Bednal Green, and gave him charge
To fasten padlocks with Antarctic food.

The end will be the Mill ponds must be laded,
To fish for white pots in a Country dance;
So they that suffered wrong and were upbraided
Shall be made friends in a left-handed Trance.

Anonymous

My Dream

I dreamed a dream next Tuesday week,
  Beneath the apple trees;
I thought my eyes were big pork pies,
  And my nose was Stilton cheese.
The clock struck twenty minutes to six,
  When a frog sat on my knee;
I asked him to lend me eighteenpence,
  But he borrowed a shilling of me.

Anonymous

The Sorrows of Werther

Werther had a love for Charlotte
  Such as words could never utter;
Would you know how first he met her?
  She was cutting bread and butter.

Charlotte was a married lady,
  And a moral man was Werther,
And for all the wealth of Indies,
  Would do nothing for to hurt her.

So he sigh'd and pined and ogled,
  And his passion boil'd and bubbled,
Till he blew his silly brains out,
  And no more was by it troubled.

Charlotte, having seen his body
  Borne before her on a shutter,
Like a well-conducted person,
  Went on cutting bread and butter.

W. M. Thackeray

The Society upon the Stanislaus

I reside at Table Mountain, and my name is Truthful James;
I am not up to small deceit, or any sinful games;
And I'll tell in simple language what I know about the row
That broke up our Society upon the Stanislow.

But first I would remark, that it is not a proper plan
For any scientific gent to whale his fellow-man,
And, if a member don't agree with his peculiar whim,
To lay for that same member for to "put a head" on him.

Now nothing could be finer or more beautiful to see
Than the first six months' proceedings of that same Society,

Till Brown of Calaveras brought a lot of fossil bones
That he found within a tunnel near the tenement of Jones.

Then Brown he read a paper, and he reconstructed there,
From those same bones, an animal that was extremely rare;
And Jones then asked the Chair for a suspension of the rules,
Till he could prove that those same bones was one of his lost
    mules.

Then Brown he smiled a bitter smile, and said he was at fault,
It seemed he had been trespassing on Jones's family vault;
He was a most sarcastic man, this quiet Mr. Brown,
And on several occasions he had cleaned out the town.

Now I hold it is not decent for a scientific gent
To say another is an ass—at least, to all intent;
Nor should the individual who happens to be meant
Reply by heaving rocks at him to any great extent.

Then Abner Dean of Angel's raised a point of order, when
A chunk of old red sandstone took him in the abdomen,
And he smiled a kind of sickly smile, and curled up on the floor,
And the subsequent proceedings interested him no more.

For, in less time than I write it, every member did engage
In a warfare with the remnants of a palaeozoic age;
And the way they heaved those fossils in their anger was a sin,
Till the skull of an old mammoth caved the head of Thomp-
    son in.

And this is all I have to say of these improper games,
For I live at Table Mountain, and my name is Truthful James;
And I've told in simple language what I know about the row
That broke up our Society upon the Stanislow.

                                        Bret Harte

A Voice Speaks from the Well

Fair maiden, white and red,
Comb me smooth, and stroke my head;
And thou shalt have some cockle bread.
Gently dip, but not too deep,
For fear thou make the golden beard to weep.
Fair maid, white and red,
Comb me smooth, and stroke my head;
And every hair a sheave shall be,
And every sheave a golden tree.

George Peele

Tom o' Bedlam

From the hag and hungry goblin
That into rags would rend ye
And the spirit that stan' by the naked man
In the Book of Moons defend ye!
That of your five sound senses
You never be forsaken
Nor travel from yourselves with Tom
Abroad to beg your bacon.

Chorus: Nor never sing "Any food, any feeding,
          Money, drink or clothing":
          Come dame or maid, be not afraid,
          Poor Tom will injure nothing.

Of thirty bare years have I
Twice twenty been enragéd
And of forty bin three times fifteen
In durance soundly cagéd
In the lordly lofts of Bedlam
On stubble soft and dainty,
Brave bracelets strong, sweet whips ding dong,
With wholesome hunger plenty.

With a thought I took for Maudlin
And a cruse of cockle pottage
With a thing thus—tall, (sky bless you all),
I fell into this dotage.
I slept not since the conquest,
Till then I never wakéd
Till the roguish boy of love where I lay
Me found and stripped me naked.

When short I have shorn my sowce face
And swigged my hornéd barrel
In an oaken inn do I pawn my skin
As a suit of gilt apparel.
The moon's my constant mistress
And the lonely owl my marrow
The flaming drake and the night-crow make
Me music to my sorrow.

The palsy plague these pounces,
When I prig your pigs or pullen,
Your culvers take, or mateless make
Your chanticlere, and sullen.
When I want provant with Humfrey
I sup, and when benighted
To repose in Paul's with waking souls
I never am affrighted.

I know more than Apollo,
For oft when he lies sleeping
I behold the stars at mortal wars
And the wounded welkin weeping;
The moon embrace her shepherd
And the queen of love her warrior,
While the first doth horn the star of the morn
And the next the heavenly Farrier.

The Gipsy Snap and Tedro
Are none of Tom's comrados.
The punk I scorn and the cutpurse sworn
And the roaring-boys bravadoes.
The sober, white, and gentle,
Me trace, or touch, and spare not;
But those that cross Tom's Rhinoceros
Do what the panther dare not.

With an host of furious fancies
Whereof I am commander
With a burning spear, and a horse of air,
To the wilderness I wander.
By a knight of ghosts and shadows
I summoned am to tourney
Ten leagues beyond the wide world's end.
Me thinks it is no journey.

Anonymous

Tom of Bedlam

From the top of high Caucasus,
        To Pauls-wharf near the Tower,
                In no great haste
                I easily past
        In less than half an hour.
The gates of old Bizantium,
        I took upon my shoulders,
                And them I bore
                Twelve leagues and more
        In spight of Turks and soldiers.

Chorus: Sigh, sing and sob, sing, sigh and be merry,
        Sighing, singing and sobbing,
                Thus naked Tom
                Alway doth run,
        And fears no cold nor robbing.

From monsieur Tillies army
        I took two hundred bannors,
                And brought them all
                To "Leaden"-hall,
        In sight of all the tannors.
I passed Parnassus-ferry.
        By the hill call'd "Aganippé,"
                From thence, on foot,
                Without shoe or boot,
        I past to the Isle of "Shippey."

O'er the Pirènean valley
        'Twixt Europe and Saint-Giles
                I walkt one night
                By sun-shine light,
        Which fifteen thousand miles is:
I landed at White-chappel,
        Near to Saint-Edmonds-berry
                From thence I stept,
                While Charon slept,
        And stole away his ferry.

One Summers day at Shrove-tide,
        I met old January,
                Being malecontent
                With him I went
        To weep o'er old Canary,
The man i' th' moon, at Pancrass
        Doth yield us excellent claret,

Having steel'd my nose,
I sung, *Old Rose;*
Tush! greatness cannot carry't.

I met the Turkish sulton
At Dover, near Saint-Georges,
His train and him
Did to Callis swim
Without ships, boats or barges.
I taught the King of Egypt
A trick to save his cattle;
I'le plough with dogs
And harrow with hogs;
You'd think it I do prattle.

In boat I went on dry land,
From Carthage to Saint-Albons
I sail'd to Spain
And back again.
In a vessel made of whalebones.
I met Diana hunting,
With all her nymphs attending
In Turnball-street
With voices sweet,
That honest place commending.

Diogenes, the belman,
Walkt with his lanthorn duely,
I'th'term among
The lawyers throng,
To find one that "spoke" truly.
The Sun and Moon eclipsed
I, very friendly, parted,
And made the Sun
Away to run,
For fear he should be carted.

Long time have I been studying,
My brains with fancies tearing
How I might get
Old Pauls a hat,
And cross-cloth for old Charing.
Thus to give men and women
In cloaths full satisfaction,
These fruitless toyes,
"Rob" me of joyes,
And "keep" my brains in action.

Anonymous, 1660

Mad Maudlin to Find Out Tom of Bedlam

To find out Tom of Bedlam ten thousand years I'll travel,
Mad Maudlin goes with dirty toes to save her shoes from
    gravel.

Chorus: Yet will I sing Bonny Boys, bonny mad boys, Bedlam
            Boys are bonny;
            They still go bare and live by the air, and want no
            drink nor money.

I now repent that ever poor Tom was so disdain'd,
My wits are lost since him I crost, which makes me go thus
    chain'd:

My staff hath murder'd gyants, my bag a long knife carries,
To cut mince pyes from children's thighs, with which I feast
    the faries:

My horn is made of thunder, I stole it out of heav'n,
The rainbow there is this I wear, for which I thence was driven:

I went to Pluto's kitchin, to beg some food one morning,
And there I got souls piping hot, with which the spits were
    turning:

Then took I up a cauldron where boiled ten thousand harlots,
'Twas full of flame, yet I drank the same to the health of all
    such varlets:

A spirit as hot as lightning, did in that journey guide me,
The sun did shake, and the pale moon quake, as soon as e'er
    they spi'd me:

And now that I have gotten a lease, than Dooms-day longer,
To live on earth with some in mirth, ten whales shall feed my
    hunger:

No gipsie, slut or doxy, shall win my mad Tom from me,
We'll weep all night, and with the stars fight, the fray will well
    become me:

And when that I have beaten the man i' th' moon to powder,
His dog I'll take, and him I'll make as could no Daemon
    louder:

A health to Tom of Bedlam, go fill the sea in barrels,
I'll drink it all, well brew'd with gall, and maudlin drunk, I'll
    quarrel.

From Thomas d'Urfey's "Pills to Purge Melancholy," 1719

The Owl and the Pussy-cat

The Owl and the Pussy-cat went to sea
   In a beautiful pea-green boat:
They took some honey, and plenty of money
   Wrapped up in a five-pound note.
The Owl looked up to the stars above,
   And sang to a small guitar,
"O lovely Pussy, O Pussy, my love,
   What a beautiful Pussy you are,
       You are,
       You are!
   What a beautiful Pussy you are!"

Pussy said to the Owl, "You elegant fowl,
   How charmingly sweet you sing!
Oh! let us be married; too long we have tarried:
   But what shall we do for a ring?"
They sailed away, for a year and a day,
   To the land where the bong-tree grows;
And there in a wood a Piggy-wig stood,
   With a ring at the end of his nose,
       His nose,
       His nose,
   With a ring at the end of his nose.

"Dear Pig, are you willing to sell for one shilling
   Your ring?" Said the Piggy, "I will."
So they took it away, and were married next day
   By the turkey who lives on the hill.
They dined on mince and slices of quince,
   Which they ate with a runcible spoon;
And hand in hand, on the edge of the sand,
   They danced by the light of the moon,
       The moon,
       The moon,
   They danced by the light of the moon.

Edward Lear

Three Jovial Welshmen

There were three jovial
    Welshmen,
As I have heard men say,
And they would go a-hunting
Upon St. David's Day.

All the day they hunted
And nothing could they find,
But a ship a-sailing,
A-sailing with the wind.

One said it was a ship,
The other he said, Nay;
The third said it was a house,
With the chimney blown
    away.

And all the night they hunted
And nothing could they find,
But the moon a-gliding,
A-gliding with the wind.

One said it was the moon,
The other he said, Nay;
The third said it was a cheese
And half of it cut away.

And all the day they hunted
And nothing could they find,
But a hedgehog in a bramble
    bush

And that they left behind.

The first said it was a hedge-
    hog
The second he said, Nay;
The third said it was a pin-
    cushion
And the pins stuck in wrong
    way.

And all the night they hunted
And nothing could they find,
But a hare in a turnip field,
And that they left behind.

The first said it was a hare,
The second he said, Nay;
The third said it was a calf,
And the cow had run away.

And all the day they hunted
And nothing could they find,
But an owl in a holly tree,
And that they left behind.

One said it was an owl,
The other he said, Nay;
The third said 'twas an old
    man
And his beard growing gray.

Anonymous

The Lemmings: *A Philosophical Poem*

Let readers say (description or abuse),
"Pure were his morals, though his verse was loose."
The technical end I blame on Robert Frost,
On Butler, Skelton, and others whose names I've lost,
And, though this debt isn't very hard to find,
I blame it on W. H. Auden—he won't mind—
On Catullus, and Robert Bridges, I am afraid,

And really a host of others whose names I've mislaid:
For just as a Cavalier lyric shows good breeding
A reflective poem must demonstrate wide reading.
In such verse, too, a poet is at a loss if he
Doesn't remind the reader he knows philosophy.
Provided only they see that this poem is deep,
I don't care how many people it puts to sleep.
The special subject is lemmings, the pity of lemmings.
(Whenever I use that word I shall skip the rhyme,
And I think I'll have to use it time after time.)
If I knew what a lemming was, it would help a lot,
For I certainly can't list all things which it is NOT.
But sympathy shall make up for lack of science,
And ignorance be replaced by self-reliance.
After all, this is less like a monograph than a chat:
It is only a poem—philosophical, at that.
It will not be so long as Lucretius' *De Rerum Natura*,
And barely as long as Juvenal's smallest *satura*.
Though briefness seem unphilosophical to some,
I think that's the way philosophy ought to come.
I shall view the result with something akin to pride
If I make you *feel* the lemmings from the inside.

This is the end of the proem
And the beginning of the poem.

At a sharp, mysterious call, as though in a dream,
The lemmings move, and down to the ocean they stream.
From the Urals, and the Carpathians, and the plains
Of Prussia, or Lapland, on they come in trains.
Or secretly, through the silent forests, the hordes
Rush to the sea in the tallest of Norway's fjords.
For them, the whole world beckons and is on fire,
So add what geographical names you desire:
To say the Ganges, Peru, the Cape of Good Hope,
Though it blur our accuracy, increases our scope.
And here I shall use T. S. Eliot's famed device
Of allusion to gain intensity—it's nice!
Read over Browning's *Piper of Hamelin*, please,
Read it slowly, with care, and at your ease,
And wherever he talks about either rats or mice
Just substitute lemmings. Isn't *that* a device?
You will then have sizes and colors of all sorts
And grotesque detail that fascinates as it distorts,
And all of the lemmings streaming in grave glee—
Not after the Piper, mind, but toward the sea.

We've now saved a hundred lines by referring to Browning
And have got to the crucial part where the lemmings start
  drowning.
Each one making his certain and positive lunge,
Into the black and freezing waters they plunge.
And from their noses, the ripples in endless V's
Complicate webs and woofs on the flux of the seas.
Like flocks of starlings, or minnows in lucent shoals,
Infinite atoms move towards communal goals.
The northern night is above, and the water beneath,
(How far off now is the nest on the rock-strewn heath!)
And all are swimming together in regular tread
As the strokes of their feet keep pulsing their noses ahead.
Beyond, and straight, and sure, and together they swim.
Where they are when the sun looks over the ocean's rim
Nobody knows. I would like to say, if I dare,
That the point of this poem is: *Nobody ought to care.*
So far I could have prettied this up a lot
If this had been a descriptive poem. It's not.
Or I might have given you facts that were terrific,
Provided my aim were solely scientific.
As it is, unless I hear some better suggestions,
We will open this poem to philosophical questions.

But one thing first: I admit I admire the lemmings.
Together plunging far out to sea by night—
How express and admirable! how lemming! how right!
That one act only I know in the lemmings' history;
And although its end may always remain a mystery,
The lemmings fill me with gratitude and cheer
For acting one act that is so sure and clear.
There must be a thousand species of rodents and stoats,
Fieldmice, moles, muskrats, hedgehogs, mink, dwarf goats,
That live the humdrum life of the seasons through:
Gray dawns, gray fear, gray sleep, and little to do.
Even Noah forgot them, above or under the ground.
But we remember the lemmings, because they drowned.
A species famous abroad for a single act
Wins glory that less energetic fauna have lacked.
How various beasts are bigger, stronger, older,
More popular, quicker on trigger, longer, bolder;
But in praise of the lemmings, by all beasts this is allowed:
No other landlubbers swim out to sea in a crowd.
Here let us cease this unreasoning panegyric
And back to our deep and philosophical lyric.
If the lemmings unite to swim out to sea and die,

The inevitable and perplexing question is *Why?*
We might as well face it squarely and on the spot
Without a flippant or cynical asking *Why not?*
(a) Perhaps the lemming race is by nature joyous
And cannot conceive of the ocean flood as noyous.
(b) Their cosmic outlook, perhaps, is far from wide
So that they know of waves, but ignore the tide,
And do not believe that it's leagues from this side to that side.
(c) Some people think that the race as a whole is feckless
And kills itself off for the pleasure of being reckless.
(d) Still more maintain that the lemming brain is blighted;
(e) While some physiologists hold that the creature's near-
  sighted.
(f) Surroundings and habit, say others, have made them fools:
The lemmings come from countries of lakes and of pools;
They cannot adapt to new places, they are so fond,
And jump in the ocean as if it could be but a pond.
(g) One theory runs that deep in the past of the race
On Atlantis the lemmings were happy all over the place,
And, when that continent sank at some black touch of magic,
The end of the lemmings was comprehensively tragic.
Ancestral mourning now leads them shorewards to weep
And they find the golden age thousand fathoms deep.
This theory, though, I shan't even bother to mention,
For it bears in itself the marks of a febrile invention.
And blaming one's gloom on the dead—on a lot of dead, too—
Is one of the things that a gentleman doesn't do.
(h) A further hypothesis leads to many confusions
Because it supposes the lemmings are conscious Malthusians,
And if these wee beasts have practiced his laws for so long
Then Malthus and countless lemmings can't be wrong.
It holds that lemmings, viewed in their breeding habits,
Are as sanguine, redundant, prolific, and careless as rabbits,
And knowing that population outstrips supply,
A certain proportion resolves, quite wisely, to die.
This sort of thing should appeal to G. B. Shaw:
Good sense, you see, no fuss, and community law.
The unemployed, unwanted, unloved, and unwed,
Swim out to ocean, and never a tear is shed;
Or if a tear falls, it mixes quick with the brine
And loses all personal sense of yours and mine.
The Greek youth shipped for the Minotaur's delectation
Is a more romantic means of saving a nation;
But I much prefer this classical lemming way
(As Vigny might put it) of "Nages, et meurs sans parler."
It avoids the melodramatically pathetic

And isn't, like Jude the Obscure's hanged children, frenetic;
Yet Hardy's words fit, for the lemmings, as well as any,
And perhaps the last thought of each lemming is "WE WAS
  TOO MANY."

All of these explanations that don't explain
You may, with my kindest permission, throw down the drain.
They cannot illumine, or mar, in the least degree
The simple fact of the lemmings and the sea.
I sometimes think we'd be further out of the wood
If we didn't believe our brains were so frightfully good.
The last infirmity of the noble mind
Is its faith that the noble mind leaves all else behind.
To believe anything which is not the product of reason
Is, to the human race in its latest development, treason.
And thanks to the Russells, the Huxleys, the Deweys and
  Shaws,
We'll all soon be rescued from Superstition's jaws.
Those ultimate secrets of mystery or of sorrow
That we don't grasp today, will be clear as crystal tomorrow.
The fear and the ecstasies that our grandfathers share
Come from another world that isn't there.
Let us endure, our new wise men say, for a season,
For all will be clarified soon in the light of pure reason.

But the lemmings' acts may be past reach of our brain,
Perhaps we had better accept what we can't explain.
Instincts within us are fixed so central and certain
That our tampering minds cannot pull aside the curtain.
And still, though we prove that it should or it shouldn't be,
The lemmings continue their progress out to sea.
I know this amounts almost to accepting God
And know also today such belief is most certainly odd.
Yet I would prefer, when we look at human behavior,
If we must be saved, to have God—not man—for a savior.
Give us a bit less pride and a little more trust:
We but guess we are terribly clever; we know we are dust.
Grace is a ware which should be on the front of our shelves,
And we have most grace when we don't try to make it our-
  selves.
After all, reflective verse shouldn't give the answers.
It should merely set the questions moving like dancers,
And should leave us, where we began, with the excellent notion
Of the lemmings moving in unison toward the ocean.

                                        Donald A. Stauffer

PART TEN

Animal Fair

Animals

I think I could turn and live with animals, they are so placid
    and self-contained;
I stand and look at them long and long,
They do not sweat and whine about their condition;
They do not lie awake in the dark and weep for their sins;
They do not make me sick discussing their duty to God;
Not one is dissatisfied—not one is demented with the mania of
    owning things;
Not one kneels to another, nor to his kind that lived thousands
    of years ago;
Not one is respectable or industrious over the whole earth.

Walt Whitman

The Answers

"When did the world begin and how?"
    I asked a lamb, a goat, a cow:

"What's it all about and why?"
    I asked a hog as he went by:

288

"Where will the whole thing end and when?"
I asked a duck, a goose, a hen:

And I copied all the answers too,
A quack, a honk, an oink, a moo.

Robert Clairmont

Advices from Rexroth's Bestiary

I: KANGAROO

As you know, the kangaroo
Has a pocket, but *all* she
Puts in it is her baby.
Never keep a purse if *all*
You can find to put in it
Is additional expense.
(The reception of these words
Will also serve to warn you:
Never make fun of babies!)

II: RACOON

The racoon wears a black mask,
And he washes everything
Before he eats it. If you
Give him a cube of sugar,
He'll wash it away and weep.
Some of life's sweetest pleasures
Can be enjoyed only if
You don't mind a little dirt.
Here a false face won't help you.

III: TROUT

The trout is taken when he
Bites an artificial fly.
Confronted with fraud, keep your
Mouth shut and don't volunteer.

IV: WOLF

Never believe all you hear.
Wolves are not as bad as lambs.
I've been a wolf all my life,
And have two lovely daughters
To show for it, while I could
Tell you sickening tales of
Lambs who got their just desserts.

Kenneth Rexroth

The Auld Seceder Cat

There was a Presbyterian cat
Went forth to catch her prey;
She brought a mouse intill the house,
Upon the Sabbath day.
The minister, offended
With such an act profane,
Laid down his book, the cat he took,
And bound her with a chain.

Thou vile malicious creature,
Thou murderer, said he,
Oh do you think to bring to Hell
My holy wife and me?
But be thou well assured,
That blood for blood shall pay,
For taking of the mouse's life
Upon the Sabbath day.

Then he took doun his Bible,
And fervently he prayed,
That the great sin the cat had done
Might not on him be laid.
Then forth to exe-cu-ti-on,
Poor Baudrons she was drawn,
And on a tree they hanged her hie,
And then they sung a psalm.

Anonymous

The Sloth

In moving-slow he has no Peer.
You ask him something in his ear;
He thinks about it for a Year;

And then, before he says a Word
There, upside down (unlike a Bird)
He will assume that you have Heard—

A most Ex-as-per-at-ing Lug.
But should you call his manner Smug,
He'll sigh and give his Branch a Hug;

Then off again to Sleep he goes,
Still swaying gently by his Toes,
And you just know he knows he knows.

Theodore Roethke

The Flea

Mark but this flea, and mark in this,
How little that which thou deny'st me is;
It sucked me first, and now sucks thee,
And in this flea our two bloods mingled be;
Thou know'st that this cannot be said
A sin, nor shame, nor loss of maidenhead;
 Yet this enjoys before it woo,
 And pampered swells with one blood made of two,
 And this, alas, is more than we would do.

Oh stay, three lives in one flea spare,
Where we almost, yea, more than married are.
This flea is you and I, and this
Our marriage bed, and marriage temple is;
Though parents grudge, and you, we're met,
And cloistered in these living walls of jet.
 Though use make you apt to kill me,
 Let not to that, self-murder added be,
 And sacrilege, three sins in killing three.

Cruel and sudden, hast thou since
Purpled thy nail in blood of innocence?
Wherein could this flea guilty be,
Except in that drop which it sucked from thee?
Yet thou triumph'st and say'st that thou
Find'st not thyself, nor me the weaker now;
 'Tis true, then learn how false fears be:
 Just so much honor, when thou yield'st to me,
 Will waste, as this flea's death took life from thee.

John Donne

To a Louse, on Seeing One on a Lady's Bonnet at Church

Ha! whare ye gaun, ye crowlan ferlie!
Your impudence protects you sairly:
I canna say but ye strunt rarely,
 Owre gawze and lace;
Tho' faith, I fear ye dine but sparely,
 On sic a place.

Ye ugly, creepan, blastet wonner,
Detested, shunn'd, by saunt an' sinner,
How daur ye set your fit upon her,
 Sae fine a Lady!
Gae somewhere else and seek your dinner,
 On some poor body.

Swith, in some beggar's haffet squattle;
There ye may creep, and sprawl, and sprattle,
Wi' ither kindred, jumping cattle,
        In shoals and nations;
Whare horn nor bane ne'er daur unsettle
        Your thick plantations.

Now haud you there, ye're out o' sight,
Below the fatt'rels, snug and tight,
Na faith ye yet, ye'll no be right,
        Till ye've got on it,
The vera tapmost, towrin height
        O' Miss's bonnet.

My sooth! right bauld ye set your nose out,
As plump an' gray as onie grozet:
O for some rank, mercurial rozet,
        Or fell, red smeddum,
I'd gie you sic a hearty dose o't,
        Wad dress your droddum!

I wad na been surpriz'd to spy
You on an auld wife's flainen toy;
Or aiblins some bit duddie boy,
        On's wylecoat;
But Miss's fine Lunardi, fye!
        How daur ye do't?

O Jenny dinna toss your head,
An' set your beauties a' abread!
Ye little ken what cursed speed
        The beastie's makin!
Thae winks and finger-ends, I dread,
        Are notice takin!

O wad some Pow'r the giftie gie us
To see oursels as ithers see us!
It wad frae monie a blunder free us
        An' foolish notion:
What airs in dress an' gait wad lea'e us,
        And ev'n Devotion!

                                    Robert Burns

Drodum: breech	Flainen: flannel	Rozet: rosin
Fatt'rels: folderols	Grozet: gooseberry	Smeddum: powder
Ferlie: wonder	Haffet: temple	Toy: old-fashioned
		headdress

I Wish I Were

I wish I were a
Elephantiaphus
And could pick off the coconuts with my nose.
But, oh! I am not,
(Alas! I cannot be)
An Elephanti—
Elephantiaphus.
But I'm a cockroach
And I'm a water-bug,
I can crawl around and hide behind the sink.

I wish I were a
Rhinoscerèeacus
And could wear an ivory toothpick in my nose.
But, oh! I am not,
(Alas! I cannot be)
A Rhinoscōri—
Rhinoscerèeacus—
But I'm a beetle
And I'm a pumpkin-bug,
I can buzz and bang my head against the wall.

I wish I were a
Hippopōpotamus
And could swim the Tigris and the broad Gangès.
But, oh! I am not,
(Alas! I cannot be)
A hippopōpo—
Hippopōpotamus—
But I'm a grasshopper
And I'm a katydid,
I can play the fiddle with my left hind-leg.

I wish I were a
Levileviathan
And had seven hundred knuckles in my spine.
But, oh! I am not,
(Alas! I cannot be)
A Levi-ikey—
A Levi-ikey-mo.
But I'm a firefly
And I'm a lightning-bug,
I can light cheroots and gaspers with my tail.

Anonymous

The Ram

As I was going to Derby,
    Upon a market day,
I met the finest ram, sir,
    That ever was fed on hay.

This ram was fat behind, sir,
    This ram was fat before,
This ram was ten yards high, sir,
    Indeed he was no more.

The wool upon his back, sir,
    Reached up unto the sky,
The eagles built their nests there,
    For I heard the young ones cry.

The space between the horns, sir,
    Was as far as man could reach,
And there they built a pulpit,
    But no one in it preached.

This ram had four legs to walk upon,
    This ram had four legs to stand,
And every leg he had, sir,
    Stood on an acre of land.

Now the man that fed the ram, sir,
    He fed him twice a day,
And each time that he fed him, sir,
    He ate a rick of hay.

The man that killed this ram, sir,
    Was up to his knees in blood,
And the boy that held the pail, sir,
    Was carried away in the flood.

Indeed, sir, it's the truth, sir,
    For I never was taught to lie,
And if you go to Derby, sir,
    You may eat a bit of the pie.

Anonymous

The Death and Burial of Cock Robbin

Here lies Cock Robbin dead
  and cold:
His end this book will soon
  unfold.

"Who did kill Cock Robbin?"
"I" said the sparrow, "with
  my bow and arrow,
I did kill Cock Robbin."

"Who did see him die?"
"I" said the fly, "with my
  little eye,
And I did see him die."

"And who catch'd his blood?"
"I" said the fish, "with my
  little dish,
And I catch'd his blood."

"And who did make his
  shroud?"
"I" said the beetle, "with my
  little needle,
And I did make his shroud."

"Who'll dig his grave?"
"I" said the owl,
"With my spade and show'l,
And I'll dig his grave."

"Who'll be the parson?"
"I" said the rook,
"With my little book,
And I'll be the parson."

"Who'll be the clerk?"
"I" said the lark,
"If 'tis not in the dark,
And I'll be the clerk."

"Who'll carry him to the
  grave?"
"I" said the kite,
"If 'tis not in the night,
And I'll carry him to the
  grave."

"Who'll carry the link?"
"I" said the linnet,
"I'll fetch it in a minute,
And I'll carry the link."

"Who'll be chief mourner?"
"I" said the swan,
"I'm sorry he's gone,
And I'll be chief mourner."

"Who'll bear the pall?"
"We" said the wren,
Both the cock and the hen,
"And we'll bear the pall."

"Who'll run before?"
"I" said the deer,
"I run fast for fear,
And I'll run before."

"Who'll sing a psalm?"
"I" said the thrush,
As she sat in a bush,
"And I'll sing a psalm."

"Who'll throw in the dirt?"
"I" said the fox,
"Though I steal hens and
  cocks,
I'll throw in the dirt."

"And who'll toll the bell?"
"I" said the bull,
"Because I can pull,
And so, Cock Robbin, fare-
  well!"

All the birds of the air
Fell to sighing and sobbing,
When they heard the bell toll
For poor Cock Robbin.
          Anonymous

My Cat Jeoffry

For I will consider my cat Jeoffry.

For he is the servant of the Living God, duly and daily serving him.

For at the first glance of the glory of God in the East he worships in his way.

For is this done by wreathing his body seven times round with elegant quickness.

For then he leaps up to catch the musk, which is the blessing of God upon his prayer.

For he rolls upon prank to work it in.

For having done duty and received blessing he begins to consider himself.

For this he performs in ten degrees.

For first he looks upon his fore-paws to see if they are clean.

For secondly he kicks up behind to clear away there.

For thirdly he works it upon stretch with the fore-paws extended.

For fourthly he sharpens his paws by wood.

For fifthly he washes himself.

For sixthly he rolls upon wash.

For seventhly he fleas himself, that he may not be interrupted upon the beat.

For eighthly he rubs himself against a post.

For ninthly he looks up for his instructions.

For tenthly he goes in quest of food.

For having consider'd God and himself he will consider his neighbor.

For if he meets another cat he will kiss her in kindness.

For when he takes his prey he plays with it to give it chance.

For one mouse in seven escapes by his dallying.

For when his day's work is done his business more properly begins.

For [he] keeps the Lord's watch in the night against the adversary.

For he counteracts the powers of darkness by his electrical skin and glaring eyes.

For he counteracts the Devil, who is death, by brisking about the life.

For in his morning orisons he loves the sun and the sun loves him.

For he is of the tribe of Tiger.

For the Cherub Cat is a term of the Angel Tiger.

For he has the subtlety and hissing of a serpent, which in goodness he suppresses.

For he will not do destruction, if he is well-fed, neither will he spit without provocation.

For he purrs in thankfulness, when God tells him he's a good Cat.

For he is an instrument for the children to learn benevolence upon.

For every house is incompleat without him and a blessing is lacking in the spirit.

For the Lord commanded Moses concerning the cats at the departure of the Children of Israel from Egypt.

For every family had one cat at least in the bag.

For the English Cats are the best in Europe.

For he is the cleanest in the use of his fore-paws of any quadruped.

For the dexterity of his defense is an instance of the love of God to him exceedingly.

For he is the quickest to his mark of any creature.

For he is tenacious of his point.

For he is a mixture of gravity and waggery.

For he knows that God is his Saviour.

For there is nothing sweeter than his peace when at rest.

For there is nothing brisker than his life when in motion.

For he is of the Lord's poor and so indeed is he called by benevolence perpetually—Poor Jeoffry! poor Jeoffry! the rat has bit thy throat.

For I bless the name of the Lord Jesus that Jeoffry is better.

For the divine spirit comes about his body to sustain it in compleat cat.

For his tongue is exceeding pure so that it has in purity what it wants in musick.

For he is docile and can learn certain things.

For he can set up with gravity which is patience upon approbation.

For he can fetch and carry, which is patience in employment.

For he can jump over a stick which is patience upon proof
    positive.
For he can spraggle upon waggle at the word of command.
For he can jump from an eminence into his master's bosom.
For he can catch the cork and toss it again.
For he is hated by the hypocrite and miser.
For the former is afraid of detection.
For the latter refuses the charge.
For he camels his back to bear the first notion of business.
For he is good to think on, if a man would express himself
    neatly.
For he made a great figure in Egypt for his signal services.
For he killed the Icneumon-rat very pernicious by land.
For his ears are so acute that they sting again.
For from this proceeds the passing quickness of his attention.
For by stroaking of him I have found out electricity.
For I perceived God's light about him both wax and fire.
For the Electrical fire is the spiritual substance, which God
    sends from heaven to sustain the bodies both of man and
    beast.
For God has blessed him in the variety of his movements.
For, tho he cannot fly, he is an excellent clamberer.
For his motions upon the face of the earth are more than
    any other quadruped.
For he can tread to all the measures upon the musick.
For he can swim for life.
For he can creep.

Christopher Smart

The Pig

The pig, if I am not mistaken,
Supplies us sausage, ham, and bacon.
Let others say his heart is big—
I call it stupid of the pig.

Ogden Nash

The Common Cormorant

The common cormorant or shag
Lays eggs inside a paper bag
The reason you will see no doubt
It is to keep the lightning out.
But what these unobservant birds
Have never noticed is that herds
Of wandering bears may come with buns
And steal the bags to hold the crumbs.

Anonymous

The Rabbit

The rabbit has a charming face:
Its private life is a disgrace.
I really dare not name to you
The awful things that rabbits do;
Things that your paper never prints—
You only mention them in hints.
They have such lost, degraded souls
No wonder they inhabit holes;
When such depravity is found
It only can live underground.   *Anonymous*

The Firefly

The firefly's flame
Is something for which science has no name.
I can think of nothing eerier
Than flying around with an unidentified glow on a person's
  posteerier.   *Ogden Nash*

A Melancholy Lay

Three Turkeys fair their last have breathed,
And now this world for ever leaved,
Their Father and their Mother too,
Will sigh and weep as well as you,
Mourning for their offspring fair,
Whom they did nurse with tender care.
Indeed the rats their bones have crunch'd,
To eternity are they launch'd;
Their graceful form and pretty eyes
Their fellow fowls did not despise,
A direful death indeed they had,
That would put any parent mad,
But she was more than usual calm
She did not give a single dam.
Here ends this melancholy lay:
Farewell poor Turkeys I must say.
          Marjory Fleming, Age 8

The Turtle

The turtle lives 'twixt plated decks
Which practically conceal its sex.
I think it clever of the turtle
In such a fix to be so fertile.

Ogden Nash

The Sea-Gull

Hark to the whimper of the sea-gull;
He weeps because he's not an ea-gull.
Suppose you were, you silly sea-gull,
Could you explain it to your she-gull?

Ogden Nash

The Happy Bounding Flea

And here's the happy bounding flea—
You cannot tell the he from she.
The sexes look alike, you see,
But she can tell, and so can he!

Roland Young

Milk for the Cat

When the tea is brought at five o'clock,
And all the neat curtains are drawn with care,
The little black cat with bright green eyes
Is suddenly purring there.

At first she pretends, having nothing to do,
She has come in merely to blink by the grate,
But, though tea may be late or the milk may be sour,
She is never late.

And presently her agate eyes
Take a soft large, milky haze
And her independent casual glance
Becomes a stiff, hard gaze.

Then she stamps her claws or lifts her ears,
Or twists her tail and begins to stir,
Till suddenly all her lithe body becomes
One breathing, trembling purr.

The children eat and wriggle and laugh,
The two old ladies stroke their silk:
But the cat is grown small and thin with desire,
Transformed to a creeping lust for milk.

The white saucer like some full moon descends
At last from the clouds of the table above;
She sighs and dreams and thrills and glows,
Transfigured with love.

She nestles over the shining rim,
Buries her chin in the creamy sea;
Her tail hangs loose; each drowsy paw
Is doubled under each bending knee.

A long, dim ecstasy holds her life;
Her world is an infinite shapeless white,
Till her tongue has curled the last holy drop,
Then she sinks back into the night,

Draws and dips her body to heap
Her sleepy nerves in the great armchair,
Lies defeated and buried deep
Three or four hours unconscious there.

Harold Monro

The Song of the Mischievous Dog

There are many who say that a dog has his day,
And a cat has a number of lives;
There are others who think that a lobster is pink,
And that bees never work in their hives.
There are fewer, of course, who insist that a horse
Has a horn and two humps on its head,
And a fellow who jests that a mare can build nests
Is as rare as a donkey that's red.
Yet in spite of all this, I have moments of bliss,
For I cherish a passion for bones,
And though doubtful of biscuits, I'm willing to risk it,
And love to chase rabbits and stones.
But my greatest delight is to take a good bite
At a calf that is plump and delicious;
And if I indulge in a bite at a bulge,
Let's hope you won't think me too vicious.

Dylan Thomas, Age 11

The Song of Quoodle

They haven't got no noses,
The fallen sons of Eve;
Even the smell of roses
Is not what they supposes;
But more than mind discloses
And more than men believe.

They haven't got no noses,
They cannot even tell
When door and darkness closes
The park a Jew encloses,
Where even the law of Moses
Will let you steal a smell.

The brilliant smell of water,
The brave smell of a stone,
The smell of dew and thunder,
The old bones buried under,
Are things in which they blunder
And err, if left alone.

The wind from winter forests,
The scent of scentless flowers,
The breath of brides' adorning,
The smell of snare and warning,
The smell of Sunday morning,
God gave to us for ours.

And Quoodle here discloses
All things that Quoodle can,
They haven't got no noses,
They haven't got no noses,
And goodness only knowses
The Noselessness of Man.

G. K. Chesterton

the honey bee

the honey bee is sad and cross
and wicked as a weasel
and when she perches on you, boss,
she leaves a little measle

Don Marquis

The Frog

What a wonderful bird the frog are—
When he stand he sit almost;
When he hop, he fly almost.
He ain't got no sense hardly;
He ain't got no tail hardly either.
When he sit, he sit on what he ain't got almost.

Anonymous

As I Went to Bonner

As I went to Bonner,
I met a pig
Without a wig,
Upon my word and honor.

Anonymous

The Fleas

Great fleas have little fleas upon their backs to bite 'em,
And little fleas have lesser fleas and so *ad infinitum*.
And the great fleas themselves, in turn, have greater fleas
to go on;
While these again have greater still, and greater still, and so on.

A. de Morgan

Beginning of an Undergraduate Poem

When the sun's perpendicular rays
Illumine the depths of the sea—
The fishes, beginning to sweat,
Cry, *Damn it, how hot we shall be!*

Anonymous

The Mosquito

When did you start your tricks,
Monsieur?

What do you stand on such high legs for?
Why this length of shredded shank,
You exaltation?

Is it so that you shall lift your center of gravity upwards
And weigh no more than air as you alight upon me,
Stand upon me weightless, you phantom?

I heard a woman call you the Winged Victory
In sluggish Venice.
You turn your head towards your tail, and smile.

How can you put so much devilry
Into that translucent phantom shred
Of a frail corpus?

Queer, with your thin wings and your streaming legs,
How you sail like a heron, or a dull clot of air,
A nothingness.

Yet what an aura surrounds you;
Your evil little aura, prowling, and casting a numbness on
    my mind.

That is your trick, your bit of filthy magic:
Invisibility, and the anesthetic power
To deaden my attention in your direction.

But I know your game now, streaky sorcerer.
Queer, how you stalk and prowl the air
In circles and evasions, enveloping me,
Ghoul on wings
Winged Victory.

Settle, and stand on long thin shanks
Eyeing me sideways, and cunningly conscious that I am aware,
You speck.

I hate the way you lurch off sideways into air
Having read my thoughts against you.

Come then, let us play at unawares,
And see who wins in this sly game of bluff.
Man or mosquito.

You don't know that I exist, and I don't know that you exist.
Now then!
It is your trump,
It is your hateful little trump,
You pointed fiend,
Which shakes my sudden blood to hatred of you:
It is your small, high, hateful bugle in my ear.

Why do you do it?
Surely it is bad policy.
They say you can't help it.

If that is so, then I believe a little in Providence protecting
    the innocent.
But it sounds so amazingly like a slogan,
A yell of triumph as you snatch my scalp.

Blood, red blood
Super-magical
Forbidden liquor.
I behold you stand
For a second enspasmed in oblivion,
Obscenely ecstasied
Sucking live blood,
My blood.
Such silence, such suspended transport,
Such gorging,
Such obscenity of trespass.

You stagger
As well as you may.
Only your accursed hairy frailty,
Your own imponderable weightlessness
Saves you, wafts you away on the very draught my anger
    makes in its snatching.

Away with a paean of derision,
You winged blood-drop.
Can I not overtake you?
Are you one too many for me,
Winged Victory?
Am I not mosquito enough to out-mosquito you?

Queer, what a big stain my sucked blood makes
Beside the infinitesimal faint smear of you!
Queer, what a dim dark smudge you have disappeared into!

                    D. H. Lawrence

A Sonnet on a Monkey

O lovely O most charming pug
Thy graceful air and heavenly mug
The beauties of his mind do shine
And every bit is shaped so fine
Your very tail is most divine
Your teeth is whiter than the snow
You are a great buck and a bow
Your eyes are of so fine a shape
More like a christian's than an ape
His cheeks is like the rose's blume
Your hair is like the raven's plume
His nose's cast is of the roman
He is a very pretty woman
I could not get a rhyme for roman
And was obliged to call him woman.

Marjory Fleming, Age 8

Heaven

Fish (fly-replete, in depth of June,
Dawdling away their wat'ry noon)
Ponder deep wisdom, dark or clear,
Each secret fishy hope or fear.
Fish say, they have their Stream and Pond;
But is there anything Beyond?
This life cannot be All, they swear,
For how unpleasant, if it were!
One may not doubt that, somehow, Good
Shall come of Water and of Mud;
And, sure, the reverent eye must see
A purpose in Liquidity.
We darkly know, by Faith we cry,
The future is not Wholly Dry.
Mud unto mud!—Death eddies near—

Not here the appointed End, not here!
But somewhere, beyond Space and Time,
Is wetter water, slimier slime!
And there (they trust) there swimmeth One
Who swam ere rivers were begun,
Immense, of fishy form and mind,
Squamous, omnipotent, and kind;
And under that Almighty Fin,
The littlest fish may enter in.
Oh! never fly conceals a hook,
Fish say, in the Eternal Brook,
But more than mundane weeds are there,
And mud, celestially fair;
Fat caterpillars drift around,
And Paradisal grubs are found;
Unfading moths, immortal flies,
And the worm that never dies.
And in that Heaven of all their wish,
There shall be no more land, say fish.

Rupert Brooke

Pigeons

On the crooked arm of Columbus, on his cloak,
they mimic his blind and statuary stare,
and the chipped profiles of his handmaidens
they adorn with droppings. Over the loud square,
from all the arms and ledges of their rest,
only a breadcrust or a bell unshelves them.
Adding to Atlas' globe, they dispose themselves
with a portly propriety, and pose as garlands
importantly about his burdened shoulders.
Occasionally a lift of wind uncarves them.

Stone becomes them; they, in their turn, become it.
Their opal eyes have a monumental cast.
And in a maze of noise
their quiet *croomb croomb* dignifies the spaces,
suggesting the sound of silence. On cobbled islands,
marooned in tantrums of traffic, they know their place
—the faithful anonymity of servants—
and never beg, but properly receive.

All praise to them who nightly in the parks
keep peace for us; who, cosmopolitan,
patrol and people all cathedraled places,
and easily, lazily, haunt and inhabit
St. Paul's, St. Peter's, or the Madeleine,
the paved courts of the past, pompous as keepers
—a sober race of preservers and messengers,
neat in their international uniforms,
alighting with a word perhaps from Rome.
Permanence is their business, space and time
their special preservations; and wherever
the great stone men we save from death are stationed,
appropriately on the head of each is perched,
as though forever, his appointed pigeon.

Alastair Reid

Animal Fair

I went to the animal fair,
The birds and beasts were there.
The big baboon, by the light of the moon,
Was combing his auburn hair.
The monkey, he got drunk,
And sat on the elephant's trunk.
The elephant sneezed and fell on his knees,
And what became of the monk, the monk?

Anonymous

mind your p's & q's Harry

Ely

PART ELEVEN

Your P's and Q's and Haitches

Spelling Bee

I

A handsome young gent down in Fla.
Collapsed in a hospital ca.
    A young nurse from Me.
    Sought to banish his pe.
And shot him. Now what could be ha.?

II

There is an old Cook in N. Y.
Who insists you should always st. p.;
    He says he once tried
    To eat some that was fried,
And claims he would rather ch. c.

III

There once was a boring young Rev.
Who preached till it seemed he would nev.
    His hearers, en masse
    Got a pain at this farce
And prayed for relief of their neth.

IV

A lady who liked to crochet
Had a manner vivacious and get.
    People's names she forgot,
    But this bothered her not,
For she calmly addressed them as "set."

V

There was an old man of Hawaii,
Who ate too much whale and shark paii;
    So he quaffed some sperm-oil,
    And quitted life's termoil
Without even saying "Good-baii!"

VI. THE AMERICAN INDIAN

There once were some people called Sioux
Who spent all their time making shioux
Which they colored in various hioux;
    Don't think that they made them to ioux.
    Oh! no, they just sold them for bioux.

VII

Once a Frenchman who'd promptly said "Oui"
To some ladies who'd asked him if houi
    Cared to drink, threw a fit
    Upon finding that it
Was a tipple no stronger than toui.

VIII

When you think of the hosts without no.
Who are made sick by the deadly cuco.,
    It's quite a mistake
    Of such food to partake:
It results in a permanent slo.

Anonymous

O I C

I'm in a 10der mood today
  & feel poetic, 2;
4 fun I'll just — off a line
  & send it off 2 U.

I'm sorry you've been 6 o long;
  Don't B disconsol8;
But bear your ills with 42de,
    & they won't seem so gr8.

Anonymous

Haitches!

*Old English Cockney's Explanation of How to Become Very
Famous*

Halways sound your Haitches,
Haspirate your Haitches,
Hif you want to get hon in this world.
Show the Haitch in helephant; study haspiration,
Show you've a Heaton or a Hoxford heducation.

Halways sound your Haitches.
Remember hall your Haitches,
Then famous you will surely be.
Hand maybe the Queen will take you by the 'and,
Saying " 'Enery, there's kippers for tea!"

Anonymous

To a Thesaurus

O precious codex, volume, tome,
  Book, writing, compilation, work
Attend the while I pen a pome,
  A jest, a jape, a quip, a quirk.

For I would pen, engross, indite,
  Transcribe, set forth, compose, address,
Record, submit—yea, even write
  An ode, an elegy to bless—

To bless, set store by, celebrate,
  Approve, esteem, endow with soul,
Commend, acclaim, appreciate,
  Immortalize, laud, praise, extol

Thy merit, goodness, value, worth,
  Expedience, utility—

O manna, honey, salt of earth,
   I sing, I chant, I worship thee!

How could I manage, live, exist,
   Obtain, produce, be real, prevail,
Be present in the flesh, subsist,
   Have place, become, breathe or inhale,

Without thy help, recruit, support,
   Opitulation, furtherance,
Assistance, rescue, aid, resort,
   Favor, sustention, and advance?

Alas! alack! and well-a-day!
   My case would then be dour and sad,
Likewise distressing, dismal, gray,
   Pathetic, mournful, dreary, bad.

.   .   .   .

Though I could keep this up all day,
   This lyric, elegiac song.
Meseems hath come the time to say
   Farewell! adieu! good-by! so long!

Franklin P. Adams

All Awry

I want to know, am I the only stooge
Who has this trouble between "gauge" and "gouge"?
Or is it "*gowge*"? Am I a problem child
Because, to me, "misled" is always "misled"?
Does one pronounce the "Mall" as I do, "Mall,"
Or does it rhyme with "shall"; or not at all?
I have—I think I have—my "orgy" taped
But "prosecute" is still not firmly shaped
And gets mixed up with "persecute" at times.
I can't divorce "executor" from crimes,
And have internal struggles when I say
"Quayside"—I want to call it "quay"—
Do there exist some types who, without fail,
Can spot the winner between "goal" and "gaol,"
Unerring supermen who know their stuff
And call it "slough"? (or, dammit, is it "slough"?)
I hope there are, to prove it *can* be done;
Meanwhile, I ask again, am I the one—
The *only* one in our rough island story—
Who always gets such words as these all awry?

Justin Richardson

Please Excuse Typing

If you have ever, like me,
Missed the "r" and hit the "t,"
Addressing some fat blister
As "Mt." instead of "Mr.,"
I trust you left it unamended?

Splendid.

J. B. Boothroyd

My Own Simplified Spelling

(I cannot be bothered with other people's systems, new or old. I have chosen what I liked from any source that suited me. I have tried to clarify not only pronunciation but sense. And to make things easier I have omitted punctuation, always a nuisance to children and often, no doubt, to foreigners.)

Awltho I no how 2 and fro
Sum peepul go with spade and ho
   And doutless have gud reason

I doo not so
I plahnt no ro
I neether dig nor proon nor mo
   Throo awl the singing season

If ruff winds sow
Across the slow
They cannot cow my glad hart now
   To werk wer well ni treason

Come with me Flo
Thine ainshent bo
Wair hi and lo we yoost 2 go
   Wair virelets bloom in every coom

Wair leeps from lair
The startuld hair
Wair springs from brake the trembling do
   Wile yet the yung yere fleas on

Wot ho dust thow
Or I need now
Amungst the ferze beneeth the bow
Wen brites the sun weel cair for nun
   But wonder wudlands throo

No racking coff shall keep us off
   Nor trace of winters floo
Wot not shall not
   Our troo luv twine
In cops or grot
   Thi hand in mine
By sum trees bole weel make our gole
Sole speek to sole time onwud role
   And hevvn luk down benine

Wile mounts the lark
In that hi ark
Weel from the bark
Cut out the names
Of Flo and James
   With tangled harts for sine

Is life not 0 and 2 sho
Wen browze b lined with ankshus tho
   And cairs 2 closely clinging

Wot ho wot ho
Need we to no
Wen wites the blossum on the slo
   And meeds with joy r springing

Wot sox 2 nit
Wen skize r lit
And down on floury banx we sit
   With larx awl round us singing
                      Evoe (E. V. Knox)

Lama

The one-l lama,
He's a priest.
The two-l llama,
He's a beast.
And I will bet
A silk pajama
There isn't any
Three-l lllama.
                      Ogden Nash

For Loose Tongues

I

Betty Botter bought some butter,
But, she said, the butter's bitter;
If I put it in my batter
It will make my batter bitter,
But a bit of better butter
Will make my batter better.
So she bought a bit of butter

Better than her bitter butter,
And she put it in her batter
And the batter was not bitter.
So 'twas better Betty Botter bought a bit
  of better butter.

II

Peter Piper picked a peck of pickled pepper;
A peck of pickled pepper Peter Piper picked;
If Peter Piper picked a peck of pickled pepper,
Where's the peck of pickled pepper Peter Piper picked?

III. THE BAKER'S REPLY TO THE NEEDLE PEDDLER

I need not your needles, they're needless to me;
For kneading of needles were needless, you see;
But did my neat trousers but need to be kneed,
I then should have need of your needles indeed.

IV

Celia sat beside the seaside,
Quite beside herself was she
For beside her on the leeside
No one sat beside her, see?

V. A TWISTER

The twain that, in twining, before in the twine
As twines were intwisted; he now doth untwine;
'Twixt the twain inter-twisting a twine more between,
He, twirling his twister, makes a twist of the twine.

When a Twister a-twisting will twist him a twist,
For the twisting of his twist, he three twines doth intwist;
But if one of the twines of the twist do untwist,
The twine that untwisteth, untwisteth the twist.

Untwirling the twine that untwisteth between,
He twirls, with his twister, the two in a twine;
Then, twice having twisted the twines of the twine,
He twitcheth, the twice he had twined, in twain.

                                        Anonymous

A New Song of New Similes

My passion is as mustard strong;
  I sit all sober sad;
Drunk as a piper all day long,
  Or like a March-hare mad.

Round as a hoop the bumpers flow;
  I drink, yet can't forget her;
For, though as drunk as David's sow,
  I love her still the better.

Pert as a pear-monger I'd be,
  If Molly were but kind;
Cool as a cucumber could see
  The rest of womankind.

Like a stuck pig I gaping stare,
  And eye her o'er and o'er;
Lean as a rake with sighs and care,
  Sleek as a mouse before.

Plump as a partridge was I known,
  And soft as silk my skin,
My cheeks as fat as butter grown;
  But as a groat now thin!

I, melancholy as a cat,
  And kept awake to weep;
But she, insensible of that,
  Sound as a top can sleep.

Hard is her heart as flint or stone,
  She laughs to see me pale;
And merry as a grig is grown,
  And brisk as bottled ale.

The God of Love at her approach
  Is busy as a bee;
Hearts, sound as any bell or roach,
  Are smit and sigh like me.

Ay me! as thick as hops or hail,
  The fine men crowd about her;
But soon as dead as a door nail
  Shall I be, if without her.

Straight as my leg her shape appears;
    O were we join'd together!
My heart would be scot-free from cares,
    And lighter than a feather.

As fine as fivepence is her mien,
    No drum was ever tighter;
Her glance is as the razor keen,
    And not the sun is brighter.

As soft as pap her kisses are,
    Methinks I taste them yet;
Brown as a berry is her hair,
    Her eyes as black as jet:

As smooth as glass, as white as curds,
    Her pretty hand invites;
Sharp as a needle are her words;
    Her wit, like pepper, bites:

Brisk as a body-louse she trips,
    Clean as a penny drest;
Sweet as a rose her breath and lips,
    Round as the globe her breast.

Full as an egg was I with glee;
    And happy as a king.
Good Lord! how all men envy'd me!
    She lov'd like any thing.

But false as hell! she, like the wind,
    Chang'd, as her sex must do;
Though seeming as the turtle kind,
    And like the gospel true.

If I and Molly could agree,
    Let who would take Peru!
Great as an emperor should I be,
    And richer than a Jew.

Till you grow tender as a chick,
    I'm dull as any post;
Let us, like burs, together stick,
    And warm as any toast.

You'll know me truer than a dye;
    And wish me better speed;

Flat as a flounder when I lie,
  And as a herring dead.

Sure as a gun, she'll drop a tear,
  And sigh, perhaps, and wish,
When I am rotten as a pear,
  And mute as any fish.

John Gay

Varialtk

When Very was a celibate
It meant "in high degree";
Its emphasis was moderate
But quite enough for me.
It never thumped its little chest
Or raised its voice unduly,
And always looked its level best
When flanked by Yours and Truly.

But in an age of shrill extremes
One adverb's ineffective,
So now the Verys trot in teams
To gain the same objective,
And no one can be mortified,
Or sad, or shy, or merry,
Unless the mood is fortified
By Very comma Very.

I hope this twosome will suffice
For purposes emphatic.
But mated words may breed like mice
Sequestered in an attic.
And thus produce a corollary
—the intensified intensive—
A triple threat that makes me Very
Very, *Very* apprehensive.

Weare Holbrook

An Austrian Army

An Austrian army awfully array'd,
Boldly by battery besieged Belgrade.
Cossack commanders cannonading come
Dealing destruction's devastating doom:
Every endeavor engineers essay,

For fame, for fortune fighting—furious fray!
Generals 'gainst generals grapple, gracious God!
How Heaven honors heroic hardihood!
Infuriate—indiscriminate in ill—
Kinsmen kill kindred—kindred kinsmen kill:
Labor low levels loftiest, longest lines,
Men march 'mid mounds, 'mid moles, 'mid murd'rous mines:
Now noisy noxious numbers notice nought
Of outward obstacles, opposing ought—
Poor patriots—partly purchased—partly press'd,
Quite quaking, quickly "Quarter! quarter!" quest:
Reason returns, religious right redounds,
Suwarrow stops such sanguinary sounds.
Truce to thee, Turkey, triumph to thy train,
Unwise, unjust, unmerciful Ukraine!
Vanish, vain victory! Vanish, victory vain!
Why wish we warfare? Wherefore welcome were
Xerxes, Ximenes, Xanthus, Xavier?
Yield, yield, ye youths, ye yeomen, yield your yell:
Zeno's, Zimmermann's, Zoroaster's zeal,
Again attract; arts against arms appeal!

Alaric A. Watts

Bonne Entente

The advantages of living with two cultures
Strike one at every turn,
Especially when one finds a notice in an office building:
"This elevator will not run on Ascension Day";
Or reads in the *Montreal Star*:
"Tomorrow being the Feast of the Immaculate Conception,
There will be no collection of garbage in the city";
Or sees on the restaurant menu the bilingual dish:

DEEP APPLE PIE

TARTE AUX POMMES PROFONDES   *F. R. Scott*

Enigma

'Twas whispered in Heaven, 'twas muttered in Hell,
And echo caught softly the sound as it fell;
In the confines of earth 'twas permitted to rest,
And the depth of the ocean its presence confessed;
'Twas seen in the lightning, 'twas heard in the thunder,
'Twill be found in the spheres when they're riven asunder;
'Twas given to man with his earliest breath,
It assists at his birth and attends him in death,
Presides o'er his happiness, honor, and health,
'Tis the prop of his house and the end of his wealth;
It begins every hope, every wish it must bound,
With the husbandman toils, and with monarchs is crowned;
In the heaps of the miser 'tis hoarded with care,
But is sure to be lost in the prodigal heir;
Without it the soldier and sailor may roam,
But woe to the wretch who expels it from home;
In the whispers of conscience it there will be found,
Nor e'er in the whirlwind of passion be drowned;
It softens the heart, and though deaf to the ear,
It will make it acutely and instantly hear;
But in shades let it rest, like an elegant flower,
Oh! breathe on it softly, it dies in an hour.

C. M. Fanshawe

PART TWELVE

The Children's Playground

The Children's Playground

This is the children's playground, the home of the inner eye,
Surrounded by the fences and benches against the unbridled
    dark,
Where the prodigious exuberance of the miniature human
    beings
Tests the chutes of gravitation, seventeen trees from the zoo.

This is the place where the adults are grotesquely overgrown,
Where other children's parents are statues out of their niches,
Where the tree of plurals grows, where time is over forever,
A sea of all directions for the wayward paddling of childhood.

This is the children's playground, the tenderest part of the park,
Where home buzzes behind a bush and nurse is a hillside of
    don'ts,
Where every pigeon rolls along like a slowly stopping ball
And glittering birds fall from the hairy lips of fountains.

The squirrels adorn the trees with the scrolls of their tails,
And sparrows, those crumbs of birds, dart for their dots of
    bread;
The buildings stand in a crowded parade to see above each
    other,
The ambush of the everywhere is crowded with elbows, hats
    and toes.

With daylight, a common denominator, entering everything
    easily
The cars the day long on the streets play games of north-&-
    south,
The grown-up people sit all alone in the middle of their shops,
But this is the children's playground, seventeen aeons from
    lunch.

Oscar Williams

There Was a Naughty Boy

There was a naughty Boy
A naughty Boy was he
He would not stop at home
He could not quiet be—
    He took
    In his Knapsack
    A Book
    Full of vowels
    And a shirt
    With some towels—
    A slight cap
    For night cap—
    A hair brush
    Comb ditto
    New Stockings
    For old ones
    Would split O!
    This Knapsack
    Tight at 's back
    He riveted close
And follow'd his Nose
    To the North
    To the North
And follow'd his nose
    To the North.

There was a naughty Boy
And a naughty Boy was he
He ran away to Scotland
The people for to see—
    There he found
    That the ground
    Was as hard
    That a yard
    Was as long,
    That a song
    Was as merry,
    That a cherry
    Was as red—
    That lead
    Was as weighty
    That fourscore
    Was as eighty
    That a door
    Was as wooden
    As in England—
    So he stood in
    His shoes
    And he wonder'd
    He stood in his
    Shoes and he wonder'd.

John Keats

A Butcher's Dozen of Children's Rhymes

I

I asked my mother for fifty cents
To see the elephant jump the fence.
He jumped so high he reached the sky,
And didn't get back till the Fourth of July.

II

Said the monkey to the donkey,
"What'll you have to drink?"
Said the donkey to the monkey,
"I'd like a swig of ink."

III

I'm a little Hindoo.
I do all I kindoo.
Where my pants and shirt don't meet
I make my little skindoo.

IV

I'd like a little
Of that nourishing victual,
But I'll take a lot
From the candy pot.

V

My father owns the butcher shop,
My mother cuts the meat,
And I'm the little hot dog
That runs around the street.

VI

I stood on the bridge at midnight,
When the clock was striking in town;
I stood on the bridge at midnight—
Because I couldn't sit down.

VII

Sam, Sam, the butcher man,
Washed his face in a frying pan,
Combed his hair with a wagon wheel,
And died with a toothache in his heel.

VIII

A horse and a flea and three blind mice
Sat on a curbstone shooting dice.
The horse he slipped and fell on the flea.
The flea said, "Whoops, there's a horse on me."

IX

I like coffee, I like tea,
I like the boys and the boys like me.
Tell your mother to hold her tongue,
For she did the same when she was young.
Tell your father to do the same,
For he was the one who changed her name.

X

Charlie Chaplin went to France
To teach the ladies how to dance.
Heel, toe, and around we go;
Salute to the captain,
Bow to the queen,
Turn your back
On the old submarine.

XI

You're a poet.
You don't know it,
But your feet show it—
LONGFELLOW!

Anonymous

A Round Dozen Just for Fun

I

Roses are red,
Violets are blue,
What you need
Is a good shampoo.

II

Mary had a little lamb,
She set it on the shelf;
And every time it wagged its tail,
It spanked its little self.

III

Star light, star bright,
First star I've seen tonight,
Wish I may, wish I might
Have this wish I wish tonight.

IV

Needles and pins, needles and pins,
When you get married your trouble begins.

V

Oh, you may drive a horse to water,
But a pencil must be lead.

VI

Do you carrot all for me?
My heart beets for you,
With your turnip nose
And your radish face.

You are a peach.
If we canteloupe
Lettuce marry;
Weed make a swell pear.

VII

Did he say I said you said she said that?
He said you said I said she said that!
Well, I didn't, and that's that!

VIII

There's music in a hammer,
There's music in a nail,
There's music in a pussy cat,
When you step upon her tail.

IX

I had a nickel and I walked around the block.
I walked right into a baker's shop.
I took two doughnuts right out of the grease;
I handed the lady my five-cent piece.
She looked at the nickel and she looked at me,
And said, "This money's no good to me.
There's a hole in the nickel, and it goes right through."
Says I, "There's a hole in the doughnut, too."

X

If you and your folks like me and my folks
Like me and my folks like you and your folks,
Then me and my folks like you and your folks
Like you and your folks like me and my folks.

XI

Do you love me,
Or do you not?
You told me once,
But I forgot.

XII

Some write for pleasure,
Some write for fame,
But I write only
(to sign my name).

Anonymous

Mrs. Mother Has a Nose

What a big nose Mrs. Mother has,
the better to smell her dear.
Sniff sniff sniff it comes round the door,
detective of everything queer.

Two big noses Mrs. Mother has,
the better to quell her dear.
"I smell something odd, I smell something bad,
what is that smell in here?"

Three big noses Mrs. Mother has,
they grow and grow in the night.
Sniff sniff sniff her naughty naughty dear!
And she also can smell with her ears.

James Broughton

The Pretty Maid

Where are you going to, my pretty maid?
I'm going a-milking, sir, she said,
Sir, she said, sir, she said,
I'm going a-milking, sir, she said.

May I go with you, my pretty maid?
You're kindly welcome, sir, she said.

Say, will you marry me, my pretty maid?
Yes, if you please, kind sir, she said.

What is your father, my pretty maid?
My father's a farmer, sir, she said.

What is your fortune, my pretty maid?
My face is my fortune, sir, she said.

Then I can't marry you, my pretty maid.
Nobody asked you, sir, she said.

Anonymous

A Little Woman

There was a little woman,
　As I have heard tell,
She went to market
　Her eggs for to sell;
She went to market
　All on a market day,
And she fell asleep
　On the king's highway.

There came by a peddler,
　His name was Stout,
He cut her petticoats
　All round about;
He cut her petticoats
　Up to her knees;
Which made the little woman
　To shiver and sneeze.

When this little woman
　Began to awake,
She began to shiver,
　And she began to shake;

She began to shake,
　And she began to cry,
Lawk a mercy on me,
　This is none of I!

But if this be I,
　As I do hope it be,
I have a little dog at home
　And he knows me;
If it be I,
　He'll wag his little tail,
And if it be not I
　He'll loudly bark and wail!

Home went the little woman
　All in the dark,
Up starts the little dog,
　And he began to bark;
He began to bark,
　And she began to cry,
Lawk a mercy on me,
　This is none of I!

Anonymous

A Little Man

There was a little man,
　And he wooed a little maid,
And he said, Little maid, will you wed, wed, wed?
　I have little more to say,
　Than will you, yea or nay?
For the least said is soonest mended, ded, ded.

Then this little maid she said,
　Little sir, you've little said,
To induce a little maid for to wed, wed, wed;
　You must say a little more,
　And produce a little ore,
Ere I to the church will be led, led, led.

Then the little man replied,
　If you'll be my little bride,
I will raise my love notes a little higher, higher, higher;
　Though I little love to prate
　Yet you'll find my heart is great,
With the little God of Love all on fire, fire, fire.

Then the little maid replied,
If I should be your bride,
Pray, what must we have for to eat, eat, eat?
Will the flames that you're so rich in
Make a fire in the kitchen,
And the little God of Love turn the spit, spit, spit?

Then the little man he sighed,
And some say a little cried,
And his little heart was big with sorrow, sorrow, sorrow;
I'll be your little slave,
And if the little that I have,
Be too little, little dear, I will borrow, borrow, borrow.

Then the little man so gent,
Made the little maid relent,
And set her little soul a-thinking, king, king;
Though his little was but small,
Yet she had his little all,
And could have of a cat but her skin, skin skin.

Anonymous

The House That Jack Built

This is the house that Jack built.

This is the malt
That lay in the house that Jack built.

This is the rat,
That ate the malt
That lay in the house that Jack built.

This is the cat,
That killed the rat,
That ate the malt
That lay in the house that Jack built.

This is the dog,
That worried the cat,
That killed the rat,
That ate the malt
That lay in the house that Jack built.

This is the cow with the crumpled horn,
That tossed the dog,

That worried the cat,
That killed the rat,
That ate the malt
That lay in the house that Jack built.

This is the maiden all forlorn,
That milked the cow with the crumpled horn,
That tossed the dog,
That worried the cat,
That killed the rat,
That ate the malt
That lay in the house that Jack built.

This is the man all tattered and torn,
That kissed the maiden all forlorn,
That milked the cow with the crumpled horn,
That tossed the dog,
That worried the cat,
That killed the rat,
That ate the malt
That lay in the house that Jack built.

This is the priest all shaven and shorn,
That married the man all tattered and torn,
That kissed the maiden all forlorn,
That milked the cow with the crumpled horn,
That tossed the dog,
That worried the cat,
That killed the rat,
That ate the malt
That lay in the house that Jack built.

This is the cock that crowed in the morn,
That waked the priest all shaven and shorn,
That married the man all tattered and torn,
That kissed the maiden all forlorn,
That milked the cow with the crumpled horn,
That tossed the dog,
That worried the cat,
That killed the rat,
That ate the malt
That lay in the house that Jack built.

This is the farmer sowing his corn,
That kept the cock that crowed in the morn,
That waked the priest all shaven and shorn,

That married the man all tattered and torn,
That kissed the maiden all forlorn,
That milked the cow with the crumpled horn,
That tossed the dog,
That worried the cat,
That killed the rat,
That ate the malt
That lay in the house that Jack built.

Anonymous

Old Mother Hubbard

Old Mother Hubbard
Went to the cupboard,
To fetch her poor dog a bone;
But when she came there
The cupboard was bare
And so the poor dog had
none.

She went to the baker's
To buy him some bread;
But when she came back
The poor dog was dead.

She went to the undertaker's
To buy him a coffin;
But when she came back
The poor dog was laughing.

She took a clean dish
To get him some tripe;
But when she came back
He was smoking a pipe.

She went to the alehouse
To get him some beer;
But when she came back
The dog sat in a chair.

She went to the tavern
For white wine and red;
But when she came back
The dog stood on his head.

She went to the fruiterer's
To buy him some fruit;
But when she came back
He was playing the flute.

She went to the tailor's
To buy him a coat;
But when she came back
He was riding a goat.

She went to the hatter's
To buy him a hat;
But when she came back
He was feeding the cat.

She went to the barber's
To buy him a wig;
But when she came back
He was dancing a jig.

She went to the cobbler's
To buy him some shoes;
But when she came back
He was reading the news.

She went to the seamstress
To buy him some linen;
But when she came back
The dog was a-spinning.

She went to the hosier's
To buy him some hose;
But when she came back
He was dressed in his
clothes.

The dame made a curtsy,
The dog made a bow;
The dame said, Your servant,
The dog said, Bow-wow.

Anonymous

As I was Standing in the Street

As I was standing in the street,
    As quiet as could be,
A great big ugly man came up
    And tied his horse to me.

Anonymous

1 2 3 4 5 6 7 8 9 10 11 12 13 14 15 16 17 18 19 20

One, two,
Buckle my shoe;
Three, four,
Knock at the door;
Five, six,
Pick up sticks;
Seven, eight,
Lay them straight;
Nine, ten,
A big fat hen;

Eleven, twelve,
Dig and delve;
Thirteen, fourteen,
Maids a-courting;
Fifteen, sixteen,
Maids in the kitchen;
Seventeen, eighteen,
Maids in waiting;
Nineteen, twenty,
My plate's empty.

Anonymous

The Bells of London

Gay go up and gay go down
To ring the bells of London
    Town!

Bull's eyes and targets,
Say the bells of St. Marg'rets.

Brickbats and tiles,
Say the bells of St. Giles.

Halfpence and farthings,
Say the bells of St. Martin's.

Oranges and lemons,
Say the bells of St. Clement's.

Pokers and tongs,
Say the bells of St. John's.

Tin kettles and saucepans,

Say the bells of St. Anne's.

Old father Baldpate,
Say the slow bells of Aldgate.

You owe me ten shillings,
Say the bells of St. Helen's.

When will you pay me?
Say the bells of Old Bailey.

When I grow rich,
Say the bells of Shoreditch.

When will that be?
Say the bells of Stepney.

I'm sure I don't know,
Says the great bell at Bow.

Anonymous

A Century of Nursery Rhymes

I. TOM THUMB'S ALPHABET

A was an archer, who shot at a frog,
B was a butcher, and had a great dog.
C was a captain, all covered with lace,
D was a drunkard, and had a red face.
E was an Esquire, with pride on his brow,
F was a farmer, and followed the plow.
G was a gamester, who had but ill-luck,
H was a hunter and hunted a buck.
I was an innkeeper, who loved to carouse,
J was a joiner, and built up a house.
K was King William, once governed this land,
L was a lady, who had a white hand.
M was a miser, and hoarded up gold,
N was a nobleman, gallant and bold.
O was an oyster girl, and went about town,
P was a parson, and wore a black gown.
Q was a queen, who wore a silk slip,
R was a robber, and wanted a whip.
S was a sailor, and spent all he got,
T was a tinker, and mended a pot.
U was a usurer, a miserable elf,
V was a vintner, who drank all himself.
W was a watchman, and guarded the door,
X was expensive, and so became poor.
Y was a youth, that did not love school,
Z was a zany, a poor harmless fool.

II

How many miles to Babylon?
Three score miles and ten.
Can I get there by candlelight?
Yes, and back again;
If your heels are nimble and light,
You may get there by candlelight.

III

Jerry Hall,
He is so small,
A rat could eat him,
Hat and all.

IV

There was an old woman who lived in a shoe,
She had so many children she didn't know what to do;
She gave them some broth without any bread;
She whipped them all soundly and put them to bed.

Old woman, old woman, shall we go a-shearing?
Speak a little louder, sir, I'm very thick of hearing.
Old woman, old woman, shall I love you dearly?
Thank you, very kindly, sir, now I hear you clearly.

V

There was an old woman tossed up in a basket,
Seventeen times as high as the moon;
Where was she going I couldn't but ask it,
For in her hand she carried a broom,
Old woman, old woman, old woman, quoth I,
Where are you going to up so high?
To brush the cobwebs off the sky!
May I go with you?
Aye, by-and-by.

VI

If wishes were horses
Beggars would ride;
If turnips were watches
I would wear one by my side.

VII

Tweedledum and Tweedledee
    Agreed to have a battle,
For Tweedledum said Tweedledee
    Had spoiled his nice new rattle.
Just then flew by a monstrous crow,
    As big as tar-barrel,
Which frightened both the heroes so,
    They quite forgot their quarrel.

VIII

We are all in the dumps,
    For diamonds are trumps;
The kittens are gone to St. Paul's!
    The babies are bit,
    The moon's in a fit,
And the houses are built without walls.

IX

We're all dry with drinking on't,
We're all dry with drinking on't,
The piper kissed th fiddler's wife,
And I can't sleep for thinking on't.

X

Tom, Tom, the piper's son,
Stole a pig and away he run;
  The pig was eat
  And Tom was beat,
And Tom went howling down the street.

XI

I went to the road that lies under the wall,
I charmed him out, and he came at my call;
I scratched out the eyes of the owl before,
I tore the bat's wing: what would you have more?

XII

He that lies at the stock,
Shall have a gold rock;
He that lies at the wall,
Shall have a gold ball;
He that lies in the middle,
Shall have a gold fiddle.

XIII

Twinkle, twinkle, little star,
How I wonder what you are!
Up above the world so high,
Like a diamond in the sky.

XIV

Sing a song of sixpence,
  A pocket full of rye;
Four and twenty blackbirds,
  Baked in a pie.

When the pie was opened,
  The birds began to sing;
Was not that a dainty dish
  To set before the king?

The king was in his counting-house,
    Counting out his money;
The queen was in the parlor,
    Eating bread and honey.

The maid with in the garden,
    Hanging out the clothes,
There came a little blackbird,
    And snapped off her nose.

XV

Come, let's to bed,   Put on the pot,
Says Sleepy-head;   Says Greedy-gut,
Tarry a while, says Slow;   We'll sup before we go.

XVI

Simple Simon met a pieman
    Going to the fair;
Says Simple Simon to the pieman,
    "Let me taste your ware."

Says the pieman to Simple Simon,
    "Show me first your penny";
Says Simple Simon to the pieman,
    "Indeed I haven't any."

Simple Simon went a-fishing,
    For to catch a whale;
All the water he had got
    Was in his mother's pail.

Simple Simon went to look
    If plums grew on a thistle;
He pricked his finger very much,
    Which made poor Simon whistle.

XVII

Thirty days hath September,
April, June and November;
All the rest have thirty-one
Except February alone,
Which has four plus twenty-four
And every leap year one day more.

XVIII

If all the seas were one sea,
What a *great* sea that would be!
If all the trees were one tree,
What a *great* tree that would be!
And if all the axes were one axe,
What a *great* axe that would be!
And if the *great* man took the *great* axe,
And cut down the *great* tree,
And let it fall into the *great* sea,
What a splish-splash *that* would be!

XIX

A diller, a dollar,
A ten o'clock scholar,
What makes you come so soon?
You used to come at ten o'clock,
But now you come at noon.

XX

As I was going to St. Ives,
I met a man with seven wives,
Each wife had seven sacks,
Each sack had seven cats,
Each cat had seven kits:
Kits, cats, sacks, and wives,
How many were there going to St. Ives?

XXI

Hey! rub-a-dub, ho! rub-a-dub, three men in a tub,
And who do you think were there?
The butcher, the baker, the candlestick-maker,
And all of them gone to the fair.

XXII

The rose is red, the violet blue,
The gillyflower sweet, and so are you.
These are the words you bade me say
For a pair of new gloves on Easter day.

XXIII

Little Robin Redbreast
Sat upon a rail;
Niddle noddle went his head,
Wiggle waggle went his tail.

XXIV

Three young rats with black felt hats,
Three young ducks with white straw flats.
Three young dogs with curling tails,
Three young cats with demi-veils,
Went out to walk with two young pigs
In satin vests and sorrel wigs.
But suddenly it chanced to rain
And so they all went home again.

XXV

There was a rat, for want of stairs,
Went down a rope to say his prayers.

XXVI

The Queen of Hearts, she made some tarts,
    All on a summer's day;
The Knave of Hearts, he stole the tarts,
    And took them clean away.

The King of Hearts called for the tarts,
    And beat the knave full sore;
The Knave of Hearts brought back the tarts,
    And vowed he'd steal no more.

XXVII

Rain, rain, go away,
Come again some other day;
Little Willie wants to play.

XXVIII

Pussy cat, pussy cat, where have you been?
I've been to London to look at the queen.
Pussy cat, pussy cat, what did you there?
I frightened a little mouse under her chair.

XXIX

What is the rhyme for porringer?
What is the rhyme for porringer?
The king he had a daughter fair
And gave the Prince of Orange her.

XXX

This little pig went to market,
This little pig stayed at home,
This little pig had roast beef,
This little pig had none,
And this little pig cried, Wee-wee-wee-wee-wee,
    I can't find my way home.

XXXI

Solomon Grundy,
Born on a Monday,
Christened on Tuesday,
Married on Wednesday,
Took ill on Thursday,
Worse on Friday,
Died on Saturday,
Buried on Sunday.
This is the end
Of Solomon Grundy.

XXXII

Peter, Peter, pumpkin eater,
Had a wife and couldn't keep her;
He put her in a pumpkin shell
And there he kept her very well.

Peter, Peter, pumpkin eater,
Had another, and didn't love her;
Peter learned to read and spell,
And then he loved her very well.

XXXIII

Pease porridge hot,
Pease porridge cold,
Pease porridge in the pot
Nine days old.

Some like it hot,
Some like it cold,
Some like it in the pot
Nine days old.

XXXIV

A little cock sparrow sat on a green tree,
And he chirruped, he chirruped, so merry was he.

A naughty boy came with his wee bow and arrow,
Says he, I will shoot this little cock sparrow;
His body will make me a nice little stew,
And his giblets will make me a little pie too.
Oh, no, said the sparrow, I won't make a stew,
So he clapped his wings and away he flew.

XXXV

One-ery, two-ery, ickery, Ann,
Phillisy, phollisy, Nicholas John,
Quever, quaver, Irish Mary,
Stickeram, stackeram, Buck.

XXXVI

I had a little nut tree,
    Nothing would it bear
But a silver nutmeg
    And a golden pear;

The King of Spain's daughter
    Came to visit me,
And all for the sake
    Of my little nut tree.

XXXVII

Little Nancy Etticoat,
With a white petticoat,
And a red nose;
She has no feet or hands,
The longer she stands
The shorter she grows.

XXXVIII

For want of a nail, the shoe was lost,
For want of a shoe, the horse was lost,
For want of a horse, the rider was lost,
For want of a rider, the battle was lost,
For want of a battle, the kingdom was lost.
And all for the want of a horseshoe nail.

XXXIX

Old Mother Twitchett has but one eye,
And a long tail which she can let fly,
And every time she goes over a gap,
She leaves a bit of her tail in a trap.

XL

Little Miss Muffet
Sat on a tuffet,
Eating her curds and whey;
There came a big spider,
Who sat down beside her
And frightened Miss Muffet away.

XLI

Cackle, cackle, Mother Goose,
Have you any feathers loose?
Truly have I, pretty fellow,
Half enough to fill a pillow.
Here are quills, take one or two,
And down to make a bed for you.

XLII

Mother, may I go and swim?
Yes, my darling daughter.
Hang your clothes on yonder limb,
But don't go near the water.

XLIII

My mother said that I never should
Play with the gypsies in the wood;
If I did, she would say,
"Naughty girl to disobey."

XLIV

Monday's child is fair of face,
Tuesday's child is full of grace,
Wednesday's child is full of woe,
Thursday's child has far to go,
Friday's child is loving and giving,
Saturday's child works hard for his living,
And the child that is born on the Sabbath day
Is bonny and blithe, and good and gay.

XLV

Three blind mice, see how they run!
They all ran after the farmer's wife,
Who cut off their tails with a carving knife,
Did you ever see such a thing in your life,
     As three blind mice?

XLVI

Matthew, Mark, Luke and John
Bless the bed that I lie on.
     Four corners to my bed,
     Four angels round my head;
     One to watch and one to pray
     And two to bear my soul away.

XLVII

Mary, Mary, quite contrary,
     How does your garden grow?
With silver bells and cockle shells,
     And pretty maids all in a row.

XLVIII

Mary had a little lamb,
     Its fleece was white as snow;
And everywhere that Mary went
     The lamb was sure to go.

XLIX

The man in the moon
     Came down too soon,
And asked his way to Norwich;
     He went by the south,
     And burnt his mouth
With supping cold plum porridge.

L

There was an old man
And he had a calf,
　And that's half;
He took him out of the stall,
And put him on the wall,
　And that's all.

LI

There was a crooked man, and he walked a crooked mile,
He found a crooked sixpence against a crooked stile;
He bought a crooked cat, which caught a crooked mouse,
And they all lived together in a little crooked house.

LII

A man in the wilderness asked me,
How many strawberries grow in the sea?
I answered him, as I thought good,
As many as red herrings grow in the wood.

LIII

There was a man, he went mad,
He jumped into a paper bag;
The paper bag was too narrow,
He jumped into a wheelbarrow;
The wheelbarrow took on fire,
He jumped into a cow byre;
The cow byre was too nasty,
He jumped into an apple pasty;
The apple pasty was too sweet,
He jumped into Chester-le-Street;
Chester-le-Street was full of stones,
He fell down and broke his bones.

LIV

There was a little maid, and she was afraid
That her sweetheart would come unto her;
So she went to bed, and covered up her head,
And fastened the door with a skewer.

LV

Lucy Locket lost her pocket,
Kitty Fisher found it;
Not a penny was there in it,
Only ribbon round it.

LVI

As I was going o'er London Bridge
  I heard something crack;
Not a man in all England
  Can mend that!

LVII

The lion and the unicorn
  Were fighting for the crown;
The lion beat the unicorn
  All round about the town.

Some gave them white bread,
  And some gave them brown;
Some gave them plum cake
  And drummed them out of town.

LVIII

Two legs sat upon three legs
With one leg in his lap;
In comes four legs
And runs away with one leg;
Up jumps two legs,
Catches up three legs,
Throws it after four legs,
And makes him bring back one leg.

LIX

Ladybird, ladybird, fly away home,
Your house is on fire and your children all gone;
All except one and that's little Ann
And she has crept under the warming pan.

LX

Jack Sprat could eat no fat,
  His wife could eat no lean,
And so between them both, you see,
  They licked the platter clean.

LXI

Now what do you think
  Of little Jack Jingle?
Before he was married
  He used to live single.

LXII

Little Jack Horner
Sat in the corner,
Eating a Christmas pie;
He put in his thumb,
And pulled out a plum,
And said, What a good boy am I!

LXIII

I'll tell you a story
About Jack a Nory,
And now my story's begun;
I'll tell you another
About Jack and his brother,
And now my story is done.

LXIV

Jack be nimble,
Jack be quick,
Jack jump over
The candle stick.

LXV

Now I lay me down to sleep,
I pray the Lord my soul to keep;
And if I die before I wake,
I pray the Lord my soul to take.

LXVI

Oh that I were where I would be,
Then would I be where I am not;
But where I am there I must be,
And where I would be I can not.

LXVII

Jack and Jill went up the hill
To fetch a pail of water;
Jack fell down and broke his crown,
And Jill came tumbling after.

Up Jack got, and home did trot,
As fast as he could caper,
To old Dame Dob, who patched his nob
With vinegar and brown paper.

LXVIII

As I went over the water,
    The water went over me.
I saw two little blackbirds
    Sitting on a tree;
One called me a rascal,
    And one called me a thief,
I took up my little black stick
    And knocked out all their teeth.

LXIX

As I walked by myself
And talked to myself,
    Myself said unto me,
Look to thyself,
Take care of thyself,
    For nobody cares for thee.

I answered myself,
And said to myself
    In the self-same repartee,
Look to thyself,
Or not to thyself,
    The self-same thing will be.

LXX

Humpty Dumpty sat on a wall,
Humpty Dumpty had a great fall.
    All the king's horses,
    And all the king's men,
Couldn't put Humpty together again.

LXXI

Thirty white horses
    Upon a red hill.
    Now they tramp,
    Now they champ,
    Now they stand still.

LXXII

Hickory, dickory, dock,
The mouse ran up the clock.
    The clock struck one,
    The mouse ran down,
Hickory, dickory, dock.

LXXIII

I had a little hobby horse
And it was dapple gray,
Its head was made of pea-straw,
Its tail was made of hay.
I sold him to an old woman
For a copper groat,
And I'll not sing my song again
Without a new coat.

LXXIV

Hey diddle diddle,
The cat and the fiddle,
The cow jumped over the moon;
The little dog laughed
To see such sport,
And the dish ran away with the spoon.

LXXV

Oh, rare Harry Parry,
When will you marry?
When apples and pears are ripe.
I'll come to your wedding
Without any bidding,
And dance and sing all the night.

LXXVI

Hannah Bantry, in the pantry,
Gnawing at a mutton bone;
How she gnawed it,
How she clawed it,
When she found herself alone.

LXXVII

In marble halls as white as milk,
Lined with a skin as soft as silk,
Within a fountain crystal-clear,
A golden apple doth appear.
No doors there are to his stronghold,
Yet thieves break in and steal the gold.

LXXVIII

Grandfa' Grig
Had a pig,
In a field of clover;
Piggie died,
Grandfa' cried,
And all the fun was over.

LXXIX

Three wise men of Gotham,
They went to sea in a bowl,
And if the bowl had been stronger,
My song had been longer.

LXXX

Goosey Goosey Gander, where shall we wander,
Up stairs and down stairs and in my Lady's chamber.
Old father long legs will not say his prayers,
Take him by the left leg and throw him down the stairs.

LXXXI

Georgie Porgie, pudding and pie,
Kissed the girls and made them cry;
When the boys came out to play,
Georgie Porgie ran away.

LXXXII

If you are a gentleman,
As I suppose you be,
You'll neither laugh nor smile
At the tickling of your knee.

LXXXIII

Put your finger in Foxy's hole,
Foxy's not at home;
Foxy's at the back door
Picking at a bone.

LXXXIV

Doctor Foster went to Gloucester
In a shower of rain
He stepped in the puddle,
Right up to his middle,
And never went there again.

LXXXV

Fiddle-de-dee, fiddle-de-dee,
The fly shall marry the bumblebee.
They went to the church, and married was she:
The fly has married the bumblebee.

LXXXVI

My father died a month ago
And left me all his riches;
A feather bed, a wooden leg,
And a pair of leather breeches.
He left me a teapot without a spout,
A cup without a handle,
A tobacco pipe without a lid,
And half a farthing candle.

LXXXVII

Flour of England, fruit of Spain,
Met together in a shower of rain;
Put in a bag, tied round with a string;
If you'll tell me this riddle,
I'll give you a ring.

LXXXVIII

Eena, meena, mina, mo,
Catch a nigger by his toe;
If he hollers let him go,
Eena, meena, mina, mo.

LXXXIX

Mr. East gave a feast;
Mr. North laid the cloth;
Mr. West did his best;
Mr. South burnt his mouth
With eating a cold potato.

XC

Hark, hark,
The dogs do bark,
The beggars are coming to town;
Some in rags,
And some in jags,
And one in a velvet gown.

XCI

Ding, dong, bell,
Pussy's in the well.
Who put her in?
Little Johnny Green.
Who pulled her out?
Little Tommy Stout.
What a naughty boy was that,
To try to drown poor pussy cat,
Who never did any harm,
And killed the mice in his father's barn.

XCII

I had a little pony,
    His name was Dapple Gray;
I lent him to a lady
    To ride a mile away.
She whipped him, and she slashed him,
    She rode him through the mire;
I would not lend my pony now,
    For all the lady's hire.

XCIII

Cross-patch,
    Draw the latch,
Sit by the fire and spin;
    Take a cup,
    And drink it up,
Then call your neighbors in.

XCIV

Ride a cock-horse to Banbury Cross,
To see a fine lady upon a white horse;
Rings on her fingers and bells on her toes,
And she shall have music wherever she goes.

XCV

Barney Bodkin broke his nose,
Without feet we can't have toes;
Crazy folks are always mad,
Want of money makes us sad.

XCVI

As I suppose, and as I suppose,
    The barber shaved the Quaker,
And as I suppose, he cut off his nose,
    And lap't it up in a paper.

XCVII

When shall we be married,
    Billy, my pretty lad?
We'll be married tomorrow,
    If you think it good.
Shall we be married no sooner,
    Billy, my pretty lad?
Would you be married tonight?
    I think the girl is mad.

XCVIII

Baa, baa, black sheep,
    Have you any wool?
Yes, sir, yes, sir,
    Three bags full;
One for the master,
    And one for the dame,
And one for the little boy
    Who lives down the lane.

XCIX

Old King Cole
Was a merry old soul,
And a merry old soul was he;
    He called for his pipe,
    And he called for his bowl,
And he called for his fiddlers three.

C

There was an old crow
    Sat upon a clod;
That's the end of my song.
    That's odd.

Anonymous

Warning to Children

Children, if you dare to think
Of the greatness, rareness, muchness,
Fewness of this precious only
Endless world in which you say
You live, you think of things like this:
Blocks of slate enclosing dappled
Red and green, enclosing tawny
Yellow nets, enclosing white
And black acres of dominoes,
Where a neat brown paper parcel
Tempts you to untie the string.
In the parcel a small island,
On the island a large tree,
On the tree a husky fruit.
Strip the husk and cut the rind off:
In the center you will see
Blocks of slate enclosed by dappled
Red and green, enclosed by tawny
Yellow nets, enclosed by white
And black acres of dominoes,
Where the same brown paper parcel—
Children, leave the string untied!
For who dares undo the parcel
Finds himself at once inside it,
On the island, in the fruit,
Blocks of slate about his head,
Finds himself enclosed by dappled
Green and red, enclosed by yellow
Tawny nets, enclosed by black
And white acres of dominoes,
But the same brown paper parcel
Still untied upon his knee.
And, if he then should dare to think
Of the fewness, muchness, rareness,
Greatness of this endless only
Precious world in which he says
He lives—he then unties the string.

Robert Graves

PART THIRTEEN

Sally in Our Alley

Sally in Our Alley

Of all the girls that are so smart
  There's none like pretty Sally;
She is the darling of my heart,
  And she lives in our alley.
There is no lady in the land
  Is half so sweet as Sally;
She is the darling of my heart,
  And she lives in our alley.

Her father he makes cabbage nets,
  And through the streets does cry 'em;
Her mother she sells laces long
  To such as please to buy 'em;
But sure such folks could ne'er beget
  So sweet a girl as Sally!
She is the darling of my heart,
  And she lives in our alley.

When she is by, I leave my work,
    I love her so sincerely;
My master comes like any Turk,
    And bangs me most severely:
But let him bang his bellyful,
    I'll bear it all for Sally;
She is the darling of my heart,
    And she lives in our alley.

Of all the days that's in the week
    I dearly love but one day—
And that's the day that comes betwixt
    A Saturday and Monday;
For then I'm dressed all in my best
    To walk abroad with Sally;
She is the darling of my heart,
    And she lives in our alley.

My master carries me to church,
    And often am I blamèd
Because I leave him in the lurch
    As soon as text is namèd;
I leave the church in sermon-time
    And slink away to Sally;
She is the darling of my heart,
    And she lives in our alley.

When Christmas comes about again,
    O, then I shall have money;
I'll hoard it up, and box it all,
    I'll give it to my honey:
I would it were ten thousand pound,
    I'd give it all to Sally;
She is the darling of my heart,
    And she lives in our alley.

My master and the neighbors all
    Make game of me and Sally,
And, but for her, I'd better be
    A slave and row a galley;
But when my seven long years are out,
    O, then I'll marry Sally;
O, then we'll wed, and then we'll bed—
    But not in our alley!

Henry Carey

The Milkmaid

Under a daisied bank
There stands a rich red ruminating cow,
    And hard against her flank
A cotton-hooded milkmaid bends her brow.

The flowery river-ooze
Upheaves and falls; the milk purrs in the pail;
    Few pilgrims but would choose
The peace of such a life in such a vale.

The maid breathes words—to vent,
It seems, her sense of Nature's scenery,
    Of whose life, sentiment,
And essence, very part itself is she.

She bends a glance of pain,
And, at a moment, lets escape a tear;
    Is it that passing train,
Whose alien whirr offends her country ear?—

Nay! Phyllis does not dwell
On visual and familiar things like these;
    What moves her is the spell
Of inner themes and inner poetries:

Could but by Sunday morn
Her gay new gown come, meads might dry to dun,
    Trains shriek till ears were torn,
If Fred would not prefer that Other One.

Thomas Hardy

The Hour Glass

Consider this small dust, here in the glass,
    By atoms moved:
Could you believe that this the body was
    Of one that loved;
And in his mistress' flame playing like a fly,
Was turned to cinders by her eye:
Yes; and in death, as life unblessed,
    To have it expressed,
Even ashes of lovers find no rest.

Ben Jonson

Iambica

Unhappy Verse, the witness of my unhappy state,
Make thyself flutt'ring wings of thy fast flying
Thought, and fly forth unto my Love, wheresoever she be:
Whether lying restless in heavy bed, or else
   Sitting so cheerless at the cheerful board, or else
   Playing alone careless on her heavenly virginals.
If in bed, tell her, that my eyes can take no rest;
   If at board, tell her, that my mouth can eat no meat;
   If at her virginals, tell her, I can hear no mirth.
Askéd, why? say: Waking love suffereth no sleep:
   Say, that raging love doth appal the weak stomach:
   Say, that lamenting love marreth the musical.
Tell her, that her pleasures were wont to lull me asleep:
   Tell her, that her beauty was wont to feed mine eyes:
   Tell her, that her sweet tongue was wont to make me mirth.
Now do I nightly waste, wanting my kindly rest:
   Now do I daily starve, wanting my lively food:
   Now do I always die, wanting thy timely mirth.
And if I waste, who will bewail my heavy chance?
   And if I starve, who will record my curséd end?
   And if I die, who will say: "This was, Immerito"?

Edmund Spenser

Fife Tune

(6/8) for Sixth Platoon, 308th I.T.C.

One morning in spring
We marched from Devizes
All shapes and all sizes
Like beads on a string,
But yet with a swing
We trod the bluemetal
And full of high fettle
We started to sing.

She ran down the stair
A twelve-year-old darling
And laughing and calling
She tossed her bright hair;

Then silent to stare
At the men flowing past her—
There were all she could
   master
Adoring her there.

It's seldom I'll see
A sweeter or prettier;
I doubt we'll forget her
In two years or three.
And lucky he'll be
She takes for a lover
While we are far over
The treacherous sea.

John Manifold

For Anne Gregory

"Never shall a young man,
Thrown into despair
By those great honey-colored
Ramparts at your ear,
Love you for yourself alone
And not your yellow hair."

"But I can get a hair-dye
And set such color there,
Brown, or black, or carrot
That young men in despair
May love me for myself alone
And not my yellow hair."

"I heard an old religious man
But yesternight declare
That he had found a text to prove
That only God, my dear,
Could love you for yourself alone
And not your yellow hair."

William Butler Yeats

The Trees So High

All the trees they are so high,
  The leaves they are so green,
The day is past and gone, sweetheart,
  That you and I have seen.
      It is cold winter's night,
      You and I must bide alone:
        Whilst my pretty lad is young
        And is growing.

In a garden as I walked,
  I heard them laugh and call;
There were four and twenty playing there,
  They played with bat and ball.
      O the rain on the roof,
      Here and I must make my moan:
        Whilst my pretty lad is young
        And is growing.

I listen'd in the garden,
  I lookèd over the wall;
'Midst five and twenty gallants there
  My love exceedeth all.
      O the wind on the thatch,
      Here and I alone must weep:
        Whilst my pretty lad is young
        And is growing.

O father, father dear,
  Great wrong to me is done,
That I should married be this day,
  Before the set of sun.
      At the huffle of the gale,
      Here I toss and cannot sleep:
        Whilst my pretty lad is young
        And is growing.

My daughter, daughter dear,
  If better be, more fit,
I'll send him to the court awhile,
  To point his pretty wit.
      But the snow, snowflakes fall,
      O and I am chill as dead:
        Whilst my pretty lad is young
        And is growing.

To let the lovely ladies know
　　They may not touch and taste,
I'll bind a bunch of ribbons red
　　About his little waist.
　　　　　But the raven hoarsely croaks,
　　　　　And I shiver in my bed;
　　　　　　　Whilst my pretty lad is young
　　　　　　　And is growing.

I married was, alas,
　　A lady high to be,
In court and stall and stately hall,
　　And bower of tapestry.
　　　　　But the bell did only knell,
　　　　　And I shudder as one cold:
　　　　　　　When I wed the pretty lad
　　　　　　　Not done growing.

At fourteen he wedded was,
　　A father at fifteen,
At sixteen's face was white as milk,
　　And then his grave was green;
　　　　　And the daisies were outspread,
　　　　　And buttercups of gold,
　　　　　　　O'er my pretty lad so young
　　　　　　　Now ceased growing. *Anonymous*

Madrigals

I

Since Bonny-boots was dead, that so divinely
　　Could toot and foot it, (O he did it finely!)
　　　　We ne'er went more a-Maying
　　　　Nor had that sweet fa-laing.
　　　　　　　Anthony and William Holborne

II

O I do love, then kiss me;
And after I'll not miss thee
With bodies' lovely meeting
To dally, pretty sweeting.
Though I am somewhat agéd,
Yet is not love assuagéd:
But with sweet ardent clips,
I'll lay thee on the lips,
And make thee ever swear:
Farewell, old bachelor.　　　　*Robert Jones*

III

Ay me, alas, heigh ho, heigh ho!
Thus doth Messalina go
Up and down the house a-crying,
For her monkey lies a-dying.
Death, thou art too cruel
To bereave her jewel,
Or to make a seizure
Of her only treasure.
If her monkey die,
She will sit and cry,
Fie fie fie fie fie!   *Thomas Weelkes*

IV

Ha ha! ha ha! This world doth pass
  Most merrily I'll be sworn,
For many an honest Indian ass
  Goes for a unicorn.
          Fara diddle dyno,
          This is idle fyno.

Tie hie! tie hie! O sweet delight!
  He tickles this age that can
Call Tullia's ape a marmasyte
  And Leda's goose a swan.
          Fara diddle dyno,
          This is idle fyno.

So so! so so! Fine English days!
  For false play's no reproach,
For he that doth the coachman praise
  May safely use the coach.
          Fara diddle dyno,
          This is idle fyno.   *Thomas Weelkes*

V

My mistress is as fair as fine,
  Milk-white fingers, cherry nose.
Like twinkling day-stars looks her eyne,
  Lightening all things where she goes.
Fair as Phoebe, though not so fickle,
Smooth as glass, though not so brickle.

My heart is like a ball of snow
  Melting at her lukewarm sight;
Her fiery lips like night-worms glow,
  Shining clear as candle-light.
Neat she is, no feather lighter;
Bright she is, no daisy whiter.
                              Thomas Ravenscroft

VI

My mistress frowns when she should play;
I'll please her with a Fa la la.
Sometimes she chides, but I straightway
Present her with a Fa la la.

You lovers that have loves astray
May win them with a Fa la la.
Quick music's best, for still they say
None pleaseth like your Fa la la.

John Hilton

To Ladies' Eyes

To ladies' eyes around, boy,
    We can't refuse, we can't refuse,
Tho' bright eyes so abound, boy,
    'Tis hard to choose, 'tis hard to choose.
For thick as stars that lighten
    Yon airy bow'rs, yon airy bow'rs,
The countless eyes that brighten
    This earth of ours, this earth of ours.
But fill the cup—where'er, boy,
    Our choice may fall, our choice may fall,
We're sure to find love there, boy,
    So drink them all! so drink them all!

Some looks there are so holy,
    They seem but giv'n, they seem but giv'n
As shining beacons, solely
    To light to heav'n, to light to heav'n.
While some—oh! ne'er believe them—
    With tempting ray, with tempting ray,
Would lead us (God forgive them!)
    The other way, the other way.
But fill the cup—where'er, boy,
    Our choice may fall, our choice may fall,
We're sure to find love there, boy,
    So drink them all! so drink them all!

In some, as in a mirror,
    Love seems portray'd, love seems portray'd,
But shun the flattering error,
    'Tis but his shade, 'tis but his shade.
Himself has fix'd his dwelling
    In eyes we know, in eyes we know,

And lips—but this is telling—
  So here they go! so here they go!
Fill up, fill up—where'er, boy,
  Our choice may fall, our choice may fall,
We're sure to find love there, boy,
  So drink them all! so drink them all!

Thomas Moore

Out upon It, I Have Lov'd

Out upon it, I have lov'd
  Three whole days together;
And am like to love three more,
  If it prove fair weather.

Time shall molt away his wings
  Ere he shall discover
In the whole wide world again
  Such a constant lover.

But the spite on't is, no praise
  Is due at all to me:
Love with me had made no stays
  Had it any been but she.

Had it any been but she
  And that very face,
There had been at least ere this
  A dozen dozen in her place.

Sir John Suckling

To His Coy Mistress

Had we but world enough, and time,
This coyness, lady, were no crime.
We would sit down, and think which way
To walk, and pass our long love's day.
Thou by the Indian Ganges' side
Should'st rubies find: I by the tide
Of Humber would complain. I would
Love you ten years before the Flood,
And you should, if you please, refuse
Till the conversion of the Jews.
My vegetable love should grow
Vaster than empires, and more slow.
An hundred years should go to praise

Thine eyes, and on thy forehead gaze:
Two hundred to adore each breast:
But thirty thousand to the rest;
An age at least to every part,
And the last age should show your heart.
For, lady, you deserve this state,
Nor would I love at lower rate.
  But at my back I always hear
Time's wingèd chariot hurrying near:
And yonder all before us lie
Deserts of vast eternity.
Thy beauty shall no more be found;
Nor, in thy marble vault, shall sound
My echoing song: then worms shall try
That long-preserved virginity,
And your quaint honor turn to dust,
And into ashes all my lust.
The grave's a fine and private place,
But none, I think, do there embrace.
  Now, therefore, while the youthful hue
Sits on thy skin like morning dew,
And while thy willing soul transpires
At every pore with instant fires,
Now let us sport us while we may;
And now, like amorous birds of prey,
Rather at once our Time devour,
Than languish in his slow-chapt power.
Let us roll all our strength and all
Our sweetness up into one ball,
And tear our pleasures with rough strife
Thorough the iron gates of life.
Thus, though we cannot make our sun
Stand still, yet we will make him run.

Andrew Marvell

There Is a Garden in Her Face

There is a garden in her face
Where roses and white lilies grow;
A heavenly paradise is that place
Wherein all pleasant fruits do flow.
   There cherries grow which none may buy,
   Till "Cherry ripe" themselves do cry.

Those cherries fairly do enclose
Of orient pearl a double row,
Which when her lovely laughter shows,
They look like rosebuds filled with snow;
   Yet them nor peer nor prince can buy,
   Till "Cherry ripe" themselves do cry.

Her eyes like angels watch them still,
Her brows like bended bows do stand,
Threatening with piercing frowns to kill
All that attempt, with eye or hand,
   Those sacred cherries to come nigh
   Till "Cherry ripe" themselves do cry.

Thomas Campion

Song to Celia

Come, my Celia, let us prove,
While we may, the sports of love;
Time will not be ours for ever:
He at length our good will sever.
Spend not then his gifts in vain:
Suns that set, may rise again;
But if once we lose this light,
'Tis with us perpetual night.
Why should we defer our joys?
Fame and rumor are but toys.
Cannot we delude the eyes
Of a few poor household spies?
Or his easier ears beguile,
Thus removèd by our wile?
'Tis no sin love's fruits to steal,
But the sweet theft to reveal:
To be taken, to be seen,
These have crimes accounted been.

Ben Jonson

Song

Go and catch a falling star,
    Get with child a mandrake root,
Tell me where all past years are,
    Or who cleft the Devil's foot,
Teach me to heare Mermaids singing,
Or to keep off envy's stinging,
                    And finde
                    What winde
Serves to advance an honest minde.

If thou beest born to strange sights,
    Things invisible to see,
Ride ten thousand days and nights,
    Till age snow white haires on thee,
Thou, when thou return'st, wilt tell me
All strange wonders that befell thee,
                    And sweare
                    No where
Lives a woman true and faire.

If thou findst one, let me know,
    Such a pilgrimage were sweet;
Yet do not, I would not go,
    Though at next doore we might meet;
Though she were true when you met her,
And last till you write your letter,
                    Yet she
                    Will be
False, ere I come, to two or three.

                            John Donne

O Western Wind

O western wind, when wilt thou blow,
That the small rain down can rain?
Christ, if my love were in my arms
And I in my bed again!

Anonymous

Love Not Me

Love not me for comely grace,
For my pleasing eye or face,
Nor for any outward part:
No, nor for a constant heart!
For these may fail or turn to ill:
    So thou and I shall sever.
Keep therefore a true woman's eye,
And love me still, but you know not why!
So hast thou the same reason still
    To doat upon me ever.

Anonymous

There Is a Lady Sweet and Kind

There is a Lady sweet and kind,
Was never face so pleased my mind;
I did but see her passing by,
And yet I love her till I die.

Her gesture, motion, and her smiles,
Her wit, her voice my heart beguiles,
Beguiles my heart, I know not why,
And yet I love her till I die.

Cupid is wingèd and doth range,
Her country so my love doth change:
But change she earth, or change she sky,
Yet will I love her till I die.

Anonymous

My Love in Her Attire

My love in her attire doth show her wit,
    It doth so well become her:
For every season she hath dressings fit,
    For winter, spring, and summer.
    No beauty she doth miss,
    When all her robes are on:
    But Beauty's self she is,
    When all her robes are gone.

Anonymous

The Passionate Shepherd to His Love

Come live with me and be my love,
And we will all the pleasures prove,
That valleys, groves, hills and fields,
Woods or steepy mountains yields.

And we will sit upon the rocks,
Seeing the shepherds feed their flocks
By shallow rivers, to whose falls
Melodious birds sing madrigals.

And I will make thee beds of roses,
And a thousand fragrant posies,
A cap of flowers and a kirtle
Embroidered all with leaves of myrtle;

A gown made of the finest wool,
Which from our pretty lambs we pull;
Fair-linèd slippers for the cold,
With buckles of the purest gold;

A belt of straw and ivy buds,
With coral clasps and amber studs;
And if these pleasures may thee move,
Come live with me and be my love.

The shepherd swains shall dance and sing
For thy delight each May morning;
If these delights thy mind may move,
Then live with me and be my love.
Christopher Marlowe

The Nymph's Reply to the Shepherd

If all the world and love were young
And truth in every shepherd's tongue,
These pretty pleasures might me move
To live with thee and be thy love.

Time drives the flocks from field to fold
When rivers rage and rocks grow cold,
And Philomel becometh dumb;
The rest complain of cares to come.

The flowers do fade, and wanton fields
To wayward winter reckoning yields;

A honey tongue, a heart of gall,
Is fancy's spring, but sorrow's fall.

Thy gowns, thy shoes, thy beds of roses,
Thy cap, thy kirtle, and thy posies
Soon break, soon wither, soon forgotten,
In folly ripe, in reason rotten.

Thy belt of straw and ivy buds,
Thy coral clasps and amber studs,
All these in me no means can move
To come to thee and be thy love.

But could youth last and love still breed,
Had joys no date nor age no need,
Then these delights my mind might move
To live with thee and be thy love.

Sir Walter Raleigh

Song

I can't be talkin' of love, dear,
I can't be talkin' of love.
If there be one thing I can't talk of
That one thing do be love.

But that's not sayin' that I'm not lovin'—
Still water, you know, runs deep,
An' I do be lovin' so deep, dear,
I be lovin' you in my sleep.

But I can't be talkin' of love, dear,
I can't be talkin' of love,
If there be one thing I can't talk of
That one thing do be love.

Esther Mathews

Woman

Woman, beguiling man, herself beguiles
  With hopes that all too quickly turn to fears.
She lights a conflagration with her smiles
  And vainly seeks to quench it with her tears.

C. D. B. Ellis

An Immorality

Sing we for love and idleness,
Naught else is worth the having.

Though I have been in many a land,
There is naught else in living.

And I would rather have my sweet,
Though rose-leaves die of grieving,

Than do high deeds in Hungary
To pass all men's believing.

Ezra Pound

Kissin'

Some say kissin's ae sin,
  But I say, not at a';
For it's been in the warld
  Ever sin' there were twa.
If it werena lawfu',
  Lawyers wadna' 'low it;
If it werena haly,
  Meenisters wadna' dae it;
If it werena modest,
  Maidens wadna' taste it;
If it werena plenty,
  Puir folk couldna' hae it.

Anonymous

Jenny Kiss'd Me

Jenny kiss'd me when we met,
  Jumping from the chair she sat in;
Time, you thief, who love to get
  Sweets into your list, put that in!
Say I'm weary, say I'm sad,
  Say that health and wealth have miss'd me,
Say I'm growing old, but add,
  Jenny kiss'd me.

Leigh Hunt

PART FOURTEEN

Songs, Lyrics, and Ballads
for the Weekend

Mademoiselle from Armentières

Two German officers crossed the Rhine,
Parlez vous,
Two German officers crossed the Rhine,
Parlez vous,
Two German officers crossed the Rhine,
To kiss the women and drink the wine,
Inky, dinky, parlez vous.

They came to an inn at the top of the rise,
Parlez vous,
A famous French inn of enormous size,
Parlez vous,

They saw a maiden all dimples and sighs,
Then both together said, "Damn her eyes."
    Inky, dinky, parlez vous.

Oh, landlord, have you a daughter fair,
            Parlez vous,
Oh, landlord, have you a daughter fair,
            Parlez vous,
Oh, landlord, have you a daughter fair,
With lily-white arm, and golden hair?
            Inky, dinky, parlez vous.

Anonymous

I Got a Robe

I got a robe, you got a robe;
All of God's children got a robe;
When I get to Heaven goin' to put on my robe,
Goin' to shout all over God's Heav'n.

Chorus: Heav'n n n n, Heav'n n n n
        (Ev'ry body talkin' 'bout heav'n ain't goin'
            there!)
        Heav'n, Heav'n—Goin' to shout all over
        God's Heav'n.

I got a shoes, you got a shoes,
All of God's children got a shoes;
When I get to Heav'n goin' to put on my shoes,
Goin' to walk all over God's Heav'n.

I got a harp, you got a harp,
All of God's children got a harp;
When I get to Heav'n goin' to play on my harp,
Goin' to play all over God's Heav'n.

I got a song, you got a song,
All of God's children got a song;
When I get to Heav'n goin' to sing a new song,
Goin' to sing all over God's Heav'n.

Anonymous

Billy Boy

Where have ye been all the day, Billy Boy, Billy Boy?
Where have ye been all the day, me Billy Boy?
        I've been walking all the day
        With me charming Nancy Grey
        And me Nancy kittled me fancy, Oh, me charming
            Billy Boy.

Can she cook a bit o' steak, Billy Boy?
Can she cook a bit o' steak, me Billy Boy?
    She can cook a bit o' steak,
    Aye, and make a girdle cake.
    And me Nancy kittled me fancy, Oh me charming
        Billy Boy.

Is she fit to be your wife, Billy Boy, Billy Boy?
Is she fit to be your wife, me Billy Boy?
    She's as fit to by my wife
    As the fork is to the knife,
    And me Nancy kittled me fancy, Oh, me charming
        Billy Boy.

Did she lie close unto thee, Billy Boy, Billy Boy?
Did she lie close unto thee, me Billy Boy?
    Yes, she lay close unto me
    As the bark is to the tree.
    And me Nancy kittled me fancy, Oh, me charming
        Billy Boy.

Anonymous

John Kinsella's Lament for Mrs. Mary Moore

A bloody and a sudden end,
    Gunshot or a noose,
For death who takes what man would keep,
    Leaves what man would lose.
He might have had my sister,
    My cousins by the score,
But nothing satisfied the fool
    But my dear Mary Moore,
None other knows what pleasures man
    At table or in bed.
What shall I do for pretty girls
    Now my old bawd is dead?

Though stiff to strike a bargain,
    Like an old Jew man,
Her bargain struck we laughed and talked
    And emptied many a can;
And O! but she had stories,
    Though not for the priest's ear,
To keep the soul of man alive,
    Banish age and care,

And being old she put a skin
   On everything she said.
What shall I do for pretty girls
   Now my old bawd is dead?

The priests have got a book that says
   But for Adam's sin
Eden's Garden would be there,
   And I there within.
No expectation fails there,
   No pleasing habit ends,
No man grows old, no girl grows cold,
   But friends walk by friends.
Who quarrels over halfpennies
   That plucks the trees for bread?
What shall I do for pretty girls
   Now my old bawd is dead?

                        William Butler Yeats

One More River

  The animals came in two by two,
     Vive la compagnie.
  The centipede with the kangaroo,
     Vive la compagnie.

Chorus: One more river, and that's the river
        of Jordan,
        One more river. There's one more
        river to cross.

  The animals came in three by three,
     Vive la compagnie.
  The elephant on the back of the flea,
     Vive la compagnie.

  The animals came in four by four,
  The camel, he got stuck in the door.
  Some had water and some had wine.
  If you want any more you must sing it again.
                        Anonymous

Sumer Is Icumen In

Sumer is icumen in,
    Lhudè sing cuccu;
Groweth sed and bloweth med
    And springth the wudè nu.
        Sing cuccu!
Awè bleteth after lomb,
    Lhouth after calvè cu;
Bulluc sterteth, buckè verteth;
    Murie sing cuccu.
        Cuccu, cuccu,
    Wel singès thu, cuccu,
    Ne swik thu naver nu.
Sing cuccu nu! Sing cuccu!
Sing cuccu! Sing cuccu nu!

Anonymous

They Were Only Playing Leapfrog

They were only playing leapfrog,
They were only playing leapfrog,
They were only playing leapfrog,
When one grasshopper jumped up on the other grasshopper's
    back.

Anonymous

Foggy, Foggy Dew

When I was a bachelor, I lived by myself
And I worked at the weaver's trade;
The only, only thing that I ever did wrong
Was to woo a fair young maid.
I wooed her in the winter time,
And in the summer too;
And the only, only thing that I ever did wrong
Was to keep her from the foggy, foggy dew.

One night she came to my bedside
Where I lay fast asleep;
She laid her head upon my bed,
And then began to weep.
She sighed, she cried, she damn near died,
She said—"What shall I do?"—
So I hauled her into bed and I covered up her head,
Just to save her from the foggy, foggy dew.

Oh, I am a bachelor, I live with my son,
And we work at the weaver's trade;
And every, every time that I look into his eyes,
He reminds me of that maid.
He reminds me of the winter time,
And of the summer too;
And the many, many times that I held her in my arms,
Just to keep her from the foggy, foggy dew.

Anonymous

Oh, Give Me a Home Where the Buffalo Roam

Oh, give me a home where the buffalo roam,
Where the deer and the antelope play,
Where seldom is heard a discouraging word,
And the skies are not cloudy all day.

Chorus: Home, home on the range,
   Where the deer and the antelope play,
   Where seldom is heard a discouraging word,
   And the skies are not cloudy all day.

How often at night when the heavens are bright
With the light of the glittering stars,
Have I stood there amazed and ask'd as I gazed,
If their glory exceeds that of ours.

Anonymous

Cocaine Lil and Morphine Sue

Did you ever hear about Cocaine Lil?
She lived in Cocaine town on Cocaine hill,
She had a cocaine dog and a cocaine cat,
They fought all night with a cocaine rat.

She had cocaine hair on her cocaine head.
She had a cocaine dress that was poppy red:
She wore a snowbird hat and sleighriding clothes,
On her coat she wore a crimson, cocaine rose.

Big gold chariots on the Milky Way,
Snakes and elephants silver and gray.
Oh the cocaine blues they make me sad,
Oh the cocaine blues make me feel bad.

Lil went to a snow party one cold night,
And the way she sniffed was sure a fright.
There was Hophead Mag with Dopey Slim,
Kankakee Liz and Yen Shee Jim.

There was Morphine Sue and the Poppy Face Kid,
Climbed up snow ladders and down they slid;
There was the Stepladder Kit, a good six feet,
And the Sleighriding Sister who were hard to beat.

Along in the morning about half-past three
They were all lit up like a Christmas tree;
Lil got home and started for bed,
Took another sniff and it knocked her dead.

They laid her out in her cocaine clothes:
She wore a snowbird hat with a crimson rose;
On her headstone you'll find this refrain:
"She died as she lived, sniffing cocaine."

Anonymous

Annie Laurie

Maxwelton's braes are bonnie
Where early fa's the dew,
And it's there that Annie Laurie
Gie'd me her promise true;
Gie'd me her promise true,
Which ne'er forgot will be;
And for bonnie Annie Laurie
I'd lay me doun and dee.

Her brow is like the snaw drift;
Her throat is like the swan;
Her face it is the fairest
That e'er the sun shone on—
That e'er the sun shone on—
And dark blue is her ee;
And for bonnie Annie Laurie
I'd lay me doun and dee.

Like dew on the gowan lying
Is the fa' o' her fairy feet;
And like the winds in summer sighing,
Her voice is low and sweet—
Her voice is low and sweet—
And she's a' the world to me;
And for bonnie Annie Laurie
I'd lay me doun and dee.

William Douglas

Down in the Valley

Down in the valley,
   Valley so low,
   Hang your head over,
   Hear the wind blow.
Hear the wind blow, love,
Hear the wind blow,
Hang your head over,
Hear the wind blow.

If you don't love me,
   Love whom you please,
   But throw your arms
      around me,
   Give my heart ease.
Give my heart ease, dear,
Give my heart ease,
Throw your arms round
   me,
Give my heart ease.

Down in the valley
   Walking between,
   Telling our story,
   Here's what it sings—
Roses of sunshine,
Violets of dew,
Angels in heaven,
Know I love you.

Build me a castle,
   Forty feet high,
   So I can see her
   As she goes by,
As she goes by, dear,
As she goes by.
So I can see her
As she goes by.

Bird in a cage, love,
   Bird in a cage,
   Dying for freedom,
   Ever a slave.
Ever a slave, dear,
Ever a slave,
Dying for freedom,
Ever a slave.

Write me a letter;
   Send it by mail;
   And back it in care of
   The Barbourville jail.
Barbourville jail, love,
Barbourville jail,
And back it in care of
The Barbourville jail.

Anonymous

Titwillow

On a tree by a river a little tomtit
      Sang "Willow, titwillow, titwillow!"
And I said to him, "Dicky-bird, why do you sit
      Singing 'Willow, titwillow, titwillow'?
Is it a weakness of intellect, birdie?" I cried,
"Or a rather tough worm in your little inside?"
With a shake of his poor little head he replied,
      "Oh, willow, titwillow, titwillow!"

He slapped at his chest, as he sat on that bough,
      Singing "Willow, titwillow, titwillow!"
And a cold perspiration bespangled his brow,
      Oh, willow, titwillow, titwillow!
He sobbed and he sighed, and a gurgle he gave,
Then he threw himself into the billowy wave,
And an echo arose from the suicide's grave—
      "Oh, willow, titwillow, titwillow!"

Now, I feel just as sure as I'm sure that my name
      Isn't Willow, titwillow, titwillow,
That 'twas blighted affection that made him exclaim,
      "Oh, willow, titwillow, titwillow!"
And if you remain callous and obdurate, I
Shall perish as he did, and you will know why,
Though I probably shall not exclaim as I die,
      "Oh, willow, titwillow, titwillow!"

Sir W. S. Gilbert

Broom, Green Broom

There was an old man and he lived in a wood,
    And his trade it was making of broom, of broom,
And he had a naughty boy, Jack, to his son,
    And he lay in bed till 'twas noon, 'twas noon,
      And he lay in bed till 'twas noon.

The father was vext and sorely perplext,
    With passion he enters the room, the room,
"Come, sirrah," he cried, "I'll leather your hide,
    If you will not go gather green broom, green broom,
      If you will not go gather green broom."

Master Jack being sly, he got up by and by,
    And went into the town to cry, "Broom, green broom."
So loud did he call, and so loudly did bawl,

"Pretty maids, do you want any broom, green broom?
   Pretty maids, do you want any broom?"

A lady looked out of her lattice so high,
   And spied Jack a-selling of broom, green broom,
Says she, "You young blade, won't you give up your trade,
   And marry a maid in full bloom, full bloom?
     And marry a maid in full bloom?"

So they sent for the parson without more delay,
   And married they were in the room, the room,
There was eating and drink, and Jack, with a wink,
   "This is better than cutting of broom, green broom,
     This is better than cutting of broom."

Anonymous

Spring

When daisies pied and violets blue
   And lady-smocks all silver-white
And cuckoo buds of yellow hue
   Do paint the meadows with delight,
The cuckoo then, on every tree,
Mocks married men; for thus sings he,
     Cuckoo;
Cuckoo, cuckoo: O word of fear,
Unpleasing to a married ear.

When shepherds pipe on oaten straws,
   And merry larks are plowmen's clocks,
When turtles tread, and rooks, and daws,
   And maidens bleach their summer smocks,
The cuckoo then, on every tree,
Mocks married men; for thus sings he,
     Cuckoo;
Cuckoo, cuckoo: O word of fear,
Unpleasing to a married ear.

William Shakespeare

When That I Was and a Little Tiny Boy

When that I was and a little tiny boy,
  With hey, ho, the wind and the rain,
A foolish thing was but a toy,
  For the rain it raineth every day.

But when I came to man's estate
  With hey, ho, the wind and the rain,
'Gainst knaves and thieves men shut the gate,
  For the rain it raineth every day.

But when I came, alas! to wive,
  With hey, ho, the wind and the rain,
By swaggering could I never thrive
  For the rain it raineth every day.

But when I came unto my beds,
  With hey, ho, the wind and the rain,
With tosspots still had drunken heads,
  For the rain it raineth every day.

A great while ago the world begun,
  With hey, ho, the wind and the rain,
But that's all one, our play is done,
  And we'll strive to please you every day.

William Shakespeare

Green Grow the Rashes, O!

There's nought but care on ev'ry han';
  In ev'ry hour that passes, O;
What signifies the life o' man,
  And 'twere na for the lasses, O!

Chorus: *Green grow the rashes, O;*
         Green grow the rashes, O;
         The sweetest hours that e'er I spend,
         Are spent amang the lasses, O.

The war'ly race may riches chase,
  An' riches still may fly them, O;
An' tho' at last they catch them fast,
  Their hearts can ne'er enjoy them, O.

But gie me a cannie hour at e'en,
  My arms about my dearie, O;

An' war'ly cares an' war'ly men
May a' gae tapsalteerie, O!

For you sae douce, ye sneer at this;
Ye're nought but senseless asses, O:
The wisest man that warl' e'er saw,
He dearly lov'd the lasses, O.

Auld Nature swears, the lovely dears
Her noblest work she classes, O:
Her prentice han' she try'd on man,
And then she made the lasses, O.

Robert Burns

Green Grow the Rushes, O!

I'll sing you twelve O
Green grow the rushes O
What are your twelve O?
Twelve for the twelve apostles
Eleven for the eleven that went up to heaven
Ten for the ten commandments
Nine for the nine bright shiners
Eight for the eight bold rainers
Seven for the seven stars in the sky
Six for the six proud walkers
Five for the symbol at your door
Four for the Gospel makers
Three, three for the rivals
Two, two for the lily-white boys
Clothed all in green O
One is one and all alone
And evermore shall be so.

Anonymous

It Was a Lover and His Lass

It was a lover and his lass,
   With a hey, and a ho, and hey nonino,
That o'er the green cornfield did pass
   In the spring time, the only pretty ring time,
When birds do sing, hey ding a ding, ding:
Sweet lovers love the spring.

Between the acres of the rye,
   With a hey, and a ho, and hey nonino,
These pretty country folk would lie,
   In the spring time, the only pretty ring time,
When birds do sing, hey ding a ding, ding:
Sweet lovers love the spring.

This carol they began that hour,
   With a hey, and a ho, and hey nonino,
How that a life was but a flower
   In the spring time, the only pretty ring time,
When birds do sing, hey ding a ding, ding:
Sweet lovers love the spring.

And therefore take the present time,
   With a hey, and a ho, and a hey nonino,
For love is crowned with the prime
   In the spring time, the only pretty ring time,
When birds do sing, hey ding a ding, ding:
Sweet lovers love the spring.

                                        William Shakespeare

Who Is Silvia

Who is Silvia? what is she,
   That all our swains commend her?
Holy, fair, and wise is she;
   The heaven such grace did lend her,
That she might admiréd be.

Is she kind as she is fair?
   For beauty lives with kindness.
Love doth to her eyes repair,
   To help him of his blindness,
And, being help'd, inhabits there.

Then to Silvia let us sing,
   That Silvia is excelling;

She excels each mortal thing
   Upon the dull earth dwelling:
To her let us garlands bring.

William Shakespeare

Sigh No More, Ladies

Sigh no more, ladies, sigh no more,
   Men were deceivers ever,
One foot in sea and one on shore,
   To one thing constant never:
Then sigh not so, but let them go,
   And be you blithe and bonny,
Converting all your sounds of woe
   Into Hey nonny, nonny.

Sing no more ditties, sing no more,
   Of dumps so dull and heavy;
The fraud of men was ever so,
   Since summer first was leafy:
Then sigh not so, but let them go,
   And be you blithe and bonny,
Converting all your sounds of woe
   Into Hey nonny, nonny.

William Shakespeare

Young and Old

When all the world is young, lad,
   And all the trees are green;
And every goose a swan, lad,
   And every lass a queen;
Then hey for boot and horse, lad,
   And round the world away;
Young blood must have its course, lad,
   And every dog his day.

When all the world is old, lad,
   And all the trees are brown;
And all the sport is stale, lad,
   And all the wheels run down;
Creep home, and take your place there,
   The spent and maimed among:
God grant you find one face there,
   You loved when all was young.

Charles Kingsley

To Celia

Drink to me only with thine eyes,
    And I will pledge with mine;
Or leave a kiss but in the cup
    And I'll not look for wine.
The thirst that from the soul doth rise
    Doth ask a drink divine;
But might I of Jove's nectar sup,
    I would not change for thine.

I sent thee late a rosy wreath,
    Not so much honoring thee
As giving it a hope that there
    It could not withered be;
But thou thereon didst only breathe
    And sent'st it back to me;
Since when it grows, and smells, I swear
    Not of itself but thee!

Ben Jonson

Sweet Afton

Flow gently, sweet Afton! amang thy green braes,
Flow gently, I'll sing thee a song in thy praise;
My Mary's asleep by thy murmuring stream,
Flow gently, sweet Afton, disturb not her dream.

Thou stock dove whose echo resounds thro' the glen,
Ye wild whistling blackbirds, in yon thorny den,
Thou green crested lapwing thy screaming forbear,
I charge you, disturb not my slumbering fair.

How lofty, sweet Afton, thy neighboring hills,
Far mark'd with the courses of clear, winding rills;
There daily I wander as noon rises high,
My flocks and my Mary's sweet cot in my eye.

How pleasant thy banks and green valleys below,
Where, wild in the woodlands, the primroses blow;
There oft, as mild evening weeps over the lea,
The sweet-scented birk shades my Mary and me.

Thy crystal stream, Afton, how lovely it glides,
And winds by the cot where my Mary resides;
How wanton thy waters her snowy feet lave,
As, gathering sweet flowerets, she stems thy clear wave.

Flow gently, sweet Afton, amang thy green braes,
Flow gently, sweet river, the theme of my lays;
My Mary's asleep by thy murmuring stream,
Flow gently, sweet Afton, disturb not her dream.

Robert Burns

Auld Lang Syne

Should auld acquaintance be forgot
    And never brought to mind?
Should auld acquaintance be forgot,
    And auld lang syne!

Chorus: For auld lang syne, my dear,
    For auld lang syne,
    We'll tak a cup o' kindness yet,
    For auld lang syne!

We twa hae run about the braes,
    And pu'd the gowans fine;
But we've wandered monie a weary foot
    Sin' auld lang syne.

We twa hae paidled i' the burn
    Frae mornin' sun till dine;
But seas between us braid hae roared
    Sin' auld lang syne.

And there's a hand, my trusty fiere,
    And gie's a hand o' thine;
And we'll tak a right guid-willie waught,
    For auld lang syne.

Robert Burns

The Mermaid

'Twas a Friday morn when we set sail,
And we were not far from the land,
When the captain spied a lovely mermaid
With a comb and a glass in her hand.

*Chorus: Oh the ocean waves may roll, may roll,
And the stormy winds may blow,
While we poor sailors go skipping to the tops,
And the landlubbers lie down below, below.
And the landlubbers lie down below.*

Then up spoke the captain of our gallant ship,
And a well-spoken man was he,
"I have married a wife in Salem town;
And tonight she a widow will be."

Then up spoke the boy of our gallant ship,
And a well-spoken lad was he,
"I've a father and mother in Boston City,
And tonight they childless will be."

"Oh, the moon shines bright, and the stars give light;
Oh, my mother'll be looking for me;
She may look, she may weep, she may look to the deep,
She may look to the bottom of the sea."

Then up spoke the cook of our gallant ship,
And a red-hot cook was he,
"I care more for my kettles and pots
Than I care for the bottom of the sea."

Then three times round went our gallant ship,
And three times round went she;
Then three times round went our gallant ship,
And she went to the bottom of the sea.

Anonymous

Darky Sunday School

Jonah was an immigrant, so runs the Bible tale,
 He took a steerage passage in a transatlantic whale;
Now, Jonah in the belly of the whale was quite compressed,
 So Jonah pressed the button, and the whale he did the rest.

Chorus: Young folks, old folks, everybody come,
   Join our darky Sunday School, and make yourself to
    hum.
   There's a place to check your chewing gum and razors
    at the door,
   And hear such Bible stories as you never heard before.

Adam was the first man that ever was invented.
 He lived all his life and he never was contented;
He was made out of mud in the days gone by
 And hung on the fence in the sun to get him dry.

The good book says Cain killed his brother Abel,
 He hit him on the head with a leg of a table.
Then along came Jonah in the belly of the whale,
 The first submarine boat that ever did sail.

Esau was a cowboy of the wild and woolly make,
 Half the farm belonged to him and half to Brother Jake;
Now, Esau thought his title to the farm was none too clear,
 So he sold it to his brother for a sandwich and a beer.

Noah was a mariner who sailed around the sea,
 With half a dozen wives and a big menagerie;
He failed the first season when it rained for forty days,
 For in that sort of weather no circus ever pays.

Elijah was a prophet who attended country fairs,
 He advertised his business with a pair of dancing bears;
He held a sale of prophecies most every afternoon,
 And went up in the evening in a painted fire balloon.

Then down came Peter, the Keeper of the Gates,
 He came down cheap on excursion rates.
Then along came Noah a-stumblin' in the dark,
 He found a hatchet and some nails and built himself
  an ark.

David was a shepherd and a scrappy little cuss,
 Along came Goliath, just a-spoilin' for a muss;

Now, David didn't want to fight, but thought he must or bust,
   So he cotched up a cobblestone and busted in his crust.

Ahab had a wife, and her name was Jezebel;
   She went out in the vineyard to hang the clothes and fell.
She's gone to the dogs, the people told the king,
   Ahab said he'd never heard of such an awful thing.

Samson was a strong man of the John L. Sullivan school,
   He slew ten thousand Philistines with the jawbone of a
      mule.
But Delilah captured him and filled him full of gin,
   Slashed off his hair and the coppers run him in.

Samson was a husky guy as everyone should know,
   He used to lift five hundred pounds as strong man in his
      show.
One week the bill was rotten, all the actors had a souse,
   But the strong-man act of Samson's, it just brought down
      the house.

Salome was a chorus girl who had a winning way,
   She was the star attraction in King Herod's Cabaret.
Although you can hardly say discretion was her rule,
   She's the favorite Bible figure in the Gertrude Hoffman
      school.

There are plenty of these Bible tales. I'll tell you one
      tomorrow
   How Lot, his wife and family fled from Sodom and
      Gomorrah;
But his wife she turned to rubber and got stuck upon the
      spot,
   And became a salty monument and missed a happy Lot.

Now Joey was unhappy in the bowels of the soil,
   He lost his pretty rainbow coat because he wouldn't toil.
He hollered, howled, and bellowed until far into the night,
   But of course you couldn't see him, for he was out of
      sight.

It happened that a caravan was passing by the place,
   Laden down with frankincense and imitation lace.
They heard the Sheeney yelling and pulled him from the
      well,
   If this ain't a proper ending, then you can go to Hell.

Anonymous

Believe Me, if All Those Endearing Young Charms

Believe me, if all those endearing young charms,
    Which I gaze on so fondly today,
Were to change by tomorrow, and fleet in my arms,
    Like fairy gifts fading away,
Thou wouldst still be adored, as this moment thou art,
    Let thy loveliness fade as it will,
And around the dear ruin each wish of my heart
    Would entwine itself verdantly still.

It is not while beauty and youth are thine own,
    And thy cheeks unprofaned by a tear,
That the fervor and faith of a soul can be known,
    To which time will but make thee more dear;
No, the heart that has truly loved never forgets,
    But as truly loves on to the close,
As the sunflower turns on her god, when he sets,
    The same look which she turned when he rose.

                                        Thomas Moore

Honey, Take a Whiff on Me

Oh, whiffaree an' a-whiffo-rye,
Gonna keep a-whiffin', boys, till I die.
Ho, ho, honey, take a whiff on me.

*Chorus: Take a whiff on me, take a whiff on me,
        Hi, hi, baby, take a whiff on me,
        Ho, ho, honey, take a whiff on me.*

I went down to Mister Apperson's place,
Says to Mister Apperson, right to his face—
Ho, ho, honey, take a whiff on me—

"I ain' gonna buy coke here no mo',"
An' Mister Apperson slam de do'.
Ho, ho, honey, take a whiff on me.

Went to Mister Lehman's on a lope,
Sign in de window said, "No mo' coke."
Ho, ho, honey, take a whiff on me.

Well, I wake up in de mornin' by de city clock bell,
An' de niggers up town givin' cocaine hell,
Ho, ho, honey, take a whiff on me.

Goin' up State Street, comin' down Main,
Lookin' for a woman dat use cocaine,
Ho, ho, honey, take a whiff on me.

De blacker de berry, de sweeter de juice,
Takes a brown-skin woman for my pertickeler use.
Ho, ho, honey, take a whiff on me.

I'se got a nickel, you's got a dime,
You buy de coke an' I'll buy de wine.
Ho, ho, honey, take a whiff on me.

I chew my terbacker, I spit my juice,
I love my baby, till it ain' no use,
Ho, ho, honey, take a whiff on me.

Well, de cocaine habit is mighty bad,
It kill ev'body I know it to have had.
Ho, ho, honey, take a whiff on me.

Cocaine's for hosses an' not for men,
De doctors say it'll kill you, but dey don' say when.
Ho, ho, honey, take a whiff on me.

Anonymous

This Train

This train is bound for glory, this train,
This train is bound for glory, this train,
This train is bound for glory,
If you ride in it, you must be holy, this train.
This train don' pull no extras, this train,
Don' pull nothin' but de Midnight Special.
This train don' pull no sleepers, this train,
Don' pull nothin' but the righteous people, this train.
This train don' pull no jokers, this train,
Neither don' pull no cigar smokers, this train.
This train is bound for glory, this train.
If you ride in it, you mus' be holy, this train.

Anonymous

Hell and Heaven

Chorus: I been 'buked an' I been scorned,
*   Childrens, I been 'buked an' I been scorned,*
*   Childrens, I been 'buked an' I been scorned,*
*   I been talked 'bout sure as you're born.*

I met ol' Satan on the way,
I met ol' Satan on the way,
I met ol' Satan on the way,
He says, "Young man, you're too young to pray."

Ef you want to see ol' Satan run,
Jes' fire off dat gospel gun.

Ol' Satan wears a mighty big shoe,
Ef you don' watch, gwine slip it on you.

Ol' Satan's like a snake in de grass,
Always in some Christian's pass.

What's ol' Satan grumblin' about?
He's in hell and he cain't get out.

Ol' Satan's mad, an' I am glad,
He missed de soul he thought he had.

Ol' Satan's like an ol' greyhoun',
Runnin' dem sinners roun' an' roun'.

Ol' Satan's a-settin' on a red-hot seat,
A-coolin' of his head an' a-warmin' of his feet.

I'd rather pray myself away,
Dan live an' burn in hell one day.

Oh, hell is deep an' hell is wide,
Oh, hell ain' got no bottom or side.

.   .   .   .   .   .

Two milk-white hosses, side by side,
Me an' Jesus gwinter take a ride.

King Jesus give me a little broom,
Jes' fer to sweep my heart clean.

What kin' o' shoes does de angels wear?
Don' wear none, ca'se dey walks on de air.

One o' dese mornin's bright an' fair,
Gwinter hitch my wings an' try de air.

When I gits to heaven, got nothin' to do
But fly aroun' an' sing hallelu.

Away up in heaven where I'm gwinter shout,
Nobody dere to put me out.

I haven' been to heaven, but I've been tol',
De streets in heaven are paved in gol'.

I want to go to heaven at my own expense,
Ef I cain' git through the gate, I'll jump de fence.

When I go to heaven, I want to go right,
I want to go to heaven all dressed in white.

When I git to heaven, gwinter take my stan',
Gwinter wrastle wid my Lawd like a nachul man.

When I git to heaven, gwinter sit an' tell,
Tell dem angels ring dem bells.

When I git to heaven, gwinter be at ease,
Me an' my God's gwinter do as we please!

Anonymous

Dese Bones Gwine to Rise Again

De Lord he thought he'd make a man—
Dese bones gwine to rise again;
Made him out-a dirt an' a little bit o' sand—
Dese bones gwine to rise again.

Chorus: I know it, 'deed I know it,
Dese bones gwine to rise again.

Adam was de fust he made—
He put him on de bank and lay him in de shade—

Thought He'd make a 'ooman, too—
Didn't know exactly what to do—

Took a rib from Adam's side—
Made Miss Eve for to be his bride—

Put 'em in a gyarden, rich and fair—
Tol' 'em dey might eat whatever wuz dere—

But to one tree dey mus' not go—
Mus' leave de apples dere to grow—

Ol' Miss Eve come walkin' round—
Spied a tree all loaded down—

Sarpint quoiled around a chunk—
At Miss Eve his eye he wunk—

Firs' she took a little pull—
Den she fill her apron full—

Den Adam took a little slice—
Smack his lips an' say 'twas nice—

De Lord he come a-wanderin' roun'—
Spied dem peelin's on de groun'—

De Lord he speaks wid a monstrus voice—
Shuck dis ol' worl' to its ve'y joists—

"Adam, Adam, where art thou?"
"Heah, Marse Lord, I'se a-comin' now."

"Stole my apples, I believe?"
"No, Marse Lord, but I spec' it wuz Eve."

De Lord he riz up in his wrath—
Told 'em, "Yo' beat it down de path."

"Out o' dis gyarden you mus' git.
Earn yo' living by yo' sweat."

He put an angel at de do'—
Tol' 'em not to never come dere no mo'—

Ob dis tale dere ain' no mo'—
Dese bones gwine to rise again.
Eve eat de apple, gib Adam de co'—
Dese bones gwine to rise again.

Anonymous

Dink's Song

Ef I had wings like Noah's dove,
I'd fly up the river to the man I love.
Fare thee well, O Honey, fare thee well.

I'se got a man, an' he's long and tall,
Moves his body like a cannon ball.
Fare thee well, O Honey, fare thee well.

One o' dese days, an' it won't be long,
Call my name an' I'll be gone.
Fare thee well, O Honey, fare thee well.

'Member one night, a-drizzlin' rain,
Roun' my heart I felt a pain.
Fare thee well, O Honey, fare thee well.

When I wo' my ap'ons low,
Couldn't keep you from my do'.
Fare thee well, O Honey, fare thee well.

Now I wears my ap'ons high,
Sca'cely ever see you passin' by.
Fare thee well, O Honey, fare thee well.

Now my ap'on's up to my chin,
You pass my do' an' you won' come in.
Fare thee well, O Honey, fare thee well.

Ef I had listened to whut my mama said,
I'd be at home in my mama's bed.
Fare thee well, O Honey, fare thee well.

Anonymous

The Man on the Flying Trapeze

Oh, the girl that I loved she was handsome,
I tried all I knew her to please.
But I couldn't please her a quarter as well
As the man on the flying trapeze.

*Chorus: Oh, he flies through the air with the greatest of
ease,
This daring young man on the flying trapeze.
His figure is handsome, all girls he can please,
And my love he purloined her away.*

Last night as usual I went to her home.
There sat her old father and mother alone.
I asked for my love and they soon made it known
That she-e had flown away.

She packed up her box and eloped in the night,
To go-o with him at his ease.
He lowered her down from a four-story flight,
By means of his flying trapeze.

He took her to town and he dressed her in tights,
That he-e might live at his ease.
He ordered her up to the tent's awful height,
To appear on the flying trapeze.

Now she flies through the air with the greatest of ease,
This daring young girl on the flying trapeze.
Her figure is handsome, all men she can please,
And my love is purloinèd away.

Once I was happy, but now I'm forlorn,
Like an old coat that is tattered and torn,
Left to this wide world to fret and to mourn,
Betrayed by a maid in her teens.

Anonymous

Pippa's Song

The year's at the spring,
And day's at the morn;
Morning's at seven;
The hill-side's dew-pearl'd;
The lark's on the wing;
The snail's on the thorn;
God's in His heaven—
All's right with the world!

Robert Browning

Mandalay

By the old Moulmein Pagoda, lookin' eastward to the sea,
There's a Burma girl a-settin', and I know she thinks o' me;
For the wind is in the palm-trees, and the temple-bells they say:
"Come you back, you British soldier; come you back to Man-
dalay!"
    Come you back to Mandalay,
    Where the old Flotilla lay:
    Can't you 'ear their paddles chunkin' from Rangoon to
    Mandalay?

Chorus: On the road to Mandalay,
       Where the flyin'-fishes play,
        An' the dawn comes up like thunder outer China
        'crost the Bay!

'Er petticoat was yaller an' 'er little cap was green,
An' 'er name was Supi-yaw-lat—jes' the same as Theebaw's
Queen,

An' I seed her first a-smokin' of a whackin' white cheroot,
An' a-wastin' Christian kisses on an 'eathen idol's foot:
    Bloomin' idol made o' mud—
    Wot they called the Great Gawd Budd—
    Plucky lot she cared for idols when I kissed 'er where
    she stud!

When the mist was on the rice-fields an' the sun was droppin'
    slow,
She'd git 'er little banjo an' she'd sing *"Kulla-lo-lo!"*
With 'er arm upon my shoulder an' 'er cheek again my cheek
We useter watch the steamers an' the *hathis* pilin' teak.
    Elephants a'pilin' teak
    In the sludgy, squdgy creek,
    Where the silence 'ung that 'eavy you was 'arf afraid to
    speak!

But that's all shove be'ind me—long ago an' fur away,
An' there ain't no 'busses runnin' from the Bank to Mandalay;
An' I'm learnin' 'ere in London what the ten-year soldier tells:
"If you've 'eard the East a-callin', you won't never 'eed naught
    else."
    No! you won't 'eed nothin' else
    But them spicy garlic smells
    An' the sunshine an' the palm-trees an' the tinkly temple-
    bells;

I am sick o' wastin' leather on these gritty pavin'-stones,
An' the blasted English drizzle wakes the fever in my bones;
Tho' I walks with fifty 'ousemaids outer Chelsea to the Strand,
An' they talks a lot o' lovin', but wot do they understand?
    Beefy face an' grubby 'and—
    Law! wot do they understand?
    I've a neater, sweeter maiden in a cleaner, greener land!

Ship me somewheres east of Suez, where the best is like the
    worst
Where there aren't no Ten Commandments an' a man can
    raise a thirst;
For the temple-bells are callin', an' it's there that I would be—
By the old Moulmein Pagoda, looking lazy at the sea;
    On the road to Mandalay,
    Where the old Flotilla lay,
    With our sick beneath the awnings when we went to
    Mandalay!

                                        Rudyard Kipling

Three Men of Gotham

Seamen three! What men be ye?
Gotham's three wise men we be.
Whither in your bowl so free?
To rake the moon from out the sea.
The bowl goes trim. The moon doth shine.
And our ballast is old wine.—
And your ballast is old wine.

Who art thou, so fast adrift?
I am he they call Old Care.
Here on board we will thee lift.
No: I may not enter there.
Wherefore so? 'Tis Jove's decree,
In a bowl Care may not be.—
In a bowl Care may not be.

Fear ye not the waves that roll?
No: in charmèd bowl we swim.
What the charm that floats the bowl?
Water may not pass the brim.
The bowl goes trim. The moon doth shine
And our ballast is old wine.—
And your ballast is old wine.   *T. L. Peacock*

The Wearing of the Green

Oh Paddy dear, and did you hear the news that's going round?
The shamrock is forbid by law to grow on Irish ground:
Saint Patrick's day no more we'll keep, his color can't be seen,
For there's a cruel law agin the wearing of the Green.
I met with Napper Tandy and he took me by the hand,
And said he, How's poor old Ireland, and how does she stand?
She's the most distressful country that ever yet was seen;
They're hanging men and women for the wearing of the Green.

Then since the color we must wear is England's cruel Red,
'Twill serve us to remind us of the blood that has been shed;
You may take the shamrock from your hat and cast it on the
      sod,
But never fear, 'twill take root there, though underfoot 'tis trod.
When laws can stop the blades of grass from growing as they
      grow,
And when the leaves in summertime their verdure dare not
      show,
Then I will change the color that I wear in my caubeen;
But till that day, please God, I'll stick to wearing of the Green.
                                              Anonymous

Song, Written at Sea

*In the First Dutch War, 1665,
the Night before an Engagement*

To all you ladies now at land
   We men at sea indite;
But first would have you understand
   How hard it is to write;
The Muses now, and Neptune too,
We must implore to write to you,
   With a fa, la, la, la, la.

For though the Muses should prove kind,
   And fill our empty brain;
Yet if rough Neptune rouse the wind,
   To wave the azure main,
Our paper, pen, and ink, and we,
Roll up and down our ships at sea,
   With a fa, la, la, la, la.

Then, if we write not by each post,
   Think not we are unkind;
Nor yet conclude our ships are lost
   By Dutchmen, or by wind:
Our tears we'll send a speedier way,
The tide shall bring 'em twice a day,
   With a fa, la, la, la, la.

The king with wonder, and surprise,
   Will swear the seas grow bold;
Because the tides will higher rise,
   Than e'er they used of old:
But let him know it is our tears
Bring floods of grief to Whitehall stairs.
   With a fa, la, la, la, la.

Should foggy Opdam chance to know
   Our sad and dismal story;
The Dutch would scorn so weak a foe,
   And quit their fort at Goree:
For what resistance can they find
From men who've left their hearts behind!
   With a fa, la, la, la, la.

Let the wind and weather do its worst,
   Be you to us but kind;

Let Dutchmen vapor, Spaniards curse,
   No sorrow we shall find:
'Tis then no matter how things go,
Or who's our friend, or who's our foe.
   With a fa, la, la, la, la.

To pass our tedious hours away,
   We throw a merry main;
Or else at serious ombre play;
   But, why should we in vain
Each other's ruin thus pursue?
We were undone when we left you.
   With a fa, la, la, la, la.

But now our fears tempestuous grow,
   And cast our hopes away;
Whilst you, regardless of our woe,
   Sit careless at a play:
Perhaps permit some happier man
To kiss your hand, or flirt your fan.
   With a fa, la, la, la, la.

When any mournful tune you hear,
   That dies in ev'ry note;
As if it sighed with each man's care,
   For being so remote;
Think then how often love we've made
To you, when all those tunes were played.
   With a fa, la, la, la, la.

In justice you cannot refuse
   To think of our distress;
When we for hopes of honor lose
   Our certain happiness;
All those designs are but to prove
Ourselves more worthy of your love.
   With a fa, la, la, la, la.

And now we've told you all our loves,
   And likewise all our fears;
In hopes this declaration moves
   Some pity from your tears:
Let's hear of no inconstancy,
We have too much of that at sea.
   With a fa, la, la, la, la.

Charles Sackville, Earl of Dorset

Sir Joseph's Song

When I was a lad I served a term
As office boy to an Attorney's firm.
I cleaned the windows and I swept the floor,
And I polished up the handle of the big front door.
   I polished up that handle so carefullee
    That now I am the Ruler of the Queen's Navee!

As office boy I made such a mark
That they gave me the post of a junior clerk.
I served the writs with a smile so bland,
And I copied all the letters in a big round hand—
   I copied all the letters in a hand so free,
    That now I am the Ruler of the Queen's Navee!

In serving writs I made such a name
That an articled clerk I soon became;
I wore clean collars and a brand new suit
For the pass examination at the Institute,
   And that pass examination did so well for me,
    That now I am the Ruler of the Queen's Navee!

Of legal knowledge I acquired such a grip
That they took me into the partnership.
And that junior partnership, I ween,
Was the only ship that I ever had seen.
   But that kind of ship so suited me,
    That now I am the Ruler of the Queen's Navee!

I grew so rich that I was sent
By a pocket borough into Parliament.
I always voted at my party's call,
And I never thought of thinking for myself at all.
   I thought so little, they rewarded me
    By making me the Ruler of the Queen's Navee!

Now Landsmen all, whoever you may be,
If you want to rise to the top of the tree,
If your soul isn't fettered to an office stool,
Be careful to be guided by this golden rule—
   Stick close to your desks and never go to sea,
    And you all may be Rulers of the Queen's Navee!

Sir W. S. Gilbert

Bunthorne's Song

If you're anxious for to shine in the high aesthetic line as a
    man of culture rare,
You must get up all the germs of the transcendental terms,
    and plant them everywhere.
You must lie upon the daisies and discourse in novel phrases
    of your complicated state of mind,
The meaning doesn't matter if it's only idle chatter of a tran-
    scendental kind.
    And everyone will say.
    As you walk your mystic way,
"If this young man expresses himself in terms too deep for *me,*
Why, what a very singularly deep young man this deep young
    man must be!"

Be eloquent in praise of the very dull old days which have
    long since passed away,
And convince 'em, if you can, that the reign of good Queen
    Anne was Culture's palmiest day.
Of course you will pooh-pooh whatever's fresh and new, and
    declare it's crude and mean,
For Art stopped short in the cultivated court of the Empress
    Josephine.
    And everyone will say,
    As you walk your mystic way,
"If that's not good enough for him which is good enough for
    me,
Why, what a very cultivated kind of youth this kind of youth
    must be!"

Then a sentimental passion of a vegetable fashion must excite
    your languid spleen,
An attachment *à la* Plato for a bashful young potato, or a
    not-too-French French bean!
Though the Philistines may jostle, you will rank as an apostle
    in the high aesthetic band,
If you walk down Piccadilly with a poppy or a lily in your
    medieval hand.
    And everyone will say,
    As you walk your flowery way,
"If he's content with a vegetable love which would certainly
    not suit *me,*
Why, what a most particularly pure young man this pure young
    man must be!"

Sir W. S. Gilbert

Ko-Ko's Song

As some day it may happen that a victim must be found, I've
  got a little list—I've got a little list
Of society offenders who might well be underground,
    And who never would be missed—who never would be
    missed!
There's the pestilential nuisances who write for autographs—
All people who have flabby hands and irritating laughs—
All children who are up in dates, and floor you with 'em flat—
All persons who in shaking hands, shake hands with you like
    that—
And all third persons who on spoiling *tête-à-têtes* insist—
    They'd none of 'em be missed—they'd none of 'em be
    missed!

Chorus: He's got 'em on the list—he's got 'em on the list;
        And they'll none of 'em be missed—they'll none of
        'em be missed.

There's the nigger serenader, and the others of his race,
    And the piano-organist—I've got him on the list!
And the people who eat peppermint and puff it in your face,
    They never would be missed—they never would be missed!
Then the idiot who praises, with enthusiastic tone,
All centuries but this, and every country but his own;
And the lady from the provinces, who dresses like a guy,
And who "doesn't think she waltzes, but would rather like
    to try";
And that singular anomaly, the lady novelist—
    I don't think she'd be missed—I'm *sure* she'd not be missed!

And that *Nisi Prius* nuisance, who just now is rather rife,
    That judicial humorist—I've got *him* on the list!
All funny fellows, comic men, and clowns of private life—

They'd none of 'em be missed—they'd none of 'em be missed.
And apologetic statesmen of a compromising kind,
Such as—What d'ye call him—Thing'em-bob, and likewise—
  Nevermind,
And 'St—'st—'st—and What's-his-name, and also You-know-
  who—
The task of filling up the blanks I'd rather leave to *you*.
But it really doesn't matter whom you put upon the list,
  For they'd none of 'em be missed—they'd none of 'em be
  missed!

Sir W. S. Gilbert

Yankee Doodle

Father and I went down to camp,
    Along with Cap'n Gooding;
And there we saw the men and boys,
    As thick as hasty pudding.

*Chorus: Yankee Doodle, keep it up,
        Yankee Doodle Dandy;
        Mind the music and the step,
        And with the girls be handy.*

And there we see a thousand men,
    As rich as Squire David;
And what they wasted every day,
    I wish it could be savèd.

And there was Cap'n Wellington,
    And gentle folks about him;
They say he's grown so 'tarnal proud,
    He will not ride without 'em.

I saw another snarl of men
    A-digging graves, they told me;
So 'tarnal long, so 'tarnal deep,
    They 'tended they should hold me.

It scared me so, I hooked it off,
    Nor stopped, as I remember;
Nor turned about till I got home,
    Locked up in mother's chamber.

Anonymous

John Brown's Body

John Brown's body lies a-mould'ring in the grave,
John Brown's body lies a-mould'ring in the grave,
John Brown's body lies a-mould'ring in the grave,
   His soul goes marching on!

Chorus:
  Glory, glory! Hallelujah!
  Glory, glory! Hallelujah!
  Glory, glory! Hallelujah!
  His soul is marching on!

He captured Harper's Ferry with his nineteen men so true,
And he frightened old Virginia till she trembled through and
   through.
They hung him for a traitor, themselves the traitor crew,
   But his soul is marching on!

John Brown died that the slave might be free,
John Brown died that the slave might be free,
John Brown died that the slave might be free,
   And his soul is marching on!

The stars of Heaven are looking kindly down,
The stars of Heaven are looking kindly down,
The stars of Heaven are looking kindly down,
   On the grave of old John Brown.

Now has come the glorious jubilee,
Now has come the glorious jubilee,
Now has come the glorious jubilee,
   When all mankind are free.

Anonymous

The Blue-Tail Fly

When I was young I used to wait
On master and hand him his plate,
And pass the bottle when he got dry,
And brush away the blue-tail fly.

Chorus: Jimmie crack corn and I don't care,
       Jimmie crack corn and I don't care,
       Jimmie crack corn and I don't care,
       My master's gone away!

And when he'd ride in the afternoon,
I'd follow after with a hickory broom;
The pony being like to shy
When bitten by a blue-tail fly. *(Cho.)*

One day he ride around the farm,
The flies so numerous, they did swarm.
One chanced to bite him on the thigh;
The devil take the blue-tail fly! *(Cho.)*

The pony run, he jump, he pitch;
He threw my master in the ditch.
He died—and the jury wondered why—
The verdict was the blue-tail fly. *(Cho.)*

They laid him under a 'simmon tree;
His epitaph is there to see:
"Beneath this stone I'm forced to lie,
A victim of the blue-tail fly." *(Cho.)*

Anonymous

On Top of Old Smoky

On top of old Smoky, all covered with snow,
I lost my true lover by a-courting too slow.
Now courting is pleasure, parting is grief;
But a false-hearted lover is worse than a thief.

A thief he will rob you and take what you have,
But a false-hearted lover will take you to your grave.
The grave will decay you and turn you to dust,
But where is the young man a poor girl can trust?

They'll hug you and kiss you and tell you more lies
Than the cross-ties on railroads or the stars in the skies;
They'll tell you they love you to give your heart ease,
But the minute your back's turned, they'll court who they
      please.

On top of old Smoky, all covered with snow,
I lost my true lover by courting too slow;
Bury me on old Smoky, old Smoky so high,
Where the wild birds in heaven can hear my sad cry.

Anonymous

The Twelve Days of Christmas

The first day of Christmas,
My true love sent to me
A partridge in a pear tree.

The second day of Christmas,
My true love sent to me
Two turtle doves, and
A partridge in a pear tree.

The third day of Christmas,
My true love sent to me
Three French hens,
Two turtle doves, and
A partridge in a pear tree.

The fourth day of Christmas,
My true love sent to me
Four colly birds,
Three French hens,
Two turtle doves, and
A partridge in a pear tree.

The fifth day of Christmas,
My true love sent to me
Five gold rings,
Four colly birds,
Three French hens,
Two turtle doves, and
A partridge in a pear tree.

The sixth day of Christmas,
My true love sent to me
Six geese a-laying,

Five gold rings,
Four colly birds,
Three French hens,
Two turtle doves, and
A partridge in a pear tree.

The seventh day of Christmas,
My true love sent to me
Seven swans a-swimming,
Six geese a-laying,
Five gold rings,
Four colly birds,
Three French hens,
Two turtle doves, and
A partridge in a pear tree.

The eighth day of Christmas,
My true love sent to me
Eight maids a-milking,
Seven swans a-swimming,
Six geese a-laying,
Five gold rings,
Four colly birds,
Three French hens,
Two turtle doves, and
A partridge in a pear tree.

The ninth day of Christmas,
My true love sent to me
Nine drummers drumming,
Eight maids a-milking,
Seven swans a-swimming,

Six geese a-laying,
Five gold rings,
Four colly birds,
Three French hens,
Two turtle doves, and
A partridge in a pear tree.

The tenth day of Christmas,
My true love sent to me
Ten pipers piping,
Nine drummers drumming,
Eight maids a-milking,
Seven swans a-swimming,
Six geese a-laying,
Five gold rings,
Four colly birds,
Three French hens,
Two turtle doves, and
A partridge in a pear tree.

The eleventh day of Christ-
    mas,
My true love sent to me
Eleven ladies dancing,
Ten pipers piping,

Nine drummers drumming,
Eight maids a-milking,
Seven swans a-swimming,
Six geese a-laying,
Five gold rings,
Four colly birds,
Three French hens,
Two turtle doves, and
A partridge in a pear tree.

The twelfth day of Christmas,
My true love sent to me
Twelve lords a-leaping,
Eleven ladies dancing,
Ten pipers piping,
Nine drummers drumming,
Eight maids a-milking,
Seven swans a-swimming,
Six geese a-laying,
Five gold rings,
Four colly birds,
Three French hens,
Two turtle doves, and
A partridge in a pear tree.
                    Anonymous

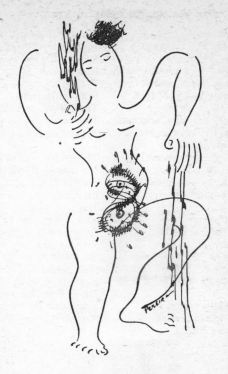

PART FIFTEEN

The Reader's Private Anthology

*This and the following pages are reserved for the favorite poems
(printable or unprintable) of, or by, the owner of this book.*

Index of Authors

(Anonymous is found throughout the book)